ACTS AGAINST GOD

ACTS
AGAINST
GOD

A SHORT HISTORY OF
BLASPHEMY

DAVID NASH

REAKTION BOOKS

For Bella, Tom and Eliza

Published by Reaktion Books Ltd
Unit 32, Waterside
44–48 Wharf Road
London N1 7UX, UK

www.reaktionbooks.co.uk

First published 2020
Copyright © David Nash 2020

Printed and bound in India
by Replika Press Pvt. Ltd

A catalogue record for this book is available from the British Library

ISBN 978 1 78914 201 3

CONTENTS

INTRODUCTION
7

ONE
BLASPHEMY IN THE ANCIENT WORLD
22

TWO
BLASPHEMY IN MEDIEVAL CHRISTENDOM
40

THREE
BLASPHEMY AND THE REFORMATION
58

FOUR
BLASPHEMY AND THE ENLIGHTENMENT
87

FIVE
BLASPHEMY IN THE NINETEENTH CENTURY
115

SIX

BLASPHEMY IN THE TWENTIETH CENTURY

139

SEVEN

BLASPHEMY IN THE CONTEMPORARY WORLD

163

REFERENCES *191*

SELECT BIBLIOGRAPHY *201*

ACKNOWLEDGEMENTS *203*

INDEX *204*

INTRODUCTION

It was a very odd thing for a seventeen-year-old to do in late 1970s west London: to sit intently ignoring my LPs to instead scrutinize endlessly the press and media coverage for still more information about a trial for blasphemy. I already knew about the moral crusader Mary Whitehouse, of course. She seemed to be little beyond a humourless killjoy, someone who had tried her best to close down and censor some of the things my adolescent mind already found funny, intriguing and sometimes both.

Mary had also just been triumphant in preventing a strange Danish man, Jens Jurgen Thorsen, from entering Britain to make a provocative film, *The Sex Life of Christ*. Thorsen himself looked, for all the world, the archetypal Scandinavian laid-back hippie, almost from another time; I remember him with a smile. I could not help feeling amused that he planned for his film to include a scene in which the figure of Christ robbed a bank and made his escape on a motor scooter. This was probably irreverent, a mildly comic or pretentiously silly film stunt rather than anything else. Certainly the idea that it could be something as grave as the offence of blasphemy, or that the film should be prevented from being made, never really occurred to me. Besides, the word blasphemy itself resonated with a strange archaic medievalism. Its appearance in the mouths of the agents of censure and cultural control only served to redouble this effect in my mind – and, indeed, the minds of others of my generation.

Thus, as Mary Whitehouse's interest in the grave and inexcusable public defacing of religion and her application for legal restitution

progressed, it just appeared to be the last gasp of a po-faced (yet ironically, save for Mary herself, also surprisingly faceless) Establishment:
one that either could not grasp that the world had moved on, or that
had decided this was a ludicrously high-stakes last pitched battle for
something important. Although young, I felt wise enough to reason
that this farcical action would fall at an early fence. As observers had
pointed out, the enduring twentieth-century image of a morally tight
and buttoned-up Britain had taken a serious humbling in both the
Lady Chatterley's Lover case in the 1960s and latterly with the *Oz* trial
of the 1970s.[1] Although evoking some distant collective memories of
crusades against unwarranted censorship, these were only vague cultural references to think about alongside the events of 1977 and '78. I
was as surprised, as so many others were, that the law of blasphemous
libel still existed in England. Soon there would be a public trial in
which a newspaper would face the apparently extensive might of the
law. The television news told of how the 'homosexual' periodical *Gay
News* had produced a poem that imagined intense and passionate
physical acts of love between Christ and other characters portrayed
in the Gospels. This culminated in a sex act between the centurion
at the crucifix and the mutilated body of the dead Christ. Despite
being, at the time, a devout and practising Catholic, my other life as
a sixth-form student of English literature had an equally compelling
influence: it led me to think of the world of poetry, metaphor and
imagination far more readily than it did the world of despicable blasphemous offence against religious ideas held sacred by many.[2] Maybe
it was because Catholicism required a seriously developed imagination for one to be devout, but certainly I could readily imagine what
James Kirkup had meant in his poem. If God was love, then this
was supposed to be there for all humanity. Given this, why had the
poem been considered as though it were a literal depiction of what
had happened? Had nobody heard of artistic creative licence? Of
metaphor? Of imagery and symbolism? It also seemed odd that an
apparently all-seeing God needed a humble (and slightly strange)
servant such as Mary Whitehouse to do his bidding on earth. Maybe
it was the Protestant world that was simply too literal, far too readily
prepared to wrap up the word of God with conceptions of morality in
the name of a Protestant ascetism that Catholics were not a part of.

Homosexuality, as well as hitting the headlines, would soon
take a prominent part in the youth culture of the period, with the

emergence of the political new wave and agitprop Tom Robinson Band. This group produced the confrontational song 'Glad to be Gay', which made many of us think of the routine injustices handed out to gay men (including our friends) in the years between decriminalization and the dawning of gradual public acceptance. The song was released just before the *Gay News* case reached the Court of Appeal, and referred to the injustice and hypocrisy that surrounded the original trial. It pointed out, quite rightly, that the concept of obscenity seemed to be a subjective tool, wielded with malice by the Establishment to prop up and sustain some dubious vested interests. Pictures of topless and naked women could appear in the red-top press without attracting condemnation or even adverse comment – yet *Gay News*, and the homosexuality it stood up for, was relentlessly vilified. This ideologically driven observation occurred in the song alongside a catalogue of wrongs perpetrated by everyone in the British Establishment, as well as those who regulated and policed society on its behalf. As such, it contributed a peculiarly influential soundtrack to the events of the *Gay News* case, something which also made the song, for some, into an inconvenient and discordant noise offstage.

And so it went on, as the public, me included, were transfixed by what gradually unfolded. The faceless Establishment that seemed to be morally bankrolling Mary Whitehouse was opposed by more recognizable and erudite members of the liberal world. John Mortimer (of *Rumpole* fame), Bernard Levin, Margaret Drabble and Geoffrey Robertson had all turned up to argue on behalf of *Gay News*. On paper it looked very much like an unfair fight that the Establishment would lose, even if few of us shed any tears over this prospect. Britain was quite obviously a liberal country with a sense of tolerance and fair play, and it had also recently joined the still more liberal European Economic Community (EEC). All this, surely, was bound to make the country conscious of how it looked to the world at large. Besides, what *were* blasphemy laws, and what were they actually for in a modern age? What a person had written could surely not be unwritten (still less unthought) and – as I was to discover was a frequent feature of the crime's modern history – the case had brought the actual blasphemous writing and utterance far more readily to public attention. It all seemed especially medieval in the age of television, radio and a press sustained by the phenomenon of mass literacy: the ongoing circulation of the blasphemous material would continue to offend – even though reporters were merely doing their job of informing the public.

But in the end, there it was in black and white – a verdict of guilty and a twelve-month suspended sentence for the editor of *Gay News*, Dennis Lemon. An abhorrence of blasphemy was surprisingly alive and well, and, going forward, would play a more significant part in my life than I had ever imagined.

Fast-forward to a summer's day in 2002 when I found myself standing on the steps of the Houses of Parliament in Westminster. By now in my early forties I was about to give evidence to the House of Lords Select Committee on Religious Offences. Many years had passed since the *Gay News* case had stirred my interest in the subject of blasphemy. By 2002 I had already written a book and several articles on the subject,[3] but what had been a pleasing academic exercise had suddenly become profoundly relevant to the contemporary world with the Salman Rushdie case of the 1990s, as we will come to in Chapter Six. By 2002 I had been approached by Keith Porteus-Wood, the secretary of the National Secular Society, to help in presenting the secularist case for a repeal of the Common Law of Blasphemous Libel. Would I write for them and speak before a House of Lords Select Committee? In the intervening years I had become convinced that blasphemy laws held a lingering and surprisingly engaged historical interest for most societies. Paradoxically, I had also become convinced that they were equally a relic of a bygone age that would too soon pass. Most subsequent experiences in dealing with laws in the contemporary context of Western nations would further confirm me in the first of these opinions, and make me unexpectedly change my mind about the second. Investigating the history of this offence also persuaded me that such laws were of extremely limited value and, in most modern societies, counterproductive. I had grown up in an era that had seen a progressive tide running against such laws, a movement that had originated in the middle of the nineteenth century. This tide had gathered pace in most Western countries, so that whatever forms blasphemy laws took, they had effectively become archaic remnants – if they had not been removed altogether by reforming governments as a part of their religious disestablishment processes.

My appearance at the House of Lords Select Committee did get these various points across, but the committee failed to reach a conclusive decision and nothing was to happen for another six years. One night in 2008, England's blasphemy law fell unexpectedly (albeit with quiet government connivance) in the context of a debate on the Criminal Justice and Immigration Act. This was one year after I had published a second book on blasphemy – this time in a more ambitious project to write a history of blasphemy encompassing the whole of the Christian world.[4] Scarcely anyone mourned blasphemy's loss in the England of 2008, and I began to think that the matter, and my involvement in it as an expert and accidental activist, might actually be over. In thinking this, I had not reckoned with certain actions of the Irish government almost a year later, which overnight created a new blasphemy law – this in a country that did not really have a conspicuous history of the crime, nor a deep cultural knowledge of it. The modern argument went that the Irish Constitution had a clause in it which required that a provision be made for the State's consideration of the crime of blasphemy. This prompted Dermot Ahern, then minister of justice, to propose an extensive blasphemy law to fill this void. The resulting law caused considerable controversy at the time and, as we shall see in the last chapter, continues to do so to this day. Thus, unexpectedly, I continued my dual career as historian and campaigner, as Irish NGOs asked for my help.

In many respects this book is an introduction to both its author and the vexing subject of blasphemy through the ages. I hope the combination proves both effective and pleasing, as well as operating in the very best traditions of engaged history. This means that the reader should hopefully find the roots of blasphemy and motivations of blasphemers in these pages, and be able to hold these up to the mirrors of both the historical past and the contemporary world. In doing so, this comparison should show a range of similar and extremely disparate images. Hopefully, this very process will also make the reader think about how and why blasphemy persists in the contemporary world, and why it is so hard to leave behind. Similarly, it should also start to become clear how it has been used and abused by societies past and present to protect, disrupt, persecute and justify. Here, far more so than in all other places I have frequented as a historical researcher, the past profoundly lives in the present – indeed, not only does it stubbornly refuse to go away, it is frequently and actively bidden back by successive contemporary worlds.

Blasphemy: Definitions and Initial Thoughts

The rudimentary definition of the offence of blasphemy in all cultures has been to see it as the wilful use of derogatory language or actions that question the existence, nature or power of sacred beings, items or texts. Sometimes, but particularly in the earlier period covered by this book, it is an expression of opinions mocking God's powers, or refers to sanctions upon individuals seeking to take such powers for themselves. Blasphemy, as a crime, appears to be primarily generated by the Abrahamic faiths. This is, perhaps, because these religions place greater emphasis on words and language, associating these more directly with religious belief and practice and the divine acts of creation and revelation. Likewise, these faiths (but particularly Islam) appear to associate blasphemy with the phenomenon of apostasy, with this distinction having been blurred sometimes in the past.[5] Blasphemy, unsurprisingly, has a history of some antiquity, emanating from different areas of the classical world. Later on it was the way that the medieval world made thought and opinion a crime. But the history of blasphemy is also about how it survived: blasphemy gives us an insight into the conception and development of censorship, how it came to silence opinion detrimental to the maintenance of authority in its widest sense, beyond even government. This also enabled it to take in beliefs that governed people's behaviour and their salvation. For something so ancient, we also need to explain why blasphemy has survived into the modern world, where it confronts very different societies and cultures. Understanding how much it has adapted through these changes is an especially pressing issue for the contemporary world, and this is one explicit function of this book. While the reader may detect a British, English-speaking world and European bias in the coverage of this book, this reflects the knowledge of the author, and I perhaps should apologize for this. Yet the book also reflects my desire to tell this little-known story to audiences in these regions, and for this I make no apology.

Introducing Blasphemy's History

So where did the justification for hunting blasphemers emerge from, and why was the crime and the acts associated with it pursued with quite such relentless vigour into modern times? From the classical to the early modern period, the issue of religious orthodoxy as a species of State security was paramount to rulers and governors. Authority nervously, and regularly, defined its clear duty to act as steward over the mechanisms of reverence and respect. Blasphemers too – sometimes through words, actions and even lifestyles – often demonstrated a worrying alternative to religious and social orthodoxy. Seeing religious dissidence as a dangerous aberration made a fear of false doctrine, corruption and evil an enduring part of the spectrum of religious belief. Given this, it is scarcely surprising that most medieval and early modern accounts of heresy emphasize the figure of the heretic as an individual corrupted by an external evil, almost as though it were a contagious disease.[6] Quite often the work of authorities and religious hierarchies was to identify the sources of this external evil, often using language describing a physical contagion to be controlled or eradicated like a pestilence. Within such a pathological model, individual heretics drawn into error were victims to be rehabilitated, saved and restored to the Christian community. This medieval vision contrasts with many early modern views of the blasphemer in which their actions are associated with sins of arrogance, pride and mental malady. Blasphemers were frequently perceived to be individuals possessing – and oft-times abusing – their own knowledge about the nature of this world and the next. Blasphemy was considered to have perpetrated violence upon concepts of the sacred and of the State. Seeing it as a species of public crime emphasized the broken peace, or the irreparably damaged respect for religious objects, persons or texts. In turn, this also invoked species of revenge and vengeance within legal systems, at the expense of restitution and rehabilitation. But the wider significance of blasphemy is that it was a specific phenomenon around which the State defined itself, and this occurs somewhat earlier than traditional history would suggest. This draws historical attention to dialogues of both godly and moral action that seek to control and civilize populations. Historians who have investigated seventeenth-century France and sixteenth-century Switzerland note that these histories place the emphasis upon impulsive acts or incidents fuelled by intoxication, for which individuals are made to feel remorse and undergo punishment or penance.[7] It is worth contrasting this with much of the work undertaken within the English-speaking world (especially around English law) that highlights more obviously a 'history of ideas' approach to the history of blasphemy. Quaker spirituality was defined as blasphemous for speaking of inner light and emphasizing personal revelation. Enlightenment deism emphasized freedom from churches and priests. In England especially, blasphemy is produced by the pen and pamphlet rather than the tavern disagreement or the rash, impulsive oath.[8] The situation in America is perhaps an antidote to the two models outlined above, since its Constitution, and commentators upon it, tried to remove the issue of blasphemy entirely from the scrutiny of the State.[9] Paradoxically, in colonial America it is individuals and communities that have initiated the informal, low-level proceedings to control opinion on the ground, something that in Europe actively inspired obvious State action.[10] All such legislative regimes worked on the premise that the blasphemer was an incorrigibly evil presence within societies at large. Here it is worth rehearsing how the process of blasphemy was produced by the mechanism of religious orthodoxy. It is not always appreciated that this seemingly precious orthodoxy in the West seemed an absolute necessity, or that its success was neither self-evident nor always a foregone conclusion.

The varieties of Christian doctrine that flourished in the first centuries of the Roman Empire bear comparison with the variety of contemporary Christian denominations. These former thrived in an atmosphere of reasonably respectful tolerance. This was only streamlined by the interested action of successive secular rulers, evident particularly in the First (325 CE) and Second (787 CE) Councils of Nicaea, through which a blueprint for Orthodox Christian doctrine (particularly in 325 about the divine nature of Christ) and for ways to worship (in 787 by permitting divine images) was created. Previously the approach to Christian doctrine had been looser and more accommodating of difference. The prescriptive approach of the Councils of Nicaea thus almost invented orthodoxy and placed a significant premium upon its preservation and desirability.[11] Paradoxically, this action gave birth to Christian religious dissidence both in the form of heresy and the much less widespread phenomenon of blasphemy.

The Contemporary World and Blasphemy

Blasphemy's power, and the taste of medieval conflict it can provide, perhaps gives us a captivating glimpse of the days before tolerance. However, an alternative reading of contemporary history provides evidence for an active revolt against the whole concept of tolerance per se as an obvious social good. In this potential scenario observers perceive that power and violence might be grasped back from the modern State for the individual to use. We might conceivably argue that all the conditions are present for this to happen. Twenty-first-century societies exhibit a growing litigiousness; a desire to explore the world of religious piety before politeness made it subservient to tolerance. We might also observe that evangelical religion's desire to recolonize public space is again on the march. There is also a persistence of popular arguments that stress the poverty of State-based solutions, alongside a more general loss of faith in the State. A new generation of experts are also now more cautious about blasphemy laws and are prepared to weigh up the good they do alongside the apparent bad. These are all attitudes that would have been wholly unexpected a generation ago.

While religion seeks to colonize public space, blasphemy is also sustained by the very privatization of religious feeling. This more modern idea of religion floats a little freer from the conceptions of doctrine that sustained belief in earlier epochs, and becomes linked to personal choice and preference. The idea of religious belief held more personally by the individual becomes central to blasphemous words and behaviour. This has eventually sustained greater capacity for interpersonal offence.

In Britain, many species of evidence submitted to the 2002–3 House of Lords Select Committee on Religious Offences reflected groups and individuals seeking protection for beliefs. These also demonstrated their own carefully nuanced capacities for genuine outrage and offence. These individuals saw the sudden arrival of blasphemy on the public agenda as a scapegoat upon which to lay their other concerns. Blasphemy and the fear of immorality allowed them to express anguish about wider European standards of behaviour and threats to national identity. Challenges to private belief were seen as a dangerous catalyst for the dissolution of national culture and civilization. Thus theories of modernization fed the secular need to explain the pernicious impact of crimes of the mind and of the identity on apparently modern societies. These were societies whose aspirations to a globalized culture tried to make these older identities seem anachronistic. Ultimately, these conflicting currents prove that people cannot be relied upon to become modern (and importantly stay modern), according to predetermined theoretical patterns or apparent trends.

At this point it seems sensible to examine how the modern State has begun to revisit some thought processes first described by the medieval world. The capacity for evil within the individual has begun to fascinate criminologists, and it is from here that whole societies and legal frameworks have become interested in the genesis of 'hate crime' as a new social concern. While governing authorities may be increasingly involved in the phenomenon, their path forward through it is often confusing, unsure and dangerous. Although states may wish to protect populations, they are also swimming against the tide of rights and responsibilities. We should also remember that this dilemma is something that liberal ideas encouraged generations of fledgling democratic citizens to adopt and defend. Freedom of thought and speech are often less easily curtailed than some libertarians fear. It is also true that Western liberal traditions are left feeling uncomfortable with what their own logic frequently tells them to defend.

THE HISTORY OF the last two centuries has shown the State retreating from the display and use of power in the area of religious conformity. Increasingly the offence of blasphemy has come to reside with the individual, and the responsibility to initiate action, too, generally lies here. This process has been aided by the measurable growth of individualism through participatory democracy, as well as the legal recognition of individual conscience and dissent. It is also a paradox that the development of the secular, and of social, cultural and religious tolerance, has also played its part: because of it, religions of the word and of the conscience were able to develop, multiply and actively flourish. Cultural trends, while not actively encouraging secularization, did make religion more malleable and more able to survive assaults upon its claims to be a universal system of values applicable to all.

In Britain, paradoxically, it is a confidence in a secular outcome to the process of toleration which enabled laws against blasphemy to survive. Home Office opinion, in the first half of the twentieth century, regularly asserted that the survival of blasphemy as a judge-made (or common) law meant it was interpreted anew for each generation. If a film, book or performance was blasphemous then it would attract prosecution, while if it was wholly tolerable or acceptable it would not. This meant that informed popular opinion was regularly empowered to speak for the public good against concepts of rights and liberties. To its practitioners this appeared wholly modern, and in keeping with the balanced logic inherent in the democracy of opinions and rights. It assumed (as it turns out, rashly) that affronts to religion would matter less and less, as Christianity and other religions adopted a more relaxed (supposedly secular) stance.

This was government giving both power and sovereignty to the individual to determine aspects of hurt, blame and culpability. Certainly this highlights that modern offences and blasphemy cases of perhaps the last 150 years have exhibited the power of the individual to intervene and restore an equilibrium unbalanced by the words of others. What is particularly striking, even into the nineteenth century, is the persistence of notions of violence in legal thinking, courtroom evidence and the pronouncements of Common Law judges on blasphemy. Policing authorities continually thought of blasphemy in a public order context, and twentieth-century conceptions of the law thus emphasized that it was a tool to prevent violence between perpetrator and victim. Actual harm, in the crime of blasphemy, has always been extraordinarily difficult to demonstrate satisfactorily. Historically, in precious few other areas of law has the magnitude of evil been assessed solely by the victim. Blasphemy has always existed as a glaring and perplexing exception.

In contemporary societies the pursuit and prosecution of offenders uses the public interest as a test of its legitimacy. Nonetheless, patterns in such decision making are rarely accompanied by plausible explanation. Alongside this we might also consider how the work of some contemporary lawyers discussing the importance of vengeance as a legitimate aim of a legal system impacts upon wider thinking in this area of attitude crime. It is also important to note that some commentators have actively rejected the tide of liberalism that loudly suggests blasphemy laws are a dangerous anachronism. Neville Cox, for example, is sceptical of the idea that blasphemy laws are inherently bad, seeing this argument as a piece of legal and cultural hegemony operated by the West that is seeking to have its views prevail to the utter exclusion of all others. Cox suggests that confrontations in this area constitute a problem for societies that face the question of whether they should exclude free speech which profoundly challenges their own moral values of tolerance. Equally, so he argues, it becomes questionable whether those producing such free speech should be permitted to damage the overall image of a minority group by focusing on the illegal and terrorist acts of some of its members.

To commentators like Cox, it seems self-evident that most people have an intrinsic sense of what they should not say, and that they exercise this type of judgement all the time. If people do actively self-censor, this opens up the suggestion that some things should thus be prohibited. Such widespread sensibilities are a reality, and it is thus true that people can be offended by observing things which do not actually affect them personally. This is because the attempt to use such words is an attack on their own perceived moral standards. Cox suggests that blasphemy laws cannot be said to be intrinsically wrong, and that our focus should instead fall beyond the different perceptions of morality in the Islamic East and the secularized West. He also reminds us of the fact that the West has a liberal rights based secularism that casts itself as an alternative to religious morality, portraying itself as the champion of the individual. This suggests that its opposite in Islamic society is a conception of the community.[12] But it remains a valid question whether it is reasonable for anyone in the contemporary world to wholly expect to go through life without any knowledge that their religion is subject to intense scrutiny, and perhaps even ridicule.[13]

Taken together these different facets provide compelling species of explanation as to why modern states have revisited their relevant laws. This occurred in Britain with a re-examination of blasphemy in the context of developing a law against incitement to religious hatred. In the Netherlands, the murder of Theo van Gogh prompted an investigation of antique laws on the statute book, which complicated further the problems caused by blasphemous utterances and portrayals. In Spain and the United Kingdom, television audiences in their thousands have reminded broadcasters that Christianity would still be defended, if necessary through the threat of court action and strident protest. Within the first months of 2005 both the *Cristofagia* controversy airing on Spanish television programme *Lo + Plus* (*The Most Plus*) and the BBC's *Jerry Springer: The Opera* brought protests literally to the door of broadcasters and television executives.

It is also necessary to explore the extent to which actions of the State itself have, in the past and the present, been characterized as evil. Since the eighteenth century many of the books and pamphlets written to support blasphemers and the positions they took tried to produce a history of development inspired by a long Enlightenment, something which saw total religious toleration as the end result. According to this argument, states and governments that stood in the way of this could very quickly be seen as anachronistic *anciens régimes*.

Paradoxically, in this area, the promises of freedoms that the United States seemed to offer the children of the Enlightenment were not fulfilled. During the twentieth century, federal government may theoretically have defended the Constitution, yet the lesser rights of individuals were regularly in danger from the more local community of believers. The Constitution established separation of Church and State, but this did not stop individual states within the union from trying to establish a viable blasphemy law and jurisprudence.[14]

A related criticism frequently levelled by those who fell foul of blasphemy laws was the suggestion that punishment for opinion was frequently unjust and inhumane. The privileging of one particular version of what constituted proper religiosity was increasingly seen as evil by those with alternative viewpoints. In this the State created an externalized 'other' from among those who might claim they were indigenous. The West, the male, the heterosexual and the orthodox were established as norms by this law. The writ of citizenship did not necessarily run to their binary opposite, creating the identity of the cultural outsider.

This then constitutes what has turned out to be the 'premature' end of our story. The devolution of power to the individual has left the State as an inevitable victim of that individual's claim to autonomy and liberty of conscience. Even strong assertions of theological neutrality leave the State open to action from groups and individuals. This has occurred in America, where the State's claims of being a secular entity and its expression of theological neutrality are precisely what has led to it being viewed as anti-religious. This perception is instrumental in creating grass-roots pressure in the United States for the State to absolve itself of any responsibility to uphold the secular.

An atmosphere of nervousness within the State also encouraged grass-roots pressure in the United Kingdom for a law against incitement to religious hatred, something which duly came in 2006. As tensions continue to rise it is no coincidence that writers and artists are producing cultural products that clash violently with religious fundamentalism. The quid pro quo for liberal democracies is that members of both religious and artistic groups ask for society and the State to defend them. Where the State once offered draconian punishment for dissent, it is now trapped between arguing for the primacy of rights, on the one hand, and responsibilities on the other, in the face of polarized views. This trap, and the resulting impotence and uncertainty that stems from it, may yet prove to be the last evil this historically challenging episode of Western cultural history has to visit upon us.

The Intention of this Book

Beyond such a gloomy prediction, this book hopes to be a simultaneously informative and entertaining short history of blasphemy, a phenomenon that has regularly produced both attention-grabbing flashpoints, and larger catastrophes in Western culture. When such events occur, they make our societies re-examine their relationship with God and religion, as well as question their ideas of freedom and rights. Throughout history, humankind has always had a conception of the sacred, and many societies have safeguarded the sacrosanct. They have also acted to protect people from the consequences of others speaking against it. This created the idea and crime of blasphemy, which has changed drastically over many centuries. From the stoning of miscreants, sanctioned in biblical times, to the discovery of heretics and later free speech advocates, right through to the return of stoning in certain countries in the late twentieth century, blasphemy has frequently been a crime that attracts the harshest penalties, particularly from frightened societies.

In more recent times, blasphemy appears, at first sight, to be a hangover from ancient ideas of the sacred and a rigid conception of the religious, something so apparently alien to the contemporary world. Yet this book seeks to explain why this phenomenon has transcended the conventional history of growing religious tolerance, surviving to be still with us in laws that prosecute individuals for transgressing against the sacred. Likewise, blasphemy survives in laws against religious hatred that people today instinctively believe to be necessary, but often scarcely understand.

This book seeks to illuminate and explain these long-standing conundrums by drawing on examples that show both how and why blasphemy has changed over many centuries. This also serves to explain why it has survived and actively flourished when so many other ancient concepts have withered and died. Beyond cases and incidents, we can examine the motivations of those who wanted to blaspheme, as well as those who wished to punish such people for doing so. This becomes a genuinely human history of this strange survival from the ancient world, and shows its impact on real people in real situations. It displays a range of people confronting and con- founding the very idea of God, often for differing reasons. Opposing them are others with an equally wide range of motives, who seek to bolster and protect such ideas and deities.

ONE

BLASPHEMY IN THE
ANCIENT WORLD

Ancient Greece used to be seen as a prototype of how later Christendom would create a relationship between religion and the supportive State. Greek society appeared to have a friendly and intimate relationship with its gods, embedding them in both epic adventures and the many tasks of everyday life. They protected routine activities such as agriculture, but also the more elevated aspects of human activity such as love and the arts, as well as longevity. Christendom supposedly envied this ideal and tried tirelessly to recreate it, even while still disparaging the gods of the Greeks and the polytheism they represented. In any case, both were societies where the control and influence of religion appeared central and complete.

In the twenty-first century, our view of Greek society is undergoing a fascinating re-evaluation. The previously established and secure history of this epoch is starting to look different through the work of a number of scholars who are prepared to look at some of the evidence with fresh eyes.[1] What emerges is not a picture of rigid conformity, something that Christianity would later refine and master, but instead a system in which twinges of doubt and even scepticism were tacitly tolerated. It is even suggested that Athenian society may have given birth to the first recognizable incarnation of a worldview we could call atheist – a characterization which, as ever, was spawned partly by the opprobrium of wider society.[2] In light of this, our earliest glimpses of blasphemy within ancient Greek society start to acquire a new significance. Indeed, blasphemy here seems to be less about belief and a little more about recognizably early-modern concerns such as public conformity; and even about more recent modern ones like State confidence and security.

Our first recognizable form of dissent that Greek society found threatening appears in the thought of the philosopher Protagoras (490–420 BCE). Sometimes styled as a forerunner of modern democracy, he saw the capacity for virtue as being inherent in the individual, and reasoned that this ought to be where power lay. A founder of the Sophists, Protagoras had a fearsome intellectual reputation and combined an astonishingly modern-looking agnosticism with ideas about the gods being experienced by their worshippers, rather than having any objective existence. He seems to have had the courage to declare: 'About the Gods, I am not able to know whether they exist or do not exist.'[3] This has made him beloved of relativizers, social constructivists, agnostics and even postmodernists. Whatever his ideas were, it seems the Athenian authorities lost patience and exiled him from the city, publicly burning his works and inaugurating a somewhat ambivalent Western tradition of authoritarian reaction to discussion and dissent. To an outsider, the twin assaults on gods and governments looked like a calculated attempt to fundamentally relocate power in society.

Protagoras was a threat, but he was followed by another Sophist, Anaxagoras (500–428 BCE), a man who seemed still more dangerous. In him we find evidence of dissent and unorthodox belief that we might now consider to be more widespread than had been originally thought. His ideas moved away from the conception of personal gods as found in the traditional Greek myths we have become used to. In some ways, this was more uncomfortable than the simple ignorance of divinity offered by Protagoras. Instead Anaxagoras thought about the forces within nature and argued that there was an intelligence operating behind them.

Many might have had similar thoughts in private, but Athenian society was to make an example of Anaxagoras. He was impeached sometime in the 430s BCE on a charge of 'not believing in the Gods', implying also that he was in 'subversion of the democratic constitution'.[4] This was an especially serious charge, which would require a hearing before a political assembly; those found guilty of the crime had frequently received a death sentence. Anaxagoras' accuser was a seer named Diopethes and many believe this was a concocted political charge to ensnare the Sophist's powerful former pupil Pericles.

Although Anaxagoras escaped a death sentence, he was banished and died in obscurity a few years later. This certainly seems like the first attempt of a state to intrude on the opinion of an individual. Chief among the reasons for believing this is that the words and actions of Diopethes resulted in the creation of a decree allowing for the regular impeachment of those who expressed scepticism about the gods or taught unorthodox religious ideas. Perhaps, without knowing it, Diopethes and those who went along with him had instigated the otherwise distant concepts of religious orthodoxy and unorthodoxy. Greek society had otherwise prided itself on its curiosity and discursive, open-minded approach to ideas.

It was only a few years later, in 415 BCE, that the poet Diagoras of Melos was also banished from Athens having been found guilty on a similar charge of impiety. Less cautious in his thought and actions than Anaxagoras, this poet seems an unregenerate unbeliever, who actively mocked the supposed powers of deities. He characterized the gods as phantoms that he saw lamentably constructed in the simplistic minds of others. In particular, he was accused of profaning sacred religious rites called the Eleusinian mysteries. It was alleged that Anaxagoras had been mocking them as being of little or no value, ideas which caused upset to others. It is also telling that sailors reputedly felt especially vulnerable when he was onboard ship. This offers us our first glimpse of the blasphemer's role as a dangerous wild card in the providential game played by each individual, alongside their own conception of what their God might do to them.

The use of this charge of impiety was part of a wider period of political crisis for Athens. Tensions were heightened on the eve of a crucial expedition to attack Sicily in 415 BCE, one that would restore power and confidence to a city state still at war with its neighbours. But this campaign was speculative and risky, and Thucydides tells us that in the tense atmosphere a wave of accusations began. Across Athens sacred statues of Hermes represented next to the sacred fertility symbol of a phallus were all suddenly defaced in a single night. This had happened before at the hands of the high-spirited and drunk, but this mutilation was taken to mean something manifestly more serious. A lack of confidence in providence, and the war's outcome, meant that this act was seen as a bad omen and a plot against Athenian democracy staged by an arrogant elite.

One individual caught up in these events was the renowned Athenian military commander Alcibiades (450–404 BCE), who also appears to have been the victim of the jealousy and personal animosity of others – this in stark contrast to the following he had among the populace. Alcibiades seems to have been drawn in largely because of his independent attitudes to most matters. The attack upon the statues was linked to continuing suspicion that many still mocked the Eleusinian mysteries. Some historians believe a hard-headed military man like Alcibiades might well have done so in a moment of bravado, or as a participant in a macho-style rite of passage for himself or others.[5] Most modern verdicts believe him guilty of the crime of mockery, but doubt his involvement in the statue mutilation. What appears crucial to this judgement is the good sense a high-ranking Athenian might have displayed in distinguishing between a private act of mocking and public vandalism of the sacred. But the indulgence of suspicion by his contemporaries, in preference to a search for meaningful proof, also displays a surprisingly modern sensibility around the privacy of one's own thoughts – as does the panicked linking of two separate events that made them appear somehow providential.

Alcibiades was considered too dangerously popular for a show trial to be successful before the expedition. Thucydides tells us that, nonetheless, he understandably wanted the trial over with before his departure on a protracted military campaign. He even recklessly implored those who tried him to hurry up and put him to death, if they could be assured of his guilt. With the atmosphere of uncertainty that prevailed, this exhortation was guaranteed to produce indecision and inertia, and the safest option was instead pursued. Alcibiades thus departed for Sicily with the accusation unresolved and still hanging over him, only for him to achieve impressive military honours away from home. Despite this, some additional evidence was offered in the case, lending further power to his opponents and ultimately resulting in a guilty verdict, with a sentence of exile and the confiscation of his property.

What emerges from these episodes is not that Greek society pioneered the policing of religious belief in a manner that medieval and early modern Christianity would approve of and emulate. Rather, these events more closely resemble modern experiences. It seems clear that dissension from orthodox religious belief was permitted in Greek society, to the extent that one could almost not even talk about such a thing as orthodox belief. Tim Whitmarsh sees an array of possibilities flourishing from what he has established as a much easier-going and discursive relationship with the gods of the Greeks and the whole notion of the divine. The gods appear in this snapshot as flawed, capricious and even potentially frail, perhaps suggesting the whole notion of worship as we would understand it should perhaps be thoroughly broadened. Certainly, without some latitude the various schools of philosophy, so beloved of medieval clerics and scholars, might not have arisen or might have failed to find purchase in the various branches of Greek culture.

This makes accusations against individuals of 'impiety' actually more surprising. If there was latitude in belief, why did such damaging accusations arise? The answer lies in the fear that public profanities would infect the population at large with panic. Thereafter, providential divine judgement would escalate into self-fulfilling prophecy as soldiers, sailors and statesmen underperformed and were undermined, while individuals would potentially flee the cities in distress. So, scarcely for the last time, accusations about what we would call blasphemy arose as a result of a political situation that threatened to provoke the population to behave in a particular and extremely unwelcome manner. Thus considerations of political expediency in the elimination of rivals, as well as considerations of public peace and order, were both part of a heady cocktail that could readily be mixed by the scared and unscrupulous, according to the particular context that arose.

The Death of Socrates and Creating a Blueprint for Martyrdom

It is the trial of Socrates, one of the closest friends of Alcibiades, that provides our modern eyes with the fullest example of how Greek society would prosecute and convict for blasphemy in the shape of impiety. Moreover, his conviction would cast a shadow over subsequent Greek philosophy and civilization, especially because it had a profound effect on Socrates' erstwhile pupil Plato (c. 429–347 BCE). Socrates had also been a close friend – and some even argue a sexual partner – of Alcibiades.[6]

Socrates readily displays many of the credentials the West came to associate with subsequent blasphemers.[7] A number of his actions showed a taste for independence and, indeed, the central core of his thought (governed as it was by incessant questioning) seemed similarly calculated to infuriate the conformist mind. Socrates came to argue that the exercise of morality should be determined by the nurturing and development of the individual conscience. This was in stark contrast to the philosophy that laws were there to enforce orderly behaviour, and that the pains and penalties for not doing so were the chief incentives for conformity. As we can see, Socrates' was a view that unfortunately seemed increasingly alien to a society that had become scared of dissent – one that instead craved the comfort blanket of unquestioning conformity.

However, the nature of the charges against Socrates seems to further enhance this perception that conformity was the be-all and end-all. This surfaced in the chief accusation that he was believed to have turned his back on the publicly acknowledged deities of the city, and instead was practising his own form of religion in private. His position as an otherwise revered teacher also resulted in the central charge having a coda of 'corrupting the young of the city'.[8] This last accusation is one levelled at many others subsequently indicted for blasphemy. These individuals are universally cast as people who appear to be wilful and arrogant – but potentially influential. Sometimes they seem to possess (like Socrates) a thinly veiled contempt for the forces of apparent order, assuming it to be wielded mindlessly in the name of the less enlightened multitude or, worse still, possibly by malevolent vested interests. Faced with these attitudes, and their consequences, authorities so often congratulated themselves, coming to see their philosophies of censorship and prosecution as wholly justified by the transgressors' actions. Such rebellious people destabilize, question, overturn and disturb – while societies time and again have to negotiate their reaction to them, for good or ill.

Worse was to come during the trial, since Socrates is credited with suggesting that he alone was privy to a powerful form of enlightenment – or was it special access to his own definition of the one true deity? From this distance in time, and considering the numerous filters his words have passed through, it is difficult to follow precisely what this meant. We might presume that he looked like a frightening blend of intellectual guerrilla and religious fanatic. Indeed, it is this that resulted in the essentially incompatible charges of unbelief and devotion to an unsanctioned and unapproved conception of deity.

In answering his accusers, Socrates posed a series of questions to authorities that generations of those in charge of blasphemy prosecutions would struggle to answer. Firstly, could any court really justifiably accuse Socrates of consciously intending to destabilize Athenian society? The intentions of any blasphemer in any blasphemy case have to be presumed, or at best inferred, from actions described in legal forms. As many would regularly answer, how justified and fair is it for the law to inquire deeply into the heart and soul of anyone who comes before it? Even if it did find its interrogations to be acceptable, how reliable were the conclusions from this intrusion? And, besides, how could Socrates possibly be held responsible for all the views and ideas that young people got into their heads? Was he responsible for all that corrupted Athenian youth? He wisely indicated that elements of his ideas were scarcely new and could readily be acquired by anyone bold and adventurous enough to scour libraries or marketplaces. As such, he was arguing that he was being made a scapegoat for the fears and concerns of his society, just as others would argue in the future. He also noted that he was stalked by society's other vested interests, declaring at his trial that he was the victim of an unlikely but potent alliance of poets, artists, politicians and rhetoricians. After this, Socrates went on the attack to argue that his teachings improved the young rather than corrupted them. In this he was creating a dialogue that later defendants would follow, when they argued their opinions and writings were a guarantor of social progress.

Although he spoke vociferously, and for a long time, Socrates was outnumbered and outflanked by his accusers, and was swimming against the tide of the wider context of the situation in Athens at the time. After he had been condemned to death, he concluded that his failure to weep and plead for mercy had been a significant reason for those seeking his death to confirm this sentence. Socrates also ominously, and prophetically, argued that his stance and stoicism would be followed by others. This was another cornerstone in the creation of free speech as both a habitable and desirable state of mind – even if one consequence was that people sometimes had to choose martyrdom.

Given these universally resonant questions, it is no surprise that Socrates has morphed into an archetype of the individual dissident hero prepared to fight – and if necessary die – for their beliefs. But what exactly did authority morph into as a result of this trial? For many of us in the modern world, just as heroic crusaders against censorship seem attractive figures, those who impose, limit and censor seem to be conservative figures of retrenchment who are scared and intolerant. These latter emerge as heavy-handed people in systems willing to use (and misuse) power to crush the lone individual who, too often, finds the odds stacked against them. Yet perhaps one of the tasks for this book is to unravel and question the truth about both of these enduring stereotypes.

Although condemned to death by the court, Socrates elected to die at his own hand. Having justified his decision to his friends, Socrates declared: 'I can therefore look with cheerfulness on my journey today, and every lover of truth may do the same, when he considers that, without purification and preparation, no free entry is permitted into the mysteries of wisdom.'[9]

A short while later he drank one measured draft of hemlock that had been brought to him and, thereafter, slowly lost all feeling in his body before unconsciousness overtook him. In this, his decision to commit suicide also robbed the jurisdiction of a direct hand in his demise. This was his ultimate act of defiance and cemented the argument that the jurisdiction had no right to punish him for this crime, and his own intervention had robbed them of this power. Thus Socrates had turned himself into a martyr who had argued that there should be no authority that may rule on such a thing. His last act would enshrine a heroic status that would thereafter be quoted by free speech advocates everywhere.

Although it is tempting to unreservedly accept this heroic status for Socrates, it is worth indulging the views of the opposition, if only for a moment. Soon after the death of Socrates one opponent, Polycrates, argued that the philosopher had been an enemy of Athenian democracy. Socrates' philosophy and methods, Polycrates argued, persuaded others to ask penetrating and searching questions that would undermine the concept of democracy. Such a view was scarcely helped by Socrates' own conviction that his explicit role was to be an annoyingly dissident and perhaps even playful voice. In his role of a malcontent, we can ask ourselves to what extent Socrates does perhaps represent the way societies characterize blasphemy as vicious, mocking and resting on an assumption of unwarranted superiority. The martyr for free speech is an enduring figure, and Socrates himself was frequently championed as an exemplary beacon shining in the dark against the twentieth century's dark episodes of totalitarianism.

It is worth also remembering that the picture created of Socrates was one orchestrated by his friends and supporters (particularly Xenophon (435–354 BCE) and Plato). This is so often the case in the history of blasphemy: those who fall foul of it are celebrated and lauded by their compatriots, while the forces ranged against them are readily associated with brutality, obstinacy and tyranny. Perhaps related to this is the fact that these oppressive forces so rarely sound as articulate and plausible as those they accuse. The authorities are trapped in a situation where the maintenance of the status quo and the minimization of harm are imperatives – scarcely an intellectually stimulating or benevolent place to be. For this reason, what we hear from this side of the blasphemy argument can very often be less distinct, and considerably less erudite, than what is said by the articulate and heroic individual in the dock.

There are wider lessons and conclusions to be drawn here, and this whole episode also plays a significant part in our history of blasphemy. As many have remarked, Socrates' prosecution was notable for being conducted in a society that contemporaries, and subsequent commentators, considered a democracy. This has shocked the sensibilities of some, while encouraging vigilance among others. It warns us, and indeed all who encounter this story, that accusations like blasphemy are not wholly dependent upon the nature of the society in which they happen. Indeed it is useful in making us accept an uncomfortable proposal – why would we imagine that there should never be prosecutions for blasphemy in a free and democratic society? Context is all, and the urge to protect established values frequently emerges as an imperative to act, every bit as much as the heady charge for freedom of thought. The fate of Socrates comes to seem increasingly unusual in the Greek world, one which filled its hours and literary works with enquiry and philosophical speculation. It was a world of variety and comparative tolerance – certainly when compared to developments within the later Judaeo-Christian world.

The Origins of Blasphemy in Islam

Experiences of blasphemy's arrival in the Islamic world sometimes appear to more readily mirror the experience of the classical than the Judaeo-Christian world. Although it is specifically mentioned in the Old Testament, the offence of blasphemy does not really feature in the Koran, at least according to some scholars. It does seem, however, to have appeared later, in subsequent descriptions of the law and prophetic sayings known as Hadith.[10] These supplemented the Koran and became a part of accepted practice for the majority of Muslims. Looking at Hadith does provide a precedent for something resembling an execution for blasphemy. A Medinan seeking to repel Muslims from his city, Ka'b ibn al-Ashraf, was supposed to have composed anti-Islamic poetry and for this reason was put to death under instructions from the Prophet. Yet, many point out that this individual's crime may not have been blasphemy, but a more obviously politically related form of treason. This in turn has been complicated since al-Ashraf's opposition to Islam came at a time when its identity as a people, and its identity as a community following one religion, were tightly fused together. Some scholars have argued that these subsequent embellishments of the Koran were produced by caliphs who had avowedly political purposes in mind. After Arabia had become Muslim, there followed a period of considerable military struggle against neighbours and opponents. Identifying religious apostasy as a form of treason against Muslims, and any state they might construct, placed a premium on supporting and upholding the State and its government. Apostasy in these instances was punishable by death, but it lacked the starkly religious nature of many subsequent blasphemy allegations in the West. This was largely because the crime seemed aimed at the community rather than at something more obviously and deeply sacred. This more narrowly political dimension also has potential parallels with some later instances in the West, occasions when rulers swiftly drew upon blasphemy as a form of offence that could capture dissidents. This approach would strengthen the power and value of adhering to a State-sponsored form of community and civil society.[11]

However, others have noted that blasphemy does actually appear more obviously in the Koran, and three incidents in particular are cited. One involves religious hypocrites teasing the Prophet; another outlines instances in which some might ridicule the call to prayer. A third describes actual instances of similar hypocrites blaspheming against God and the Prophet. In each of these instances, the Koran appears to recommend ignoring and disdaining such actions and individuals, rather than any more drastic action.[12] An authoritative encyclopaedia of Islam and the Muslim world notes that words which can be construed as indicative of proscriptions against blasphemy are clearly evident in the Koran.[13] The connection with the idea of apostasy comes from the assertion that blasphemous acts lead to apostasy from Islam itself, suggesting that this transgression looms larger as an offence. The reason for this may be the fear that such ideas would infect others, an outlook which was equally a staple of thinking around the laws within the classical world, Judaism and Christendom.

Others actively wanting to promote a liberal definition of blasphemy within the Islamic world suggest that it should be considered an alien concept. Throughout these arguments such commentators point to numerous occasions when the Prophet advocated the display of forgiveness and mercy in the face of scornful disbelief and reviling of his message. In this account, blasphemy is clearly thought to be mentioned in the Koran, but there is again the view that severe punishments for the offence were absent from it.[14] Rather than calling for punishment, there are instead warnings of what would almost certainly await such people in the afterlife. In its way, this was a variation of the later argument that it was the special preserve of deities to punish disrespect, rather than humankind. Yet this has not stopped others from seeing Koranic precedents as informing how more modern laws of blasphemy should be created to provide clear and obvious punishments.[15]

What emerges from all this is that scholars disagree about the extent to which the Koran itself is unequivocal about the precise nature of blasphemy. Most do seem to agree that it does not demand the harshest penalties for this offence, considering it as a road to apostasy rather than being a danger in itself.

This means the nature, origin and implication of both of these offences are less obvious in Islam than in the Judaeo-Christian world. In Islam, the context of armed struggle and its dangers motivated action against apostates, something which had a writ sanctioned by the emergency of the situation. It was naturally assumed, and expected, that tolerant attitudes would resume in peacetime. If blasphemy became important within Islamic law, most authorities agree this was a later development. Some scholars also suggest that revisiting uncertainty about its origins has been an important component of modern attempts to rejuvenate the status of the offence of blasphemy in Islamic societies.[16]

Blasphemy in the World of the Old Testament

While the Greek city states and the Islamic world were regularly involved in war against their neighbours and adjacent empires, generally speaking these were neither wars of religion nor for the preservation of specific identities that societies lost at the peril of their very souls. This starkly alternative world was the reality for the Kingdom of Israel portrayed in the Bible. Throughout the Scriptures, the Israelites are struggling for existence against a variety of enemies. They take possession of Israel from its previous occupants (the Canaanites) and thereafter fight off a range of warring neighbours intent upon conquest, including the Babylonians and the Assyrians. At other times, orthodox adherents of the Hebrew god have to overcome a variety of usurper deities that threaten their own existence. As the Book of Exodus tells us, the Israelites quickly took to worshipping a golden calf (Exodus 32), and subsequent generations eventually overthrew the false gods Baal and Moloch (Judges 2:10–14; Acts 7:42–4).

One cornerstone of the Israelites' struggle, which also drove them forward, was that their concept of blasphemy had effectively been handed down from Mount Sinai as part of the Ten Commandments. This produced a strong element of religious prescription and control within this society, and a later text of Mosaic law confirmed it could be used to condemn an outsider who spoke disrespectfully of the Hebrew God (Leviticus 24:10–23). By the time we reach the end of the Old Testament, many of the characteristics of the Israelites' reaction to blasphemy were in place. We can find instructions for judges to rent (tear) their clothing at the utterance of such dangerous words; and we find a biblically prescribed punishment of stoning for those found guilty of blasphemy. Like any ancient source, the biblical Scriptures can sometimes seem dubious as precise records of historical events. For some obvious reasons, we can find no record of what biblical offenders may have actually said. The focus on speech was a crucially important element here since it made the offence one of visible public order and immediately generated providential fear. It also meant that blasphemy law focused on a specific act, unlike the series of presumptions made about the ideas and private thoughts of Socrates.

The law's content also came to concentrate on the Scriptures as the authority for defining blasphemy in a wide sense. The commentaries upon Jewish law, the Talmud, merely argued that reviling the name of God was the offence of blasphemy. The Scriptures, however, contained a host of incidents of blasphemy and its punishment that almost certainly portray individuals reacting to a heightened sense of fear at what they had encountered.[17]

If we seek coherence in this it seems that the reliance on Scripture certainly extended the number and type of infractions that Judaism was prepared to take action against. Likewise, we can see some of these ideas finding their way into later Christian conceptions of the offence. While speaking ill of the Almighty was considered blasphemous in both the Talmud and the Scriptures, the latter added pronouncing the name of God in private or public to the offence. This heightened a providential fear of divine retribution and the fear of taking God's name in vain (something so shamelessly parodied in 1979 in the blaspheming 'Jehovah' sequence in the film *Monty Python's Life of Brian*). A further addition appeared in the offence of seeking to command the Almighty – something which regularly emerged, then as now, as a component of curses and swearing. Such abhorrent events and performances were given further power by the ritualized utterance of the precise words used by judges to establish the truth of the crime, whereupon all present would tear their garments in a co-ordinated and dramatic response. This sprawling definition of blasphemy as a number of different, if related, offences had a significant impact when the elders and priesthood of Israel had the figure of Jesus Christ brought before them.

Biblical scholars are greatly divided on the issue of precisely what offence the historical Jesus was found guilty of, and which of his actions and utterances were actually considered blasphemous.[18] This uncertainty is at least in part created by the conflicting accounts found in the Gospels and, as some have argued, the possibility that they were more likely to be literary (or even propagandized) creations, than the histories they are often readily taken to be. It could have been his healing the sick on the Sabbath that was considered blasphemous; it could have been his claim to be equal to God and to sit at the right hand of the Father; it could have been his more worldly concerns about protecting the Jewish people from Roman interference; or the motive for his arrest could even have been retribution in the aftermath of Jesus' refuting yet another apparently false Messiah.

Alternatively, it could be that the Sanhedrin trial of Jesus was motivated by their need to preserve their authority over the Jewish people in a time of turmoil – authority that would be overturned if even a scrap of what the man before them, claiming to be the Messiah, was suggesting were indeed to happen. It might equally be that the Jews were largely blameless, and Jesus was executed (in a Roman fashion after all) for a crime related to treason. Certainly, his assertion that he was the Messiah had dangerous political implications for Roman power in the region, something which had scarcely been left unchallenged by the Jews before this date. Eventually, high-ranking Romans would become indifferent or even cynical. Emperor Tiberius (42 BCE–37 CE) was famous for his pronouncement that mankind had no reason to punish blasphemers since supposedly all-powerful gods were quite capable of exacting their own punishment from the wilful and the guilty, if they so chose. There is no definitive explanation as to why, or even indeed if, blasphemy was the offence that resulted in the trial and death of Jesus. Nonetheless, one outcome of this action is certain: the Gospels all indicted the Jewish people for their failure to recognize Jesus as the Messiah, thereby fuelling anti-Semitism and pogroms in the ensuing centuries.

Early Christian Society and Blasphemy

Between them, Judaism and the fledgling religious groups that came to be Christianity had created the first 'religion of the Book'. This also had extremely important implications for the way that Christianity developed throughout the Mediterranean world during the centuries immediately after the crucifixion of Christ.

From a religion that conceived of blasphemy as a crime of action, of utterance and an immediately observable event occurring within an enclosed community, there was suddenly now one that seemed atomized to the four winds. In its initial phases, Christianity was spread by missionary work, and we certainly get a flavour of this when we consider the far-flung travels and long-distance letters of the Apostle St Paul. As the letters demonstrate, he visited many different corners of the Mediterranean world, from Corinth to Rome and various destinations in between. St Paul also wrote to a range of significant individuals, and his correspondence had a lasting effect and influence. It is evident from Paul's epistles that the range and scope within this canon of ideas created a religion that became adept at thinking about the nature of God and Jesus, and which could reflect on its own ability to interpret texts and pronouncements. As such, we could consider early Christianity to look more like the discursive Greek society we met earlier in this chapter. This would mean that this early Christianity more likely resembles a collection of sects than the cohesive Church that it would for a time become. These sects had grown organically, offering sincere and cogent interpretations of the Scriptures and the teachings of Jesus.

With variations upon their interpretation of the Gospels, and the precise meaning of the words of Jesus, a great number of religious sects began to proliferate in the Christian world of the Mediterranean. There were groups such as the Donatists of North Africa who refused to accept the validity of sacraments bestowed by traitorous priests – namely men who had co-operated with Roman persecution in the reign of Diocletian (244–311). There were also the more enduring Gnostics, who had turned their back on materialism and espoused considerable doubts about the idea that God was the creator of the universe. They also speculated on the role of Christ, with some relegating him to a subordinate position, while others discounted his importance altogether.

Against this backdrop of multiplying differences, figures of authority such as bishops and archbishops began to crave conformity within the growing Church. In doing so, they reached for accusations of blasphemy as a means of marginalizing some of these beliefs, such as those which denied divinity and questioned the nature of the Trinity. Very quickly, the precise nature of God the Father and God the Son had become discursive questions. Those who held earnest, but contrary, beliefs were unwilling to be shaken from them merely by bishops and churchmen flexing their muscles.

What this clearly demonstrates is that the issue of authority was becoming fundamentally important to the future of Christianity. One justification for this craving for control was an urge to preserve Christianity from its external foes, such as paganism, by limiting the power and damage done by its internal ones. There was no longer any question of tolerating dissent as though it were a harmless eccentricity or difference of opinion. Instead, the defiant contestation of official authority set religious sects into conflict with the Church.

The destination to which this conflict was heading was the convening of the great religious council. This was a place where these issues would be debated and resolved, enabling formal and final decisions to be made. Henceforth, the hoped-for result from such councils would be an accepted Church doctrine, something to which all were expected to subscribe on pain of excommunication. This draconian sentence isolated the individual from the spiritual and material comfort of the community. It was a much more feared and dangerous sentence than it sounds to modern ears, since it threatened the lasting destitution of both body and soul.

Perhaps without any having realized its ultimate consequences, this process also heralded the creation in the Christian world of something called orthodoxy, and thus of its opposite, heresy. These categories surfaced in the First Council of Nicaea in 325 CE. Among many issues discussed at this several-months-long meeting, the central one was the extremely vexed question of how to worship and perform appropriate devotions to the Christian God. One faction, the Arians, denied that the son of God could in any way himself actually also be God – indeed, to consider the Son to be God, they argued, would be to dilute God's power. Rather, Jesus must have been created or called forth by God and had not existed for all time as a part of God. As such, the Arians were ambivalent about the prescribed orders of worship. They were opposed by more mainstream groups and individuals (sometimes called 'Alexandrians'), who were insiders and much more obviously integrated into the concept of the Church as an institution.

The Alexandrian faction came to represent the views of the Emperor Constantine (272–337), a recent convert to Christianity who had already understood the potential power of Church and State combined. Constantine had also recognized that his active participation in the Council could be important, and he was determined to influence proceedings.

Contradicting the divine nature of Jesus was to deny the idea of the Trinity. When the Arians were defeated, the doctrine of Trinitarianism was to become a cornerstone of Western Christian religious belief, something embodied in a prayer with considerable significance and longevity: the Nicene Creed. The Council's long deliberations highlighted that Christianity really had problems theorizing the precise nature of Jesus, and subsequent theologians would continue to debate the point and produce different answers. These matters would never be wholly settled, even though the Church would make continued efforts to prescribe orthodox thinking about the nature of Christ, notably at the Council of Chalcedon in 451.

If thinking about Jesus was one problem, thinking about how precisely to depict him was another. This was the crucial subject discussed at another, much later, Council held in Nicaea in 787. Some had argued that producing images of Jesus would inspire unhealthy feelings of reverence that would be actively idolatrous, and would risk promoting a more primitive and heathen religious focus on objects. Such ideas were hangovers from the Arian belief in the subordination of Christ to God, and the Nestorian position which identified the separate divine and human natures of Christ. In the face of such ideas this Council began by condemning what it called 'iconoclasm' as a dangerous and pernicious form of blasphemy. Instead, it reasserted that the power and value of icons was 'in accordance with the proclamation of the gospel' and that those who venerated images were venerating the real object of devotion. This would hereafter be the central doctrine of the Church.[19]

The idea that Christ was unequivocally divine significantly triumphed at both Nicaean councils. Thereafter, this created the blueprint for how doctrinal 'trouble' would be conceived of in the Church, right up until the Reformation. A Church that thought of itself as a cohesive institution, guiding and leading its flock to heaven through the insistence on orthodoxy and the punishment of error could not rely on this benevolent view of its activities being shared by all. Dissidents who differed in their interpretation of the Gospel, or on other matters, would quickly recognize an overwhelming authoritarianism that would not simply allow them to live quietly in their communities. Indeed, nor would it even allow them to disappear and exile themselves in the name of their devotions and the shared public peace. Isolated religious groups who conceived of themselves as harmlessly separated from the Church would never see how they posed a threat to the order of the Church as an institution. Nor would they comprehend the strength and logic of secular and religious compulsion, an impetus which anxiously sought their conformity. This conformity was conceived of by the Church as something that would both save the souls of these dissidents and save the souls of those charged with seeking their restoration to the Church. By the end of this Second Council of Nicaea, the battle lines for the creation of heresy – and its heir, blasphemy – had been drawn. They would remain set for the best part of 1,100 years.

It is important to note that this decision at Nicaea effectively placed blasphemy, for a time, in the background, to be overshadowed by heresy; with blasphemy becoming an additional charge thrown in when the Church moved against heretics. This remained the case for a surprisingly long time.[20] Precise beliefs would be considered objectively heretical, but some actions and words would be blasphemous. Prosecutors would seek to discipline blasphemy, but would take more rigorous action against heresy, which was more likely to be contagious to Christian churches and populations at large. Although heresy would prove to be a problem for the late medieval Church in particular, there is a case for saying that the decision at Nicaea was successful as a form of damage limitation, something that preserved the Catholic Church's monopoly position for as long as possible.

Allowing images to be sacred and revered did focus the minds of the faithful upon orthodox places and orthodox objects that became sites and items for veneration and belief. If the early Church had chosen to deny and remove images, the faithful would arguably have been left to find their own conception of how they might imagine and communicate with their God. Would they choose to view the Almighty through images, pictures and objects and comprehend him with awe? Or would they find such things to be graven images that should be destroyed, instead to be replaced with a purity of thought and religious life that the individual would conjure within themselves? These opposing questions had now been effectively shelved, for most people, until the dawn of the Reformation.

TWO

BLASPHEMY IN MEDIEVAL CHRISTENDOM

The Christian world entered the Middle Ages with essentially two internal problems. The first was the need to control errant and heretical opinions that threatened the authority of the Church as an institution. This challenge to authority made heresy also appear to be a danger to secular rulers. The second, albeit less threatening, problem was blasphemy, with its disparaging of God and his powers, and its mocking of the sacred.

Conventional religious histories are plain about the first of these problems being the primary concern of the Christian Church. Why else had the Church organized and hosted a significant number of ecumenical councils? These were places where the issues of faith were discussed and eventually codified; they had been attempts to create unity and conformity. Unfortunately, defining conformity also defined dissidence. This meant that heresy appeared to be a constant threat and could spring from many quarters. Those who objected to the authority of the Church and where this came from – groups such as the Bogomils, Henricians and Lollards – could readily constitute one form of opposition. Equally, those who objected to the riches of the Church and of churchmen – such as the Arnoldists, Beguins and Fraticelli – would seek to stage a 'return' to poverty, the pure Christianity of the Gospels and the Acts of the Apostles.[1] Christianity, for these people, was not just a series of doctrines, but instead a blueprint for how to live peaceably and in holiness. Others would conclude that certain rites of the Church were unsanctioned by God and practised against the intention of Scripture. Still more groups continued the arguments about the precise nature of God, of Christ and of the Trinity. The last of these concepts united all facets of the Almighty and then, as now, this appeared an extremely difficult doctrine to understand, let alone believe. An enduring sticking point would be discussions about the precise nature of Christ. Was he wholly divine, wholly human, or some being that blended both aspects?[2] Throughout the Middle Ages, and even into modern times, different answers would emerge from religious thinkers driven by a sincere search for religious truth.

While the early Church was frustrated by its failure to create uniformity, the medieval period hardened this into the creation of heresy and heretics. In doing so, it created a sin and greatly stricter responses to the transgression. St Augustine (354–430), having once flirted with heresy himself in the form of Manichaeism, eventually sought to maintain the sanctity and purity of faith. For him, heretics not only threatened this sanctity, they imperilled the secular State that supported it and prevented such pure piety from withering. In his argument, Augustine showed evidence of a providentialism that emphasized protection from God's wrath as the consequence of sustained good behaviour. Those who ignored such advice, he advised, 'provoked God to fill the world with terrible disasters'.[3] Augustine himself viewed mankind as fallen and intensely in need of the redemptive power of God. Men were what Diarmaid MacCulloch, borrowing from Augustine, has called 'lumps of perdition or lostness'.[4]

Inquisitions and Embryo Machineries of Censorship

Heresy loomed larger in the medieval world than blasphemy (which was obviously seen as a component part of it), with the result that the medieval crime of heresy has thus contributed much to our modern conception of censorship and to the authoritarian control of opinion. Heretics were dissidents who stimulated in the orthodox the urge to both convert and control.

As a result of this, the heretic became a category of person that spawned a whole industry of countermeasures. The religious order of Dominicans became especially notable in their involvement in the detection and eradication of heresy. It was this order who supplied much of the personnel for the growth of one of the most famous religious institutions to have developed in the Middle Ages: the

Inquisition. The Inquisition initially evolved in localities (in the first instance in southern France) to combat the heretical Cathars and Waldensians. In later years the inquisitions became much more regularized and institutionalized, having previously had much more autonomy and operated under the names of their regions. Although initially active in France, inquisitions spread to Spain and Portugal, while a number of Italian regions and city states also had their own tribunals of the Inquisition. It was the Spanish Inquisition, and its inquisitor Tomás de Torquemada (1420–1498), that would make the institution both famous and infamous by the mid-sixteenth century.

The popularly distorted image of the Inquisition is one of reckless torture and cruelty without limits. However, even those involved in its work – driven by zeal and the urge to undertake God's work on earth – found the institution's actual value limited. It is the excesses that have hit the historical headlines and, as is most readily the case, may more obviously reflect the actions of individuals than the logic of a whole institution. While not distracting from the murderous cruelty it inflicted, we should complete our image by visualizing learned and earnest churchmen engaged in careful and detailed questioning. The most important part of this picture is to imagine a team of scribes taking copious notes of everything witnesses told them. At some point, the penny dropped for some far-sighted official within the Inquisition about the potential within what they were doing. Collecting, transcribing, cataloguing and cross-referencing this information would prove crucial to the task of the inquisitions, and eventually became the most effective method of furthering its ends. Essentially, time and again, these painstaking forensic examinations of information were more effective than any methods of torture.

Through the skilful use of this tool, officials in the various inquisitions of the age were able to build up pictures of heretical sects, and to link together groups from the same region and area. Sometimes they would be able to find links across regional and even national borders. The power of cataloguing and organizing this information also allowed for discerning connections across natural geographic and topographic barriers and inhospitable terrain. This was very much the case with the Cathar heresy which, by its very nature could otherwise avoid unwanted attention.

The Cathars of the thirteenth century were frequently itinerant, and their beliefs fitted in with their roving lifestyle. They, like some other heretics of the time, knew the mountainous areas that in medieval times often marked the borders between regions. They used this knowledge to hide when they needed to, sometimes helped by sympathetic locals.[5] Following, tracking and apprehending such people proved troublesome, unless records and procedures could be developed which addressed the problems for the maintenance of orthodoxy that these people raised.[6]

In its way, the innovative collating of testimonies simultan-eously invented cultures of information science, of surveillance and of sophisticated espionage. The wealth of this information also enabled those handling it to develop theories about how the blas-phemer was different to the heretic. Very quickly, it was recognized that the blasphemer was largely a hot-headed individual who spoke before they thought – an understanding that was clearly informed by probably the most influential theologian of the period, Thomas Aquinas (1225–1274). The punishment of those convicted of the crime so often reflected this, having a strongly penitential element attached to it. For example, blasphemers would be made to stand bound with ropes before the church door, with more severe punishments for repeat offenders. Others were made to wear distinctive cloth-ing that carried a shame element with it, such as a white sheet.[7] In many such rituals large candles were carried by the penitent blasphemer. Although these were psychologically an assault upon the individual, they often fulfilled their function handsomely, since capital punishment was rare.

Blasphemy in Everyday Life

But blasphemy in private in the medieval world may actually have been a significant threat which has left little evidence. The break between the Eastern and Western churches was to have a profound impact upon how blasphemy would be experienced by their respective populations – even continuing as late as the nineteenth century. In the East, the prohibition of 'graven', three-dimensional sculpted images meant that such images of the sacred were largely absent from the Eastern Orthodox world. Instead, the focus of religious devotion fell on two-dimensional painted icons, and it largely remains so to this day. The consequences of this are sometimes difficult for the religious in the West to grasp. Icons became an enduring presence within the ordinary lives of Eastern Orthodox populations. They were small pieces of the sacred, much smaller than many of the statues that became sites of devotion in the Christian West. They were portable and probably cheaper to make and construct, making them more likely to be owned and displayed in the homes of the faithful.

Thus, for these populations, a small part of the sacred, even in a material sense, was everywhere and many families found the resources to have an icon in their living space. The sacred gazed down upon families and received their prayers in return. But with the inevitable turbulence of family life they also witnessed fractiousness, arguments and cursing – some of which was blasphemous. Russian central courts in the eighteenth century were frequently dealing with cases in which individuals (a wife, workmates or friends) had been shocked and scandalized by the behaviour of somebody in front of the icon. Drunk and angry men, and occasionally Old Believers who had refused to accept changes in the Russian liturgy, all found themselves in trouble. They cursed and blasphemed in front of these sacred images, damaging the sense of the sacred in particular spaces. Sometimes the irate man even acted physically against the icon, thus scaring and agitating those present still further. Fear and terror would lead them to denounce the miscreant in no uncertain terms, thereby restoring sacred peace to the damaged space. Between 1746 and 1748, a woman from the Ural region was reported for swearing at an icon as she implored it to show her mercy. She was sentenced to death for this offence but eventually died in prison.[8] In St Petersburg in 1751, a soldier who was angry about money owed to him became worked up into a rage, throwing icons on the floor and stamping on them. He eventually was treated more leniently and was instructed to repent in front of the archbishop.[9] There is every reason to believe that these types of situation had been equally common in earlier centuries.

In the West, 'graven' three-dimensional statues had been allowed by the Second Council of Nicaea, and this resulted in the drunk and the undisciplined getting into trouble in much more obviously public ways. Blasphemy in the East was more prevalent within the private sphere, where icons were everywhere. In the West blasphemous mistreatment of statues was obviously more public, and we come across examples of individuals being caught profaning public statues of the Virgin, and other depictions of sacred individuals. This happened particularly in areas of Catholic Europe and the Americas – areas where such devotional sites also attracted the attention of the pro-fane. In many respects, this connection between blasphemy and poor behaviour towards publicly revered religious statues survived in the crime of sacrilege. This offence persisted in most Western codes of law until the end of the nineteenth century. The greater crime of blasphemy does appear in some very early laws in the West. A Danish legal code of 683 outlawed mockery of the Christian God, listing beheading or removal of a hand as punishments. Norway, meanwhile prohibited blasphemy under the first canonical law of 1024.[10]

The 'Blasphemy' of the Jews

The accusation of blasphemy was regularly reached for as a means of defining the position of the Jews, and the attitude of gentile populations toward them. The relationship was profoundly prob-lematic. After all, which other mainstream religion in the West had its founding beliefs defined by the persecution of its earthly founder, instigated by a group that seemed to persist in their denial of his divinity? This group compounded their folly in rejecting him and his message. However, this attitude was not constant throughout the period, and medieval history tells a story of grudging coexist-ence, punctuated with severe outbreaks of inter-religious violence. Sometimes the intolerance grew from a resentment against the prac-tice of money lending or usury, a profitable practice from which Christians were doctrinally excluded – although they could become indebted. Things could take a more sinister turn with allegations that Jewish individuals had indulged in the deliberately blasphemous treatment of Christian objects. Often these were said to have been pawned and in this way to have come into the possession of the Jews. This fed off age-old rumours that prominent Jews kept statues of the Virgin Mary in their latrines, providing ample opportunity for the defilement of sacred Christian images.[11] There were also popular stories that had increasingly linked the Jews to the image of the Christian Devil.

Although such ideas were apocryphal and popular currency, there were also sometimes more obviously official objections to the pres-ence of Jewish communities. These were often about the proximity of

Jewish places of worship, feast days and religious practices to those of Christians. An instance in the Bishopric of Sens in 1205 made Pope Innocent III so annoyed that he considered an oversized synagogue next to a Christian church to constitute blasphemy. He issued a papal bull entitled *Esti Iudeos* (Even the Jews), which stated plainly that the Jews had doomed themselves to eternal servitude through their rejection and punishment of Christ. Communal violence against Jews frequently broke the surface when Christianity entered periods of self-assertion, confidence and aggression. Although some local bishops and rulers would actively seek to protect their Jewish neighbours, they would find themselves hopelessly outnumbered by those seeking retribution. The chief cause of this desire among Christians was the crusading impulse, a devotion which made Christ and his birthplace the centre of piety.[12] This brought to the fore the problematic nature of the Jews and their actions, spawning mobs of the fervent and the enraged who would systematically slaughter the local Jewish population. In this they were sometimes aided and abetted by soldiers passing through on their way to the Holy Land. Occasionally, these people may simply have coveted the goods and provisions owned by wealthy Jews in the community, assets that could aid the march to Jerusalem and its potential conquest. On other occasions, some would claim that they were following an official indulgence that had promised forgiveness of sins as a recompense for murdering Jews.

These massacres had occurred in the context of the First Crusade of 1095 in the western German cities of Speyer, Worms, Mainz, Cologne and Trier. Jews found themselves taunted by Christians who argued that the Jewish God had forsaken them, delivering them into the hands of gentiles. Thus, the Jews were defiantly told that they should convert to Christianity, or face the terrible consequences of their sin – that had already clearly displeased God. In England at York in 1189, just as Richard I departed for the Third Crusade, there seems to be evidence that the justification for anti-Semitism had hardened, and violence was now motivated by a popular belief that the very existence of the Jews constituted blasphemy.[13]

This was to happen again later, elsewhere in Europe, with atrocities committed in Anjou and Poitou in the 1230s. In some respects, these actions also resonated with providential beliefs that Christian populations would continue to hold about blasphemy. Fear of divine retribution would often encourage actions to root out and punish the blasphemous. Sometimes this happened as a form of thanksgiving, in gratitude for a military victory. Likewise, as happened here, some could be encouraged to think such action would give them divine favour as they prepared for battle. In return, Jewish theologians would eventually argue that God would seek a providential vengeance upon those who had massacred the innocent. Their sacrifice in the West might yet overwrite and eclipse that of Christianity's founder.

While such violence was fortunately only episodic, blasphemy was a central component of how Western gentile populations viewed their relationship with the Jews. This race had executed Christ, and committed ongoing blasphemy by denying his status as the son of God and the saviour foretold in the Old Testament. In this they were an affront to assertive Christianity. Sometimes these regularly encountered attitudes spilled over into sustained action by the authorities.

European monarchs made attempts to attack Jewish writings, with the Talmud squarely in the firing line. In 1239, Pope Gregory IX instigated a campaign against this work of Jewish law in an attempt to coerce the Jews into adherence to the Bible. This eventually resulted in a show trial, held in Paris in 1240. The pope enacted this process through letters to local bishops and secular rulers; this was official recognition and endorsement of what had come to be xenophobic beliefs about Jews among Europe's population at large. In the lead-up to 1240, anti-Jewish imagery had begun circulating in Europe which described their hatred of Christians to be so prevalent that the Jewish population had resorted to murdering their gentile neighbours. This took place, the propaganda insisted, alongside the regular mocking blasphemy of Christian beliefs and rites. What brought this into focus were the numerous Jewish converts to Christianity, individuals who carried knowledge of the Jewish sacred texts with them. In embracing their new religion, they frequently came to attack their old one.

The letters instigating prosecution were to be directed through the Bishop of Paris, as the pope recognized that the most important action would be taken in France, following the offer of significant support from the French king Louis IX. Antagonism levelled against the Talmud amounted to 35 separate charges. Due to lack of evidence we can only get the merest glimpse of what these were, but they involved seeing the Talmud as a cynically constructed, man-made substitute for the legitimate law of God. It was thus argued that the Talmud blasphemed against the biblically sanctioned, written Mosaic law. It was also considered to have sections which glorified antisocial and anti-Christian behaviour – such as the breaking of oaths, which made Jews inherently untrustworthy. There were also allegations, here, that the Talmud mocked significant biblical figures, alongside the heinous crime of mocking God, the Virgin and, in particular, Jesus Christ.[14]

Although the Talmud was defended by probably the four leading Jewish scholars of the period resident in France, the tribunal found heavily against it. Eventually, the result was an officially condoned outbreak of book burning around the French capital in 1242. This was an event that consumed a considerable number of copies of the Talmud, among other sacred works.[15] We can take from this incident that attitudes to the Jews were open to sudden lapses in judgement. We can almost hear these assaults on their communities and faith being shaped by Christian exasperation in response to their dogged persistence in error, which in this instance was seen as blasphemy.

Although a dilution of the implications of the 1240 trial occurred under the subsequent pope, Innocent IV, more was to come. In July 1263, in the Spanish court of James I, a leading Jew from Barcelona, Rabbi Moses ben Nahman (commonly known as Nachmanides), found himself summoned to debate the status of the Talmud with a zealous ex-Jewish convert known as Friar Paul. While the previous generation of converts had brought a knowledge of Jewish texts that fuelled attacks on the Talmud, Friar Paul's project was rather more ambitious. Taking the implications of his knowledge of Judaism further he proposed that he had discovered strategies to ensure wholesale Jewish conversion to Christianity, and he actively wanted to try these out in public disputation. Once again, the Talmud came under fire, with attempts to 'Christianize' its contents. The king initially indulged the Dominicans, who had been behind this public disputation, by insisting the Jews be forcibly made to listen to set-piece conversion sermons. However, he quickly relented and allowed them to absent themselves from these ideological assaults, to the immense disappointment of the Dominicans.

As a species of resistance, ben Nahman would later write an account of this disputation in which he would record his alternative interpretation. He even went on the attack, with passages which pointed out the grievous errors of Christianity, and went so far as to argue that he could demonstrate its moral bankruptcy. Far from eradicating Jews from Christendom, the actions of Friar Paul made them construct an enduring, caustic and punchy critique of the faith that wanted to coercively convert them.[16]

The Medieval State and Christian Thinkers Consider Blasphemers and Heretics

As this book has suggested, the medieval Church was preoccupied with heresy, and to a large extent this overshadowed the appearance of blasphemy within this same society. Why precisely was this the case? For a start, heretics such as the Cathars, Bogomils and Waldensians, and the heresy of the Free Spirit, seemed to be organized as alternative, if chaotic, belief systems. They often shunned towns and modelled themselves as alternative communities which sought to build the world anew. This lifestyle stood in contrast to the orthodox path Western Christianity had adopted.[17]

These heretical beliefs were clearly and sincerely held and propagated. Their apparent appeal – and the heretics' desire and ability to convert new followers – also made these errant beliefs a conspicuous threat. Again, this was probably the impetus behind such dramatic State actions as the English statute *De heretico comburendo* (Regarding the Burning of Heretics) of 1401. This was aimed at the Lollards, a heretic group that shared some traits with their continental compatriots. Their title also existed in continental Europe, and may have been a synonym for those who had taken both the functions of priesthood and the interpretation of Scripture upon themselves.[18] *De heretico comburendo* declared that it sought the destruction of this sect, alongside any of their ideas and opinions that threatened the Church or the State. Those who did not instantly turn away from these beliefs after arrest, and having been shown the error of their ways, would be rapidly consigned to the flames. This was not conceived of as punishment nor cruelty, but rather as a justified action against the outpouring of the Devil. As such, heretics were not considered people but tools by which the Devil undertook his evil work.

Heretics and blasphemers were similarly seen as providential threats when the orthodox contemplated the dreadful things that could happen to Christendom if they did not take action. Blasphemy did exist as a separate offence in these times, but prosecuting simple disdain for religion, its doctrines and its sacred figures amid momentary lapses of judgement really meant society was looking for awkward individuals. These were also sometimes behaving in this manner only episodically, such as when drunk, gambling or appearing to be psychologically reckless for some other reason. The 'pure' blasphemer deserved harsh punishment, but they were an isolated individual. It was also very easy to simply consider blasphemy as a component of heresy, since it regularly seemed like an additional offence to be taken into consideration among a whole litany of related charges. In this sense, almost all heretics were blasphemers, but not all blasphemers were considered to be as dangerous to Christendom as heretics were. Many of the latter distorted the message of God, denied that he had created the world, denied the divinity of Christ, the sacred nature of baptism or the validity of the Church hierarchy.

It was through Thomas Aquinas – and the continuing spread of his thought, which became known as Thomism – that greater attention would fall on articulating what the late medieval West would think of as blasphemy. In his lengthy, but strangely lucid, *Summa Theologica*, the discussion is couched as a series of answers to obvious questions that the theologically minded might ask. The attitude of those asking the questions displays a desire to be practical and lenient. We really get a sense, here, of thinkers trying to unpick the difference between heresy and blasphemy. The questioners generally concluded that blasphemy was less of an obvious threat, but Aquinas wanted to warn them against this complacency.

Within the *Summa Theologica* these questions are aired and given quite sharp answers by Aquinas. For the most part they grab the attention of the questioner and persuade them that blasphemy is more important and worthy of punishment than they realize. The questioner had presumed that blasphemy was a species of lesser (venial) sin. They also noted, far-sightedly, that it might be unreasonable for a mortal sin to be committed suddenly and on the spur of the moment. Aquinas refuted this by saying the blasphemer denied the goodness of God, cutting themselves off from His grace. Both the act and the speech denied this goodness, making it a more serious mortal sin. Likewise, excusing the individual because their transgression occurred on the spur of the moment was the equivalent of excusing someone who had, in a fit of anger, recklessly reached out to kill the person next to them.

In the part of the *Summa* concerned with the subject of murder, the questioner asked Aquinas whether blasphemy should pale into insignificance beside the premeditated taking of life. As a sin, Aquinas saw blasphemy as more heinous than murder because it targeted God rather than another human being. However, this rather opened the door to the idea of an oversensitive deity whose hurt feelings needed regular and strenuously enacted vengeance. This seemed to undervalue the power of God, suggesting He needed a regular coterie of followers actively looking out for opportunities to avenge his honour. Aquinas had to do some nifty footwork to straighten this particular problem out. His conclusion was that we judge the two crimes by the harm done. Echoing his conclusion about the sudden impulse to murder, Aquinas argued that blasphemy's intention to harm God's honour was a greater crime. This was so even if an all-powerful God was not harmed by its impact as much as an unfortunate victim of murder. This explained why punishment should be more draconian for murder, even though Aquinas had said it was a lesser crime than blasphemy.[19]

In part, the views expressed by Aquinas explain much about how the crime of blasphemy was treated by authorities charged with punishing people they had convicted of this crime. We can find a quite staggering array of possible and actual punishments. At first sight, this variety looks strange and difficult to comprehend. This is until we remember that Aquinas has effectively told Christendom that it was a crime we should not tolerate and not let miscreants get away with, albeit that some infractions were obviously more serious than others. We can almost imagine medieval lawyers and theologians driven to highly subjective judgements about what precisely should happen to these people. This 'really serious/not quite so serious' double life of the offence explains the sheer variety of things society decided to do with those convicted.

Certainly, various societies wanted to portray to the populace at large the evil that the individual had perpetrated. This was quite obviously to punish and make an example of such individuals. The public nature of punishment also addressed the fear of providential judgement from God that actively stalked the consciences of even the innocent. Criminal blasphemy in thirteenth-century France, for example, displays this quite obviously. Such laws emanate from a statute enacted by King Louis ix after he had returned from crusade. The king wanted his kingdom purged of those who might bring down God's displeasure, and removing them also served as a method of celebrating his own religious zeal and expressing gratitude for having survived a crusade and the arduous journey back.[20] This again highlights the providential nature of how these laws were framed.

Thus, throughout Europe, we find blasphemers regularly branded on the face. Sometimes they would have their upper lip mutilated, or in some manner stapled with one of a variety of implements. Others would find their power to blaspheme further curbed by having their tongue removed, or bored through with metal objects. The papacy of Pius v codified such actions against blasphemers, and early sixteenth-century Dutch courts regularly dispensed such punishments, as did the Spanish. Physical mutilation was a feature of punishment regimes in German states and was also used in England against some high-profile blasphemers, notably the Quaker James Nayler.[21] Obviously, such punishments symbolically and practically curbed the power to further speak blasphemy. Banishment was of course another effective method of obvious punishment that made an example and profoundly appealed to the providentially minded – the blasphemer was simultaneously removed from sight, locality and memory.

In some countries we find more exotic choices of punishment, ones largely centred around the phenomenon of shame. For example, shame appeared in the decision taken at the Second Council of Ravenna in 1311, which excluded first offenders from the church for a month. The punishment escalated dramatically for second offenders who were to be denied Christian burial.[22] The pillory was ubiquitous in punishment regimes at this juncture, and the early modern period would prove to be the high tide of shame punishment for blasphemy.

Blasphemy as Expedient Political Crime –
The Case of the Knights Templar

The political value of blasphemy, in among other accusations, was evident in several instances in the medieval period. The most notable of these was its role in the persecution and dissolution of the Knights Templar. Originally comprised of warrior monks, by the mid-twelfth century these warriors constituted only a fraction of the Order, and it was widely despised in the West. The Knights Templar seemed inexplicably rich and almost superfluous once crusading zeal and opportunity had largely vanished from Europe. Once reclaiming the Holy Land had disappeared as both a practical possibility and an aspiration, the material and spiritual infrastructure that supported the crusades looked archaic.

By the start of the fourteenth century, this Europe-wide order was way beyond living on borrowed time. Unfortunately, their closeted and cosseted world would scarcely allow them to see the oncoming deluge that would engulf them. The Order's epicentre was France, and the French king Philip IV stealthily moved against the Order one dawn in October 1307, in a manner akin to a modern political purge. The hierarchy and rank and file of the order were swiftly arrested, together with their servants. Their substantial property was also covetously confiscated in a frenzy of activity that would eventually pay off handsomely for the French monarchy. King Philip himself was so desperate for money that even unbiased foreign contemporaries believed acting against the Templars was a cynical act intended to enrich the French king. Getting his hands on their wealth involved choosing the right tool to ensure the pope had no choice but to permit the destruction of the Templars. Unwittingly, a scared papacy had provided this in its independent commission given to the French monarchy to stamp out the Cathar heresy a century earlier, but within six weeks the first supportive papal bull was issued.

King Philip was acting on something outrageous and compelling that he had alluded to in conversations with the pope about the initiation rites of the Templars. Philip had strategically placed a number of spies within the Order and what they were telling him was potentially explosive. The initiation rites of the Order, from these stories, involved new initiates denying Christ as their saviour and they were then instructed to spit upon the crucifix. This was followed by total submission to the senior initiator which involved kissing him on the mouth or his intimate parts. Beyond this, regular mention was made of members of the Order worshipping a cat-like creature.

For quite a while, historians believed that these charges were simply politically expedient, and that the confessions of leading Templars had been extracted under torture. More modern opinion has speculated that such confessions reflect a mix of poor behaviour and a genuine initiation right which had been misconstrued.[23] Thus the confession of the Order's Grand Master, Jacques de Molay, that he had blasphemously denied Christ – not in his thoughts but only in his speech – actually signified something different.[24] Rather than blasphemy, it reflected Templar preparedness for the privations of faith that would befall them if they were captured, tortured and imprisoned by their Muslim enemies. The Templar Order was also caught in the middle of the struggle between the pope and the French king. While the pope, wary of Church wealth falling into secular hands, had initially sought to defend them, he eventually had no choice but to give way to pressure from King Philip.

Eventually, 54 Templars were burnt as heretics in 1310, and the final act occurred on 18 March 1314 when Jacques de Molay and three others renounced all their confessions of wrongdoing and accepted their fate as relapsed heretics. That same evening, they were burnt at the stake on Ile aux Juifs. Allegedly, de Molay cursed those who had conspired to bring about his end, fuelling providential speculation about the supernatural power the Order had access to. Certainly the Templars themselves have spawned a wealth of conspiracy literature. They have also maintained their mystique long enough to appear in adventure video games, such as Assassin's Creed, into the new millennium.

This incident, like blasphemy accusations against the Jews, shows some familiar patterns. While actions and beliefs could be portrayed as blasphemous, they more frequently than not erupted into incidents where there were other potent incentives. Politics, greed, fear and highly strained situations played their part in bringing Jews, Templars and heretics into the role of scapegoat. Whether justified or not, what is crucial here is the power of blasphemy as an accusation among others to generate a tide of fear and hatred against the perpetrator.

'Crusading' against Blasphemers in Europe

While the Templars had been the victims of greed and of suspicion about their secret practices, they were also victims of the waning of enthusiasm for crusading and jealous hostility concerning their wealth and riches. Crusading zeal did not wholly disappear, and where once the pious might have taken up arms, some other opportunities came their way in the later Middle Ages. Staying at home meant the search for purpose, piety, glory and status would have to be conducted on an individual's own doorstep.

Much of this explains the rise of the religious confraternity. These were local (but also sometimes transnational) organizations of dedicated laymen (and very occasionally women) who took on a mild form of crusading-style secular vocation. This was intended to help specific groups or individuals within the local community.[25] It was a product of laymen's desire to be involved in spiritual activism, something that was a product of the mid-thirteenth century's collective approach to worship. Some groups even grew in pious stature as a result, seeing themselves as guardians of morality and virtue, even ambitiously reproaching priests for sinful and poor behaviour.[26] The help they offered was largely spiritual, and individual Orders targeted specific groups. Some looked after pilgrims or dispensed alms to the moral and deserving poor; others administered religious comfort to criminals facing capital punishment – even encouraging them to equate their suffering with Christ's.

Again, many Dominicans were involved in founding these groups, and they sought to bring the Gospel to the populace at large, wanting to save them from sin. In doing so, many confraternities turned to religious music to educate and enlighten the populace with edifying themes, many related to the devotion of the Virgin Mary. Others developed an elaborate taste for dramatic productions which were staged for audiences on feast days, and especially in Holy Week.

Beyond providing such entertainments, these confraternities also had a sense of mission, and this seems to have stemmed from a significant urge to foreground the idea of penitence. One group, the *laudesi*, concentrated on praise and devotion; while another, the *disciplinati*, believed self-flagellation was the essential road to penitence. We start to see both of these groups from the middle of the thirteenth century in Italian cities such as Florence, Verona and

Siena. As time drew on, the *disciplinati* predominated and their particular route to penitence spawned action against spiritual indiscipline. When these groups penetrated the dark interior of religious beliefs among the population at large they found alarming levels of unorthodox and dangerous practices. Some later confraternities display something of a stark change in attitude to the poor, seeing them as a menace rather than people deserving of compassion and charity. This began in the fifteenth century when some, such as the Company of the Holy Cross, founded in Bologna in 1450, began to work alongside the Inquisition to enforce religious conformity.

Although the Inquisition was an ecclesiastical institution, one change that arrived in the later period was a growing sense that the State should be involved. Although this was obviously a part of rulers seeking to extend their own power while ensuring limits on ecclesiastical power, it is interesting that the crime of blasphemy was an area where this was obvious. Perhaps it is not difficult to see why: blasphemers, like witches two centuries later, were isolated individuals who could be moved against easily. Often, these individuals were spectacularly unpopular within their own community and action against them was biblically sanctioned. This permitted the act of protecting the community against the providential judgement of God. This period was especially prone to such providential reactions, as was evidenced by the outbreak of monastic public self-flagellation during the 1260s. The displays fulfilled a need to imitate the suffering of Christ in order to appease an angry God who had visited heretics and other evils upon the community.

But there could also be something else involved when individual cities decided to take action against the blasphemer. For example, in the Italian city of Orvieto in the 1260s, and slightly later in some German cities, the municipality began to exact heavy fines from blasphemers. A somewhat new justification for this was the presumption that blasphemy damaged God and such damage to the sacred had the power to damage solemn oaths, contracts and agreements made by individuals on earth. For these burgeoning city states, for whom trade was starting to become important, this meant the blasphemer was now a threat to earthly prosperity as well as to the wider God-fearing populace and their relationship with the creator.

This shows the very first signs of Western states wanting to involve themselves in the disciplining of those they had jurisdiction over. This meant they were coming to have a sense of the modern conception of the public peace and what would eventually come to be referred to as the commonwealth. Although so often written as a single word, it is worth splitting this compound noun into its component parts: wealth was the desire, and its pursuit was part of the common good that would enable and enrich all. Blasphemers, through their recklessness, challenged this on earth and in the hereafter. Such ideas were to be profoundly important in shaping how states were to mature and make themselves manifestly more deserving of God's favour. These ideas grew still greater in importance when two warring sides pitched their piety and ideological purity against each other in the long, drawn-out struggle of the Reformation. Such battles took place between nations, between cities, between individuals and even between the righteous and sinful parts within individuals. Discipline was to become the key weapon in this battle, and accusations of blasphemy – and the crime itself – would come to have a key role in the struggles.

THREE

BLASPHEMY AND THE REFORMATION

If blasphemy was overshadowed in the medieval period by the concept of heresy, everything began to change at the end of the fourteenth century. Tales of the heretical blasphemer stopped in their tracks by the vengeance of God had been quite prevalent in medieval times. One woman, for example, blasphemed the memory of a local saint in thirteenth-century Orvieto. She suffered an injury upon her mouth that was only alleviated by a contrite and penitential visit to the saint's tomb.[1] It is sometimes argued that the Reformation discovered the need to Christianize the lower orders, while the medieval period had been content to accept a gulf between the pious elites and the superstitious peasantry. Blasphemy's long history, stretching back long before this date, suggests a concern with policing populations and their morality had existed sporadically before the late medieval period.

Nonetheless, it is precisely at this time that an important distinction began to be drawn. Previously, the heretic had always been an individual who had been led into error either through their own thought or the actions and preaching of others. Heresy was a thing to eradicate, and the machinery of punishment associated with this was intent upon restoring the heretic to orthodoxy – even if this could only be achieved through their violent and very public death. Frequently, secular and ecclesiastical authorities would distance themselves from unofficial summary justice in this area, offering physical protection to individuals accused of heresy who would otherwise have suffered considerable violence at the hands of the local populace.[2] The Inquisition's ideal of systematizing examination was concerned with rooting out error as much as evil, and its deployment of sophisticated procedures is often seen as a milestone in the coming of a bureaucratic institutional apparatus to early modern Europe.[3]

Blasphemy and the Reformation

The Reformation really did insist upon conformity and orthodoxy. This was even true when age-old practices were altered. Leading up to the Reformation, many advanced religious thinkers had revisited the squabble over images that had occurred at the Second Council of Nicaea. Many concluded that images, whether two- or three-dimensional, were unacceptable, and a low-level campaign of iconoclasm commenced in many Western countries. We can see evidence of this in some surviving church defacement in England and Scotland, where traces remain today of the faces of saints on rood screens having been deliberately obliterated. This was to become a wholesale movement in Western Europe. This iconoclasm became a clear part of Calvinist doctrine, leading to the sudden disappearance of objects that had previously been highly venerated. A further part of the culture of militant Calvinism was to persuade people of the necessity of policing behaviour, because all humanity was in supreme danger of the dark power of sin – something Calvin called 'our miserable condition'.[4] Thus, it was imperative to persuade individuals and communities to police themselves. The Reformation, both north and south of the Alps – that is, both in the areas where it was embraced and those where it was not – represents a point of ambivalence for interpretations of blasphemy and its history. Some historians emphasize the upheaval of the Reformation as effecting a decisive break in the relationship between religious populations and perceptions of the Christian God.

What we should note here is the capacity shown by both secular and religious authorities to conceive of the blasphemer as somehow fundamentally alien, and to treat them accordingly. Where the imperative with the heretic was to rehabilitate them and return them to the community (after a fashion), priorities around the blasphemer became somewhat different. The blasphemer was now frequently characterized as an outsider and a dangerous individual intent on undermining the sacred beliefs of others, and creating the evils of discord and instability. In choosing their wayward actions, blasphemers seemed intent upon placing themselves outside of society and were thus a danger to it. Often they were not characterized as victims led astray, but instead as wilful individuals who arrogantly claimed authority and jurisdiction through their actions or pronouncements. These they would use to terrorize the society that had been foolish enough to tolerate them. They seemed to be people who had chosen their own fate, as they invariably appeared to scoff at authority, and in indulging such behaviour they presented an attitude problem that heretics did not have.

It was noted that blasphemy could be a product of anger, so that many theologians hoped to control the emotions that so affected the minds of susceptible individuals. Some rationalized blasphemous outbursts as thoughtlessness and produced manuals to warn against this. Examples include *De agnoscendis* (1572), written by an individual named Albertino, and the sixteenth-century *Irae malum*, which used pictures to depict towers, buildings and the whole infrastructure of society falling to the ground. Both of these texts circulated in colonial Mexico and other New World territories ruled by Habsburg Spain.[5] More seriously, others considered mortal souls to be in peril, believing that reckless speech constituted a sign of a person being predisposed to heresy.[6] We should remember that anger controlled, muted or hidden would be very unlikely to leave a trace in the historical record. Given this, we are also far more likely to hear of anger appearing unchecked by self-control or by works aiming to promote temperance.

This element of choice was further emphasized, especially in the early modern era, since many accused of blasphemy were those who exhibited economically and socially marginal lifestyles. Some of these were associated with particular occupational groups – French and Flemish evidence suggests sailors and soldiers were especially guilty here. In 1632, for example, the pastors administering to the navy in Ostend lamented that blasphemous speech was almost endemic in any communication that their flock undertook with their fellows or with authority. Some even claimed that serving naval officers used blasphemous talk as a tool to inspire fear and thus paid diligent attention to the behaviour of those serving under them on board ship. Such individuals were a captive audience at the mercy of these officers, as well as the potentially imminent presence of the Almighty's displeasure.[7] Some reached this situation from a more ideologically motivated position, exhibiting libertine and alternative lifestyles that could be construed as a direct consequence of their blasphemous opinions – dangerous ideas that disdained moral authority. This marginalization implies to us, as historians, that frequently the blasphemer was made uncivilized by their society's accumulating response to their social and intellectual choices.

This seems to explain the sixteenth- and seventeenth-century enthusiasm for statutes governing religious behaviour, and the quest for tighter discipline that appeared after the Council of Trent (1545– 63) kick-started the Counter Reformation in the Catholic world. It is important to note that the order to prosecute in the Holy Office contained investigation into the piety, learning and observance of those imprisoned by the Toledo Inquisition during the sixteenth century. This was common to the machinery of investigation used by the Inquisition throughout Southern Europe and constitutes evidence that the authorities felt the need to monitor behavioural propriety and lapses among the populace at large. This process of intensified Christianization gathered pace after 1650. The subsequent success of post-Tridentine Spanish Catholicism in establishing reli-gious knowledge among the populace of the empire was a road to individuals establishing a self-discipline similar to that craved by Calvinists and Reformers. It is easy to forget that the Reformation also effectively happened within Catholicism, and historians such as Diarmaid MacCulloch even suggest Catholicism emerged as far more reformed than the Church of England: 'seriousness', he argues, replaced a relaxed 'worldliness', and the instrument of this, the Council of Trent, went much further in establishing special-ist training of its clergy than would happen further north in the Protestant world.[8]

Tavern and Gambling-den Blasphemy – Playing with Providence

Blasphemy also emerged in early-modern popular culture as a com-ponent of strong feelings around gambling, bravado, intense physical and emotional trial and around intoxication. In 1597, in colonial Mexico, an individual named Diego Flores had lost a lot of money gambling. He lashed out verbally and was accused of blasphemy since he had accused God of deliberately pouring disfavour upon him. This effectively argued God was capricious, without reason and was subject to human emotions. Flores took this as a sign to disappear, and the State began hunting him in earnest, although he was never seen again.[9] In 1654, in colonial America, an individual named Benjamin Saucer actually found himself on trial for his life after he drunkenly denied God's existence. Despite the extremity of Puritan sensibilities in this case, the authorities eventually drew back from pronouncing a capital sentence upon him.[10]

The phenomenon of blasphemy could never be wholly eradicated because it clearly existed wherever profane life existed. In this respect, its status as an offence against individuals, sensibilities and society bears comparison with the offence of witchcraft, where the practices and behaviours that constituted the offence could not be wholly expunged from society, persisting as a low-level subculture of using charms, amulets and mild incantations. The historian of early modern popular culture Keith Thomas may have seen the gradual eclipse of 'magic' as evidence of long-term modernization, but it was equally clear that this eclipse was neither absolute nor immediate.[11]

Whether criminal or not, both blasphemy and witchcraft were schemes of behaviour which cultural, legal and social authorities found to be both stubborn and anathema. The actions these authorities took toward putting an end to such practices – and their real and imaginary threats – were comparatively ineffective. The punishment of blasphemy by the State was used from the earliest days of the Church as an exceptionally vivid instrument of authoritarian violence, before early modern concepts and regimes of discipline appear. Blasphemy's link to religion, and the assertion that religion underpinned the State, provided justification for this violence.

The combination of the Renaissance and the Reformation brought two new categories of knowledge and its consumption. The Renaissance brought a renewed interest in the nature of humankind and its aspirations, both secular and spiritual. This inevitably produced speculation about the previously accepted ways and ideas of the older world. The Reformation, with its confessional split, created new attitudes to older religions, as well as rejuvenating older attitudes to religious deviance.

New Heresies, New Blasphemies

Although some of these changes were innovations, some older theological positions still existed, albeit in new guises, and the denial of Christ's divinity, and the related denial of the Trinity, was reappearing in contemporary forms of Arianism.

Once again this group was considered to be anathema and their doctrines were a blasphemy, this time to the population of Reformation Europe. These people were notable and visible through their denial of the Trinitarian-inspired creeds of all conventional churches. Antitrinitarian views like those in Arianism persisted into succeeding centuries, where they would re-emerge first as Socinianism, and subsequently as Unitarianism (a movement initiated in Eastern Europe). The access these groups had to new printing technologies was an important development: preaching was no longer the sole means by which ideas would circulate around Europe. This was a clear advantage to religious reformists. To the religious conservatives it was a dangerous development, since reading an offensive passage made the ideas linger in the mind, and would likewise resonate with those shocked by them, as the materials were read and reread. Exposure to printed words happened in private, beyond a simple event or public occasion where opinions might be heard.

This was also the great age in which the very idea of the State grew in sophistication, probably at its fastest. Certainly expectations of what the State could do and achieve began to accelerate dramatically. It became something which passed and enforced laws as well as ensuring the public peace. One especially quick route to achieving the latter was to prevent religious discord, and instead assert the necessity of everyone within the community subscribing to one denomination of Christian belief. This was not so much a war upon dissidence for its own sake, but rather pointed to how far religion itself had been identified with both the providential and, increasingly, the day-to-day security of the community and State.

The Reformation also created problems for populations who sometimes had their previous beliefs questioned, altered and replaced before their very eyes. In flexing its muscles, the Christian State appears to have needed procedures and tools of enforcement, and blasphemy laws appear to have been recognized as a means that had almost been ignored, but which once again came into its own. Suppressing this crime became an important method that communities and local governors reached for to solve these problems of discord. Christianity, at least in the West, had striven to be relatively homogeneous before this and, indeed, the thrust and tenor of several ages of campaigning against heresy was bent upon protecting this status. In contrast, the Reformation produced actual lasting splits, which set religious doctrines and states in opposition to one another. The strength of religious doctrine and recent preoccupations would appear as the most determining factors when deciding whether new forms of authority would chase after blasphemers, heretics or witches – sometimes apprehending all three.

It had been easy enough, as we have seen in the previous chapter, to identify heresy – especially when those identifying it could readily consider themselves to be the 'orthodox' Church. This situation was complicated when what became the orthodox Church in a given city had broken away from Rome. It was easy enough to consider this orthodox Church within your city to be the True Church – an ideal that Roman churches had readily perverted and disgraced by their corruption and poor behaviour. However, what should one now call one's distrusted and despised opponents, especially when they had multiplied into so many different forms?

This difficult problem had initially confronted Martin Luther. He had already faced accusations of heresy for his dissent from the practice of selling indulgences, among other trappings of Rome. Luther himself actually grasped at the idea of blasphemy as the accusation with which to dismiss the claims of Catholicism and the practices that he was condemning. This was effective because Luther had rejected aspects of Catholic doctrine, such as the status of the pope and the Catholic interpretation of the sacraments. As such, his accusation of blasphemy made the Catholic actions look irreverent and mocking of what humankind's response to God really should be. In using this accusation, Luther made Catholic doctrine and practices appear distasteful and motivated by false, artificial and patently evil feelings and emotions.

Blasphemy as an accusation also cleverly made the accusers into the orthodox – people who had witnessed and lived through their true religion being mocked by the actions of another, irrespective of its claims to what seemed a spurious antiquity. In Luther's famous

Ninety-five Theses – nailed to the Wittenberg All Saints' Church door in 1517 – number 79 expressly identified Catholic practices with blasphemy. It declared, 'To say that the cross, emblazoned with the papal arms, which is set up [by the preachers of indulgences], is of equal worth with the Cross of Christ, is blasphemy.'

But when we look deeper we can also see that Luther himself increasingly equated religious peace with the tranquillity of the State. He began to use the accusation of blasphemy as a means of creating vilifying descriptions of opponents, doctrines he did not like and even lapsed or infrequent religious practice among otherwise like-minded Lutherans. In some respects, blasphemy came to resemble a catch-all term for people whose ideas and works represented a fundamental challenge to peace and stability. One of Luther's indictments of the Jews argued that they must be driven out, lest they infect good Christians – incurring God's wrath on the latter and their damnation alongside the Jews. Such views began to give blasphemy much greater dynamism and purchase than ever before in the minds of the rulers and ruled alike of Reformation Europe.

Such an intensification was not surprising, since religious dissidents of the age seemingly instinctively took on a political dimension. This was especially obvious in the case of the Anabaptists, a group who came to be seen as the dangerous religious fifth-column pariahs of their age. This rebellious sect believed in adult blasphemy and asserted that infant baptism was an evil foisted upon Christians by overmighty churches and their disciplinary regimes. This collection of people was scattered among the population of Western Europe, much as Cathars and Waldensians had been. But what was different this time was just how rapidly the widespread group became a dangerous movement of religious dissidents with thoroughly political overtones.

In addition to their beliefs about baptism, Anabaptists stood up to authority in many other ways. They instinctively despised the State and saw it as unnecessarily coercive and oppressive. Their opposition materialized in a refusal to accept or administer oaths between individuals or oaths of loyalty to the State. This placed them outside a civil society that was growing in sophistication, something which itself relied upon such forms of expression and goodwill to bind people together. Apparent disloyalty to the State also manifested as the refusal to undertake military service of any kind, supposedly in the name of conscience. This was expressed as an avowed pacifism, going further into a denial of the morality of capital punishment. The Anabaptists despised all officialdom and refused to pay for the upkeep of any institutions involved in the maintenance of civil society. They were seen as a menace to the mind, conscience and sensibility of the orthodox. However, matters reached a particularly dangerous point when Anabaptists decided to take control of the German city of Münster, in what was effectively a *coup d'état*. They set up their own 'king', John of Leyden, who thereafter exhibited licentious and eccentric behaviour until his rule was brought to a violent end. Münster was besieged and eventually captured, with considerable loss of life.[12] The surviving Anabaptists were executed, and their name thereafter tainted as dangerous and feared pariahs.

Although Catholics had seen the Anabaptists as just another group of heretics, the Protestant world much preferred to see their precise actions as blasphemous. They effectively drove Luther from being an advocate of religious toleration to argue strongly for un-deservedly harsh treatment for them. In 1530, after another challenge to authority in the shape of the so-called Knights' War, Luther came out in support of the death penalty for Anabaptists, since they wilfully chose to disregard beliefs that were otherwise cherished by all good Christians. Immediately this was an instance in which challenges to good religious order were characterized as blasphemy. Luther was to extend this logic further in 1536 by signing a document, alongside other theologians, which affirmed the duty of civil authority to root out and punish blasphemy. This was the culmination of the offence's increasingly ubiquitous and powerful nature during this period.

The statement did not exhaust Luther's thoughts on the matter, and blasphemy gradually became something of an obsession with him. As his religious tolerance came under strain and gradually deserted him, the offence of blasphemy became something which would be wheeled out against opponents of all shapes and sizes. Although, like Catholics before him, he viewed Jews as blasphem-ers, his thinking almost represented a revisiting of erratic medieval behaviour patterns towards this significant minority. Variously, he candidly called them 'a brood of vipers', quoting Matthew's Gospel, 'blind and senseless people' and 'truly stupid fools'. A previously grudging tolerance became replaced in his mind by the urge to tear down synagogues, take action against rabbis and confiscate property.

Ultimately, this was a series of steps that culminated in the desire to exile all Jews from the Christian world.

Again, looked at from the outside, this seems to resemble the piecemeal spontaneous action against Jews undertaken by the over-zealous and brutal crusading fraternity. Yet it perhaps better resembles more modern anti-Semitism and ethnic cleansing. However, it is worth remembering that such incidents were the products of fear and uncertainty as much as of conviction, confidence and bravado. In Luther's case, he readily felt embattled against the Catholics who had labelled him a heretic, against the reformed Calvinist churches further south and the obviously beyond-the-pale Anabaptists and Arians who felt like ideological traitors – evildoers who kept the godly and pious permanently awake at night.

While Luther and the pious might claim that their arguments were biblically sanctioned and demonstrable, the whole religious argument with Anabaptists – and indeed everyone else – stemmed from the fact that all by now had access to the Bible. Translation of the Bible into the vernacular tongue could be held to be the single most important event in European history, and gave a justification both to those clinging to their orthodoxy and those fuelling their dissidence. No genie could be put back into this particular bottle. Such a world created accusations and a much greater visibility for blasphemy. In the end, like other religious reformers who had con-structed godly states that they thought were in the image of God, Luther had no choice but to continue to assert his authority.

Policing Blasphemy – The State's Logic of Control

In England in the first years of the sixteenth century we can see evidence that more conventional heresies were perceived as being challenges to authority. Sometimes the challenge could be quite tell-ing in its implications. Around 1500, one individual named Thomas Keyser, about whom little else is known, rebelled and spoke out after he had been excommunicated by the Archbishop of Canterbury. He declared that although the earthly authority had dealt with him, he had not been excommunicated before God.[13] Moreover, he cleverly turned providential fear on its head by 'proving' that his own corn continued to grow as well as that of those who still enjoyed the apparent favour of the Church. For this blasphemy he was imprisoned, but the sentiments in this case and their meanings are quite striking. Very quickly, Keyser had appealed above the head of the archbishop to invoke his own relationship with God. Over the following century and a half, many would ask precisely who needed the connection to God to be blurred and interrupted by religious hierarchies and spurious declarations of power.

Further proof of this questioning of hierarchies can be found in the considerable variety of laws and statutes that appeared in almost all European countries in the years of the Reformation and the Wars of Religion. These laws simultaneously demonstrate the ability to display authority and the even deeper desire to protect it from challenges – whether these be calculated attacks or merely consequences of indiscipline. In Florence, a statute of 1415 sought to fine those guilty of blasphemy 100 lire, with a sentence of being whipped naked through the municipality of the city if they were unable to pay. By 1532 the fine for a first offence had doubled, with a further doubling for subsequent offences. These punishments were also to include, at the discretion of the authorities, boring through the tongue, a shaming parade mounted on a donkey, exile or service in the galleys of the city state.[14]

The Fifth Lateran Council of 1514 tried to codify and systematize the punishment of blasphemy as a crime by establishing standard punishments and increases for subsequent offences. Beginning with fines and penances, punishment would escalate to shaming individuals outside their place of worship. This was enforced by ensuring they wore a 'cap of infamy', a hat intended to inspire both dislike and ridicule. Severe recidivists could expect a custodial sentence in prison or a ship's galley. The desire to pursue these miscreants is also evident in the provision of very favourable indulgences for those who enforced these laws and prosecuted blasphemers.

When a northern portion of the Netherlands became Calvinist it not only retained the legal provisions of the Spanish Habsburg king Charles v, but made them yet harsher. The year 1518 saw the arrival of an edict against swearing and blasphemy, while a further police edict of 1531 displayed elements of the new religious thinking, removing the Virgin and the saints from the list of the sacred worthy of protection.

The imposition of religious discipline in the army and the fleet was also a striking feature of Dutch provision against blasphemy.

In 1590 a military ordinance showed a sliding scale of punishment for the offence. A first offence demanded three days on bread and water, a second offence was treated much more severely, with boring through the tongue and banishment from the United Provinces.

Venice deserves mention as the only jurisdiction that ever constructed a court solely and exclusively to hear cases of blasphemy. This, in itself, also indicates that this city state saw the extremely dangerous nature of the crime. It is also worth remembering that, since the late medieval period, Venice had regularly seen its financial and commercial success and lavishly wealthy society as a gift from God. For it was surely the Almighty that had placed it at the epicentre of European trade routes to the West and East, just as He had bestowed the considerable riches of the sea upon it. The Venetian blasphemy court, the Esecutori contro la Bestemmia, also readily identified the connection between gambling and blasphemy. From 1539 onwards it was entrusted with controlling gambling in the vicinity of churches, although gaming in other profane space was still permitted. In 1546 these laws saw a Jewish blasphemer condemned to six years' galley service, a sentence which was remitted for the payment of a fine of 600 ducats and five years' exile.[15]

Elsewhere in the Catholic world the Inquisition and its officers continued to exert control over blasphemy and issues surrounding it. They also still regularly sought to distinguish it from heresy. This happened in Spain after the Council of Seville in 1512, which imposed fines and imprisonment upon clerics caught blaspheming, with additional punishments for laymen. However, the discretionary approach to blasphemy that we witnessed in the medieval period continued with Spanish edicts of 1492, 1502, 1512, 1515, 1516 and 1525. In these, both the Spanish State and the Inquisition agreed that they would ignore most drink- and gambling-fuelled low-level blasphemy. These were to be the preoccupation of lesser courts. Instead they would concentrate upon much more serious incidents where important religious doctrines were questioned.

France followed the legislative trend with a considerable number of laws and edicts passed during the sixteenth century. Almost half of all laws against blasphemy in France were enacted between 1510 and 1594, and the sheer frequency of these, and their regular reconfirmation, suggests their intrinsic importance. They were also a further sign that the State was growing in sophistication.[16] More peripheral areas like Norway were comparatively late in seeing an awakening state seek to take control of blasphemy. It was only unification with the ruling power Denmark's new systematized legal code that gave impetus to this initiative in 1687.[17]

Here we have a convergence of a number of separate elements that we have noted already. First, the creation of 'opponents in thought' was a distinct characteristic of these years – the very idea of considering and reacting to other individuals with differing religious views had become a commonplace. With this, the opportunities to blaspheme unwittingly multiplied in the period of adjustment from one version of Christianity to another. The appearance of these accumulating laws also indicates the willingness of the State to flex its muscles in controlling a nuisance. However, the sheer number of these cases perhaps also indicates the limited success of such measures in stamping out this kind of disciplinary infraction. If something needs regular reconfirmation we can be relatively certain that the evil persists. But it may also be true that the lurking connection with providence, and such views of the world, meant that the restatement of such laws was supremely popular. This, in turn, meant that blasphemy strangely came to be seen as a cultural norm in societies in which religion had become considerably less stable.

While we can easily see how action by the forces of governance, law and order could prove popular in communities at large, this proved to not always be the case. In Spain and Portugal the Jews once again came under suspicion of blasphemy, but this time in an entirely new way. Numerous laws and other forms of pressure were applied to the Jews to make them leave the Iberian Peninsula or instead convert to Christianity. Many prominent Jews decided they were prepared to convert and thus retain their status and property within Iberian societies. These people became known as 'Conversos'. Yet, although they had complied with the demands of their rulers, their actions and their continued presence were far from universally popular. Many gentiles still resented the Conversos' wealth and position and saw their conversion to Christianity as nothing other than cynical expediency, inevitably doubting the sincerity of this new-found faith.

Accusations of blasphemy became immensely useful tools in a low-level religious war of attrition against the converts. Snooping members of the community would regularly denounce their

Conversos neighbours for failing to properly execute prayers and for the inadequacy of the sacred gestures that they must only have learned comparatively recently. In other instances, Conversos were regularly placed under unofficial surveillance to see if they inadvertently, or even secretly, displayed evidence of adherence to their old faith. In this respect, we must realize that a blasphemy accusation was not just about religious observance: it was as much a tool to advance petty grievances as a contemporary accusation of witchcraft was in other places and contexts.

Early modern Switzerland demonstrates especially well how blasphemy had become more important in Protestant countries. The City of Zurich's earliest laws against blasphemy dated from the 1340s, but the Reformation witnessed their sharpening. Laws created in the first quarter of the sixteenth century were effectively gathered together and strengthened in a 'Grand Mandate' of 1530, which grouped blasphemy in among other offences such as drunkenness and other forms of unseemly behaviour. A later legal provision of 1550 produced a fully codified law with a set of instructions for the community at large to follow.

Not only was blasphemy denounced as an offence in itself, but the population was lectured to on the precise nature of an upright Christian life, including clear duties and responsibilities. In observing these, the exercise of piety would supposedly drive dangerous passions and feelings out of the individual. Thus Christians had a duty to perform certain forms of behaviour as much as they had to consciously avoid others. Blasphemy, in these laws, was also to be prevented because it brought adverse providential judgements down upon the community, for example as disease epidemics and famines. The population was to be convinced of this by arguments which repeated the scriptural basis of blasphemy. This reinforced the legitimacy of the regime and confirmed in people's minds that they were living in a prototype godly state, one modelled on the best guidance the Bible had to offer.

Reforming Wicked People

The logical extension of these arguments on providence was to persuade the population that they had a vested interest in upholding and enforcing the law. This was achieved through regular public readings of the statute in churches and other public places. This strongly emphasized the duty of citizens to observe and report what they had seen and heard; and it even enabled them, as individual citizens, to extract fines from the miscreant if they were able.[18] In this manner, both the religious Reformation and the longer-term civilizing 'reformation of manners' were placed in the hands of an actively motivated and empowered populace. Not for the first time, Christianity recruited and made considerable use of its enthusiastic laity.

This points to how Calvinism had a gift for persuading populations to police themselves, and for having individuals know the nature of the sins committed by others – and know the corrosive danger of these transgressions. This is best summed up by the Scottish Confession of 1560, constructed by John Knox. It argues,

> The cause of good works, we confess, is not our free will, but the Spirit of the Lord Jesus, who dwells in our hearts by true faith, brings forth such works as God has prepared for us to walk in. For we most boldly affirm that it is blasphemy to say that Christ Jesus abides in the hearts of those in whom is no spirit of sanctification. Therefore we do not hesitate to affirm that murderers, oppressors, cruel persecutors, adulterers, filthy persons, idolaters, drunkards, thieves, and all workers of iniquity, have neither true faith nor anything of the Spirit of the Lord Jesus, so long as they obstinately continue in wickedness.

Individuals who fortunately escaped this exhaustive list were kept on the straight and narrow by a quite varied pamphlet literature. These small publications told formulaic stories about reckless and arrogant individuals who failed to heed warnings about the evils of blasphemy. The individuals were often, but not always, youthful; and were often, but not always, adolescent men.

The stories varied in detail, but the central thrust generally saw an arrogant individual denounce God, Jesus, the Virgin or the Saints, and thereafter receive the providential judgement of a vengeful God. One such incident, according to a contemporary ballad sheet from around 1600, told of Jasper Coningham from Aberdeen, who declared Christianity a story akin to the tale of Robin Hood.

He was surrounded by flames and died on the spot. Other divine judgements saw the limbs of the sinful struck off or damaged, and the tongues of perjurers turning black. Elsewhere in this literature particular occupations became synonymous with blasphemy and the dangerous public performance of blasphemous acts. A leading example of this was the publication in England of Anthony Painter's *The Blaspheming Caryar* (1613), which drew on well-established stereotypes that carters and other itinerant tradesmen (notably sailors) were especially prone to blasphemy, and that such people should be avoided by the godly and pious. This was another instance of the constructed and dangerous outsider so feared by early modern societies.

But for the general populace, cowed into conformity, all was not necessarily lost. Blasphemy could be contained and controlled by the individual through a sustained struggle to gain sovereignty over their base appetites. This seems to place blasphemy as an errant form of behaviour that the individual can control and cease if wished, making it different from the medieval view of it as a contagion.

This new conception could be used to justify the attempt to instil religious forms of manners and behaviour within religious populations. We can find this happening within Europe by the end of the Middle Ages. In the Netherlands, for example, a section of the Leiden local penal code created in 1440 was used against an unnamed individual who determinedly uttered a blasphemous oath to 'set a new God above God and to honour the Devil'. The city authorities succumbed to providentialism, believing such blasphemy would bring an outbreak of plague in the city, and hurriedly took action against the blasphemer. The man readily confessed his guilt and was fined 60 guilders, with the money diverted to the local poor. However, additional sentencing requirements forced him to embark on religious pilgrimage, and to return with concrete proof that he had reached his destination.[19]

Later the same year, also in Leiden, the authorities took action against an individual named Gerijt Jacobsz, who went by the local alias of 'the hedonist'. From this sobriquet it is clear that he already had quite a reputation for a dissolute lifestyle. It was on one of his drunken binges that he blurted out blasphemous words defaming the honour of both God and the Virgin. The inevitable happened, and after being apprehended he was sentenced to be whipped in the city prison. This was compounded by an especially eye-catching shame punishment that was also often used in Germany: Jacobz was made to walk about with a large barrel around himself. This was made especially public by the requirement that he attend church on Sunday in Leiden with the large barrel distorting the shape and size of his body, no doubt to the amusement of onlookers. It is a shame that we cannot capture the thoughts of the crowd, but with the prevalence of such punishments we can surely guess at them.

Examples abound of how the changed religious atmosphere – as well as the appearance of new doctrines and religious practices – could be equated with blasphemy. These factors provide important evidence of how religious disagreements among the population were mitigated, and how new thinking so often coexisted uneasily with old. In 1526 a roof tiler from Warmond in the Netherlands, just north of Leiden, got into an argument with his employer that eventually landed him in severe trouble. The employer stated that he was disturbed by some of the stories of reformed practice that were coming out of Germany. He declared that these amounted to wholesale abuse of sacred objects. In his reply, the roof tiler demonstrated that he was already more reform-minded. He dissented from his employer's opinion, declaring 'surely what is the sacrament? Is it any more than bread? The very bread we eat at this table is the same.' This might have been a throwaway comment were it not for the fact that the tiler supported his argument by quoting biblical texts.[20] The employer not only had to cope with religious disagreement, but also with the unedifying spectacle of being upbraided by a workman in his employment. Strangely, we might from the outside consider this to be a religious disagreement. But the fact that it ended in a trial for blasphemy indicates how this accusation and crime was used to 'control' people and opinions for a variety of reasons. Certainly upbraiding a superior was also considered an offence and a breach of discipline. Unsurprisingly, a vigorous attempt was made to convert this individual from his views. The tiler was convinced to recant his beliefs and to accept the punishment coming to him. He was sentenced to wear a chalice painted on his front and back for a year. Additionally, he was to stand on the scaffold wearing a woman's skirt, and to penitently carry a one-pound candle all the way to the Pieterskerk in Leiden each time he attended church.

Blasphemy and Piety in Renaissance Florence

Many of the component parts of blasphemy being taken seriously, and the mechanisms of how it was outlawed, detected, policed and punished, touch base with the typical victim and circumstance in the notorious case of the Florentine nobleman Antonio Rinaldeschi. This man had been out one night in the summer of 1501 and had visited a local Florence tavern called the Fig Tree. He had lost money and some clothes in the evening's gambling and, like many before and since, he was deeply irritated by this outcome. However, he did not heed, or perhaps had forgotten, the numerous Renaissance panaceas for calming an angry mind that we read about earlier. This led him into precisely the trouble and woe that their authors had ruefully predicted. Rinaldeschi had already uttered loud profanities against the name of the Virgin Mary upon stumbling out of the tavern, and left all present in no doubt about his reckless state of mind. Such knowledge would have concerned those present and their memory of this would eventually contribute to his undoing.

On his way home Rinaldeschi had cause to go past the church of S. Maria degli Alberighi and, as he did so, he remembered there was a shrine to the Virgin Mary in an alcove outside the church. Urging himself on to actively profane the sacred in revenge for what the latter had done to him, Rinaldeschi picked up a handful of horse dung and flung it at the painted image of the Virgin that oversaw the shrine. In a mixture of sustained anger and boyish sneaking satisfaction he made his escape, conceivably thinking about the rashness of his actions when a hungover head arrived with the new dawn. He may have been unmoved by what he had done, but equally he could have thought the dung would dry out completely and fall to the ground, concealing his reckless actions. However, the dung had somehow formed itself into a crescent shape which clung to the Virgin's crown, particularly unfortunate for Rinaldeschi, but conceivably a literal godsend for the providentially fearful. These fearful people began to make offerings and started to pray at the shrine. They may have experienced both relief and foreboding upon being confronted with this apparent miracle.

In a sense, like pretty well all blasphemers who received the ultimate punishment, Rinaldeschi was the victim of his own egregiously poor timing. Florence had recently experienced considerable political, cultural and religious turmoil. Its autocratic rulers, the Medici family, had been exiled in 1494, and Florence once again became a republic, inspired by the apocalyptic vision of the apparently divinely inspired monk Girolamo Savonarola (1452–1498). His influence brought a new piety to the city, which also involved restoring prohibitions on licentious publications and pictures, and gambling, as well as blasphemy.

The last of these came together, in the case of Rinaldeschi, with the Savonarola-inspired efforts of the populace to establish religious shrines in as many public places as possible and create a new pious environment, one into which the unfortunate Rinaldeschi had drunkenly stumbled. Many Florentines had taken this up and it became a veritable movement which considerably outlived its creator. Eventually Savonarola lost power after refusing to obey a papal summons, similarly falling out of favour with the Florentine government. He was arrested and executed, but the spirit and practices of his popular piety lived on. Several of these facets reveal the Rinaldeschi episode to be a product of its particular context, in particular the enduring religious devotion and popular piety of the community. This may have collided with the reckless selfishness and evil spite of an individual connected to a licentious nobility and known as a 'hedonist'. Such people readily became enemies of the community in the popular mind, and visiting the severest penalties on them would prove a popular measure, capable of both appeasing the populace and restoring the dignity of the dishonoured Virgin.

Rinaldeschi had by now almost certainly hoped his raging and indiscreet actions had remained undetected – or at least that what evidence there was could not identify him as the culprit. Unfortunately for him he had been seen by a small boy, who declared the person involved to be a grown man – something which exonerated the children and adolescent apprentices of the city. The proximity of the event to the tavern, combined with the testimony of witnesses who had heard Rinaldeschi's angry words there, pointed to him as the perpetrator. The circumstantial evidence was linked in the minds of many with his poor reputation and less-than-good name as an outsider. His actual guilt was more or less confirmed by the fact that he had fled to a Franciscan convent outside the city, where he was 'miraculously' found a few days later and apprehended.

Rinaldeschi appears to have entertained a deep fear of how he would be treated after capture, actually attempting to take his own life when he was discovered – though the dagger only penetrated as deep as his ribcage. Wounded and scared, he was brought back to the city and tried before a group of presiding magistrates called the 'Eight for Security'. This tribunal itself demonstrates for us the credentials of some of the institutions that wielded authority, whose emergence was an important feature of this period. The Eight had been created at the end of the fourteenth century, initially to regulate the activities of the Jews. By the end of the succeeding century it had gained far-reaching powers to hear cases. It also pronounced harsh sentences without even naming the crime involved, or mentioning proof, or citing the reason for its decision, or the law or authority that sanctioned its action. As such, these decisions could be arbitrary, representing the will of an elite determined to bring miscreants under the most draconian control possible.

Rinaldeschi was charged with an 'unspeakable' crime, the perpetration of which had been compelled by a supposedly diabolical force within him. The consequences of his act were also portrayed quite visually, with the charge emphasizing how the dung clinging to the Virgin's crown was a deeply felt dishonour. At his examination, Rinaldeschi's fears about his potential fate resurfaced after he rapidly decided to admit everything he was accused of. His admission was followed by a plea for a quick and clean execution, saving him from the ravenous attentions of a providentially aware populace, one that would, he feared, appease their maker by tearing Rinaldeschi limb from limb. Given this almost instantaneous admission of guilt, there was little more for the magistrates to do than to confirm the death sentence and to call for its hasty enactment that same evening.

Certainly the Florentine authorities saw the wisdom of sparing Rinaldeschi from the wrath of the urban population, and agreed to execute him by hanging. They may have been swayed by the fact that some sources identify Rinaldeschi as a nobleman, yet this same factor may equally have caused the authorities to perceive him as still more dangerous, and so to redouble their determination to remove this menace from their midst. This latter motive may have been compounded by the fact that his family were still considered outsiders to the community, having only relatively recently arrived from the Florentine subject town of Prato. Some sources also suggest

Rinaldeschi was a habitually dissolute personality, and that his flight from his crime was severely hampered by the symptoms of syphilis. These rumours point to the dangers of having outsider status, whether real or constructed: as we have noted regularly, populations were less willing to find any sympathy for outsiders accused of blasphemy.

Rinaldeschi scarcely had time to reflect on his crime, his admission of guilt or his impending execution. In the remarkably short time between his conviction and the carrying out of his sentence, he received absolution from a priest. At this point one of the institutions we have met before enters our story. Rinaldeschi was offered the comfort of a Florentine confraternity who tended to the needs of condemned prisoners facing execution: the 'Company of Blacks' (Compagnia dei Neri). This confraternity preserved evidence of what Rinaldeschi had done, which it records as dishonouring the name and image of the Virgin, as well as recording his eventual fate for the crime. The 'Company' escorted the condemned man to the windows of the Bargello Palace, rather than to the conventional place of execution, since it was thought the crowd might interfere with the process if it were performed in a public square. This was expedient, since it was the evening before the important feast day of St Mary Magdalene. At this unusual location, Rinaldeschi was executed and his body left hanging in place until the following afternoon.

The blasphemed image was subsequently cleaned, although the semicircle of dung remained – either in veneration of the miracle, or returning unbidden as a subsequent miracle. This was significant, since it prompted various responses to the outrage, something which also caused the whole Rinaldeschi event to be commemorated in a tableau showing the numerous scenes from his crime, right through to his sentence and punishment. This picture by Filippo Dolciati is still displayed in the Stibbert Museum in Florence, and until very recently was displayed on every anniversary of the blasphemous event at the shrine where Rinaldeschi's crime against the image of the Virgin had taken place.

The status of images such as the desecrated Virgin or the Dolciati and their (arguably) heightened importance was emphasized sixteen years after the Rinaldeschi case when the provisions of the Lateran Council of 1514 were reconfirmed with extra protection for sacred images and objects. These singled out images of the Virgin and of crucifixes and other artefacts that had presumably been subject to unwelcome attentions from the undisciplined. Considerable fines were to be imposed upon the nobility for such action – too late to save Rinaldeschi, however – with the lower orders receiving the 'cap of infamy' shame punishment while bound in chains. This desire to protect images was also part of a growing sensitivity to the phenomenon of iconoclasm, a tide of which was sweeping the Protestant world north of the Alps.

Iconoclasm and Blasphemy

The problem that iconoclasm represented for the Protestant world was scarcely lost on the Catholic world. The Council of Trent, which concluded in 1563, firmly reiterated this point. Its pronouncements in its 25th session made sure the Catholic world held onto its images and that the priesthood and populace at large recognized their value. This not only reasserted the authority of the Church in terms of what to believe about images, it also showed that the images themselves had a kind of authority – and that reverence was to be shown to them without reservation. Such images existed to

> instruct the faithful diligently in matters relating to intercession and invocation of the saints, the veneration of relics, and the legitimate use of images . . . due honour and veneration is to be given them; not, however, that any divinity or virtue is believed to be in them by reason of which they are to be venerated, or that something is to be asked of them, or that trust is to be placed in images . . . but because the honour which is shown them is referred to the prototypes which they represent, so that by means of the images which we kiss and before which we uncover the head and prostrate ourselves, we adore Christ and venerate the saints whose likeness they bear . . . great profit is derived from all holy images, not only because the people are thereby reminded of the benefits and gifts bestowed on them by Christ, but also because through the saints the miracles of God and salutary examples are set before the eyes of the faithful, so that they may give God thanks for those things, may fashion their own life and conduct in imitation of the saints and be moved to adore and love God and cultivate piety.

However, this declaration also recognized the abuses that had led to the heresies – and even conceivably the religious split – which had made the sixteenth century an era of such religious turmoil. It continues,

> Furthermore, in the invocation of the saints, the vener-
> ation of relics, and the sacred use of images, all superstition
> shall be removed, all filthy quest for gain eliminated, and all
> lasciviousness avoided, so that images shall not be painted
> and adorned with a seductive charm, or the celebration of
> saints and the visitation of relics be perverted by the people
> into boisterous festivities and drunkenness, as if the festivals
> in honour of the saints are to be celebrated with revelry and
> with no sense of decency.[21]

Blasphemy in the Godly States

The other major Protestant religious figure of the age, John Calvin (1509–1564), was equally responsible for cementing a central place for the crime of blasphemy in the history of the Reformation. Calvin had a highly developed sense of the power and value of godly rule, so that the concept of Church and State acting as allies effectively fused into one entity in Calvin's rule over Geneva. We know from the actions of the courts and jurisdictions in the city, and in the outlying areas around it, that blasphemy was taken seriously. Part of this was a real consequence of Calvin's doctrine of predestination, which was almost a modernized (and individualized) recasting of providentialism.

The medieval Catholic world had believed intensely in an imma-nent God dispensing earthly misfortune to the miscreant and the evildoer. This was their just reward and punishment for their pride, arrogance and failure to use their own free will to refrain from sin and instead undertake good works. Calvinist predestination insisted that God had decided already who was to be saved. Maintaining godly behaviour was a support for those unsure of their status as the elect, as was the discharge of their duties to protect the godly commonwealth. Such actions also created a significant gulf between those who upheld the law and those who appeared to break it. Those people who blasphemed became outsiders, as they always had been, but now in something of a new way. They were still enemies of the community and 'enemies of God' (a phrase used by one historian to suggest how witches were viewed in Calvinist Scotland) but there was also something else.[22] In day-to-day dealings these people could be considered to be the reprobates whom God had damned. Occasionally, this also worked instinctively within the mind of the miscreant themselves. So their quest for forgiveness and their acceptance of punishment were both atonement and rehabilitation back into the possibility of election, something that probably still hovered uncertainly in the mind of most Calvinists.

This stern and heavy-handed system of detection and policing was inextricably linked with Calvinism's worldview. Our evidence from Zurich and the surrounding cantons about its universality and effectiveness is actually quite mixed. Certainly we can find quite scrupulous individuals who regularly disciplined their friends, neighbours and family when their talk, or sudden interjections, strayed into dangerous territory. If things got out of hand, or individuals suddenly became frightened by the implications of what they had heard, an individual would readily report them to an authority or disciplinary figure. Equally, we also encounter those who sought to protect their family from the fallout of profanity and blasphemy uttered in the family home. This occurred through the use of a quiet caution, or perhaps through more animated disapproval of unacceptable behaviour from a child, spouse or servant. Although we also get glimpses of these two worlds combining, with an occasional accusation against a prominent individual, this suddenly becomes a part of a wider scrutiny of their behaviour.

Sometimes such surveillance was obviously being used as part of a power struggle or sustained attempt to discredit someone. In such instances, an accusation of blasphemy resumed its political function, albeit sometimes at a range of social levels. Doctors, schoolmasters, bailiffs and military men were all accused in small numbers, dwarfed in comparison to the numbers of artisans who were reported as having committed the crime.[23] Once knowledge of an accusation became public, past instances of unorthodox opinion, throwaway remarks and rash-sounding asides were suddenly and readily recalled and resurrected for the case against. As such, even in a seemingly overwhelmingly godly state and culture, it was still possible for individuals to discover that they had unwittingly developed something of a career as someone holding unorthodox opinions, or exercising levity in the face of the divine.

The difference between public and private utterances no longer held sway for individuals who thought they had a duty (or who harboured less savoury motives) to report what they knew. In Zurich in 1681, a butcher who regularly blasphemed was confronted by his wife, who begged him to stop because she was convinced that 'walls had ears' – there is little doubt that Calvinism wanted the godly State to be a surveillance state. Others would try and police things as best they could, even by attempting to gag a blasphemous speaker or by hurriedly placing their hands over his or her mouth. Some even rounded upon themselves when they considered they had overstepped the mark. One innkeeper from Mettmensen near Zurich was appalled to hear himself crack an inappropriate joke about how local nuns found to be pregnant must have been impregnated by the Holy Spirit, confessing this outburst to leave a trace in the legal written record.[24] Interestingly, this idea of the roaming and unlicensed Holy Spirit – without corporeal form yet a part of God – has always invited imagination and potentially blasphemous speculation. Such lewd and ribald ideas survived long enough to be a sketch in *Monty Python's Life of Brian*. Significantly it was one of the first pieces of the film to end up on the cutting room floor, when lawyers advised the Pythons that it was extremely likely to cause trouble among censorship bodies and the religious at large.

While this was the history of the numerous low-level blasphemy incidents that occupied the courts of Zurich and its environs, in Geneva Calvin himself was drawn into a more obviously high-profile case – a case both famous and infamous, which would ignite the blue touchpaper for State-sponsored blasphemy prosecution in Geneva. The individual concerned was a fellow divine, Michael Servetus, who had been born in Spain at the end of the first decade of the sixteenth century. He was scarcely a conventional theologian, making something of a career as a Renaissance polymath who dabbled in scholarly editing, mathematics, cartography, astrology and even physiology. Some scholars even argue he understood the body's circulatory system up to a century before William Harvey.[25]

Very quickly Servetus caused offence in religious circles through his opinions, which he did not hesitate to put into print. His most famous work, *Concerning the Errors of the Trinity*, was also his first and appeared in 1531. It did what its title simply claimed to do, namely undermined the doctrine of the Trinity. Servetus used a series of withering arguments that left his readers in no doubt about his views. This first publication did the demolition work and was followed by a two-volume piece the following year which again sported a self-explanatory title: *Dialogues on the Trinity*. These latter two works refined the earlier concepts and did some rebuilding of structures left in ruins by the work published a year earlier. Nonetheless, the fundamentals remained and the attack on the Trinity as a religious doctrine remained plain to see, even if attempts had been made to make it more palatable.

In the following years, Servetus further refined his thought and in 1553 eventually published a long and elaborate work entitled *The Restitution of Christianity*. In this he strived to create an all-embracing religious system and offered new interpretations of such ideas as baptism, the Second Coming and the existence of the Antichrist. Few could avoid the realization that Servetus was offering something of a third way that would lead those that might follow him away from both Rome and Geneva. Certainly, those who in more modern times became interested in radical evangelicalism often reached back to consider Servetus as a trailblazer for religious freedom. He also appears to be a forerunner of later Unitarianism, something which often liked to have its past linked both to the humanism of the Renaissance and to religious unorthodoxies that had been persecuted.

It is particularly noteworthy that some more recent commentators have seen in Servetus' writings a clear desire to create a workable and understandable theological system. As one pamphlet from an organization campaigning for toleration suggested, he 'dared to use reason and evidence to counter religious hierarchy and authority'.[26] He has garnered credentials as a forward-looking theologian and hero of radical thought; yet we can readily get a flavour of how his works were conceived of as both blasphemous and heretical by his contemporaries. He saw the doctrine of the Trinity as an out-and-out evil, while the Roman Catholic Mass was an idolatry concocted in imitation of Babylonian pagan rites, thus making it a creation in the service of the Devil.

Such ideas quickly ran into trouble. Luther had abhorred the attacks upon the Trinity and ensured that the works of Servetus were burned in Frankfurt and other towns in Germany. In letters trying to identify Servetus, who was now in hiding in France under an assumed name, Calvin noted in fear and exasperation that the *Restitution* contained

> prodigious blasphemies against God . . . Figure to yourself a rhapsody patched up from the impious ravings of all ages. There is no sort of impiety which this monster has not raked up, as if from the infernal regions.[27]

Soon the attempt by Servetus to live incognito under the name of Villeneuve was uncovered. He was arrested by the Lyon Papal Inquisition in the township of Vienne, where he stood trial with his ideas and opinions being closely scrutinized. At first, Servetus continued the imposture of pretending to be Villeneuve by referring to the author Servetus as if he were a third party. But this deception quickly melted away when contrary evidence was supplied and the Papal Guard intercepted an entire consignment of the *Restitution* en route from the publisher. The game was up and Servetus was imprisoned in Vienne in June 1553. He swiftly escaped, but the trial continued and the papacy sentenced him to a fine of 1,000 livres and to execution by fire, with his books also to be burned. In his absence, he was burned in effigy, in the traditional manner reserved for heretics.

Although Servetus was now a fugitive, it had been made clear by Calvin that, were he foolish enough to wind up in Geneva, the same fate awaited him as he had been sentenced to in Vienne. Some have even argued that it was Calvin who provided the proof against Servetus that eventually turned up. Calvin made no secret of his hostility and indeed was congratulated by the Lutheran theologian Philipp Melanchthon for his efforts to combat 'the horrible blasphemies of the Spaniard.'[28]

Servetus was on his way to apparent safety in Italy but paused at Geneva where Calvin had him arrested and tried. His trial consisted of attempts to demonstrate that his opinions had caused harm, and were infinitely likely to continue to do so – especially through his *Restitution*. This, to modern eyes, seems hard to sustain, since the entire consignment of the book languished in papal hands, with only those involved in prosecution having access to copies. Nonetheless,

Servetus was convicted and the tribunal pronounced the same sentence as the papacy had, although Calvin would thereafter be at pains to stress that he had never intended that Servetus be executed. Thus on 27 October 1553 Servetus was burned at the stake after falling foul of both the orthodox and the reforming churches of his age.

His fate serves as a reminder that, in the construction of the new confessional divide between Catholic, Lutheran and reformed Europe, there were victims, and the method of defining what one believed and came to see as orthodox would frequently use blasphemy as a medium for demarking dissent and anathema. This also indicates that such actions against heretics and blasphemers very often betray the hold certain ideas had on the creation of orthodoxy. It is clear from what happened to Servetus, and the short shrift given to his opinions, that Calvin had seen the Trinity as utterly central to his thinking as both theologian and magistrate. To shake this particular foundation was so easily liable to bring the whole edifice crashing down.

Although this might seem to close this particular narrative, the enduring picture of Servetus created by subsequent generations is quite intriguing. Seeing beyond his status as a religious radical – as some prototype of those persecuted under a religious intolerance that we have now vanquished – reminds us also that even the idea of tolerance as central to modern society has a shelf life and period of fashionability. Nonetheless, what happened to Servetus also displays, again, important elements of the debate about religious authority within the Reformation period, and who precisely was entitled to use it. Servetus was the progenitor of an alternative religious system and established his credentials as a writer and advocate of such views. This gave him a scholarly authority and his eventual role as a martyr has given him an enduring, posthumous presence among the real and imagined campaigners for toleration and religious freedom throughout the globe.

Servetus had the luxury of being merely a writer, albeit one who held contrarian opinions on religious matters. By comparison, Calvin had to ensure both religious and public peace through the strict maintenance of authority. These twin imperatives run like tributaries into the changes wrought by the wider river of the Reformation, firmly influencing how Renaissance rulers conceived of their positions and how they viewed those who encroached upon, disdained or failed to respect such authority. These misdemeanours could happen at the tavern, at the dinner table or in polite company, and they would be dealt with in summary fashion, however slightly or heavily. But those who went into print and had influence, or potential influence, were courting much more serious trouble. In all of these dealings and attempts to control, limit, prescribe and proscribe, we find blasphemy, then as now, utterly central to attempts to make individuals follow orthodoxy. Following this would create godly confessional populations devoid of sin and actions that would damn them. The centralized confessional State had arrived and blasphemy was the tool used by secular and religious authority to maintain its integrity. It was very much the case that the succeeding two centuries would work strongly to unravel this connection.

FOUR

BLASPHEMY AND THE ENLIGHTENMENT

I f the Reformation period had been characterized by the creation of new forms of authority – and the endowment of these with powers to act – the subsequent period witnessed a stark and dangerous crisis of these very same authorities. One enormous catalyst for this was the arrival of the Bible in the vernacular tongue of many Europeans. How religious crisis would involve blasphemy as its weapon is exemplified most obviously in the events that transpired in England and Scotland.

James I of England (and VI of Scotland) (1566–1625) was a pious and learned individual, and his initiative to create an officially sanctioned Bible was an attempt to spread the wisdom that could be gleaned from a closer relationship with Christianity's Holy Book. It was a measure of religious change in England that in the previous century Miles Coverdale had been forced into exile for seeking to translate the Bible into English. But now the king and his advisers were deeply involved in organizing a new translation. This was also, in an important way, indicative of how the Reformation had changed the religious landscape for many of Europe's citizens – the changes being closely connected with the issue of authority.[1] The Reformation and the Protestantism it spawned had, to varying degrees, brought about a considerably enhanced level of devotion to the Scriptures and what came to be referred to as the word of God. As we have seen, this was in stark contrast to the previous practice of the Catholic Church, which had focused much more on images as objects of devotion and reverence. These established modes of religious worship were very obviously collective practices. By

contrast, being able to commune with the word of God by interact-
ing with the printed page could be a solitary – and hence potentially
revolutionary – activity. In this way, devotion gave birth to various
species of Puritanism that had a devastating impact throughout the
seventeenth-century English-speaking world.

The Vernacular Bible – Constructing and Unravelling New Worlds of Belief

Prior to King James's commissioning of a vernacular Bible, religious
hierarchies had kept doctrine, and the Scriptures that inspired it,
firmly under lock and key. The seventeenth century essentially saw
religious doctrine being put before the eyes of the populace at large.
As a consequence of this, religious authority began to be diffused and
shared out among these very same people. This is not a very obvious
process, nor was it completed overnight, but it inspired challenges
to religious hierarchy and called into question who precisely had
possession over the word of God. In among this momentous change,
blasphemy would be used to influence both the direction and pace of
change. On some occasions, indicting people for blasphemy would
comfort authorities that had lost control of situations; at other times,
it would perplex and confuse them, as their application of biblically
sanctioned discipline sometimes failed to have the much-desired
effect. Those on the receiving end of blasphemy prosecutions and
punishments in the seventeenth century also reacted differently to
their forebears. Indeed, some of them scarcely came to see themselves as victims at all, their precise interactions with the Scriptures
seeming to enable them to plunge headlong and cheerfully into the
world of martyrdom, embracing its consequences and the apparent
salvation it offered them at every turn.

Perhaps the first flashpoint came as a result of Charles I's pre-
dilection for the neo-Catholic doctrine of the divine right of kings.
This we might consider to be a polar opposite to Calvinist predestination whereby all were equal before God until he had predestined
their fate. The concept of divine right marked kings out as manifestly
special since they were anointed by God (although still subject to
his providential judgement upon their conduct). As such they could
do no wrong and could not be questioned. This led Charles to dis-
pense with Parliament and increasingly roll back the achievements

that this institution had made over the previous hundred years. One of his measures was to install a compliant and ideologically co-operative Archbishop of Canterbury, William Laud (1573–1645). Having dispensed with some of the more obviously democratic institutions, as with Parliament, the king came to rely more heavily on those that remained, such as the Star Chamber. In most instances, these increasingly operated a much more arbitrary conception of power and justice.

In William Laud, Charles had made himself an ally. Laud began to use the ancient Court of Star Chamber and the Court of High Commission for Ecclesiastical Causes in increasingly lucrative and innovative ways. The Court of Star Chamber was autonomous and could effectively interest itself in any matter it chose to. Laud sharpened its teeth and used proceedings against seditious libel, including blasphemy, as a tool of religious governance. The poisoned atmosphere appeared to warrant this escalation, as the very arbitrariness which now clung to all the dealings of government led opponents to question if there could be any justification for this authority to behave in such a high-handed and tyrannical manner. Although Laud was thrown to the lions in a comparatively short time, the ecclesiastical court system he worked to preside over had already come to resemble the more draconian instruments of control enacted on the continent of Europe.

When the War of the Three Kingdoms (sometimes known as the British Civil Wars) started in 1639 and installed Parliament as the authority, in the absence of the king who fled the capital in 1642, both Star Chamber and the Court of High Commission for Ecclesiastical Causes soon fell victim to the new regime. Many had come to despise their arbitrariness and unfettered regulation of religious behaviour and opinion. For a time, there was a comparative power vacuum, and it became clear that some with unorthodox opinions were prepared to make the most of this.

Blasphemy as a Problem for the Commonwealth

One individual who sought to capitalize on the situation was a studious and religious former soldier named Paul Best, whose actions and experiences during these years seem representative of the various currents that contrived to produce forms of religious dissidence. His story also reinforces our picture of authority's desire to stop toleration being redefined carelessly, and to prevent this being actively abused. Best was an antitrinitarian and his writings became the conduit through which Socinian ideas from Eastern Europe reached England. His attempts to convince others of his views were rebuffed and he swiftly came to the attention of the authorities. By 1645 Best was imprisoned in York and he had been made aware that he would have to answer for his beliefs and actions to higher authorities in London.

In June of 1645, Best's beliefs were stridently condemned by the Westminster Assembly and a special commission was formed to investigate further into the matter of Socinianism in England. The commission had little trouble in establishing Best's guilt, and his fate seemed clear since blasphemy had been regularly and severely punished. But here the whole process ran into an enormous snag: the ecclesiastical court system responsible for judging and pronouncing upon such cases had itself fallen victim to Parliament's crusade against the king's arbitrary power. Thus, everyone knew about the crime and its perpetrator, but Parliament had removed the power to convict or pass sentence. In this unfortunate impasse, it was decided simply to detain Best until a solution could be reached.

Various options were mooted, including passing retrospective legislation that would see the death penalty passed down on Best. However, this process stalled and the bill for its enactment never successfully made it through the House of Commons. The focus then shifted to Best himself, as he was called to appear before the House of Commons for the first of several encounters with Members of Parliament. Best wove an elaborate argument in which he claimed not to actually deny the Trinity. This introduced an element of confusion, but more importantly it galvanized many wider arguments about liberty of religious conscience.

The shadow of ecclesiastical tyranny had only just been removed and, for some, Best personified the apparent intrusion into the hearts and souls of men that had arguably done so much to stimulate the turmoil of the 1640s. He thus languished in gaol and, with time on his hands, was able to publish a fuller exposition of his views. In doing so, he might have been considered to have increased the stakes and perils facing him. Yet the confidence he displayed in pressing ahead with his writings showed he had supporters, individuals who conveyed his manuscripts from gaol to the printers. Best's actions are also an obvious measure of how the logic of prosecuting him and seeking redress had arguably broken down. Indeed, Best himself pointed to how religious toleration had enabled the Netherlands and Poland to become flourishing societies, relatively removed from the evils of conflict. The House of Commons, by contrast, was rendered inert, unable to consider a way forward from this awkward situation. Eventually, after two years' captivity, Best was quietly released from prison. His constant presence had given his captors food for thought, while his studiousness and clever targeting of sensitive issues almost certainly saved him from a worse fate.

While in prison, Best was joined by a fellow antitrinitarian named John Biddle, a former schoolmaster from Gloucester. Biddle had independently come to the same opinions about the Trinity as Best had, and his story mirrors the latter's in many details. Biddle was imprisoned in a state of limbo as Best had been, and he was likewise able to publish his views from his prison cell. These writings, however, never saw the light of day – they were intercepted, and copies were burned by the public hangman in September 1647. Biddle's detention lasted longer than Best's and he was eventually released in 1652. Unrepentant, Biddle continued to publicize his views; he was arrested again in 1654 and received a sentence of banishment from the Commonwealth. He fared no better after the Restoration, returning to England and again being imprisoned in 1662. He died in gaol in September of that year.

In the midst of what looked like Parliamentary impotence, the detention of Biddle was one of the catalysts for eventual action. Parliament did seek to regulate religious opinion and more confidently proclaim the ideological bias of the new regime. The Blasphemy Act of 1648 affirmed what it saw as the constants of the Protestant religion, confirmed in its more Calvinist and Puritan manifestation. It did this explicitly by choosing to protect the nature of God himself, the Trinity, the resurrection and the Day of Judgement from attack. However, it also firmly set itself against the Catholicism that had effectively supported the doctrine of the divine right of kings, with a declaration that many Catholic beliefs were both heretical and blasphemous. These included the Catholic idea of the real presence of Christ's body and blood in the Eucharist, the worship of saints and relics, the belief in free will (the opposite of Calvinist predestination) and prayer for the forgiveness of sin.

The Act of 1648 also turned to face the other direction, clamping down on the vast cocktail of radical ideas some of which we have already encountered in other guises. Denial of infant baptism appeared in these provisions (invoking the spectre of Anabaptism in order to fully exorcise it), as did a number of the beliefs that suggested the Established Church was the Antichrist. The fact that this last provision appeared in the 1648 Act tells us how far religious dissent in England had matured and prospered. There had been hidden and underground congregations of advanced Puritans since the late Elizabethan period, but this signalled a significant advance upon these scattered and clandestine groups.[2] England had been largely spared the waking nightmares of Europe's organized heresies, and the sustained assault upon the very concept of government represented by the Anabaptists. But the confidence that appeared to lie behind the creation of such laws seems misplaced, and is particularly illuminated by how Parliament chose to deal with (or, rather, dither and eventually deal with) blasphemy charges brought against another, later, dissident: James Nayler (whom we will come to in due course).

Puritanism was influential and deep rooted, and it certainly recognized oppression when it encountered it. The end of the seventeenth century's first quarter saw a small but noteworthy portion of Puritans make the decision to leave an England they thought was close to oppressive. These 'Pilgrim Fathers', in search of a more sympathetic hearing, first made their home in the Netherlands in Leiden before making the arduous journey across the Atlantic to the eastern seaboard of America. Their fortunes as a society, and the conceptions of religious tolerance and freedom they took with them, will later form a significant part of our story.

The English blasphemy law of 1648, in facing up to radicalism and putting prohibitions in its way, was acknowledging that the ferment of the war, and the unseating of the king, put a question mark over the whole conception of authority as this society had known it. The deposition of the king not only destabilized authority, creating spaces and chaos that marginal groups could flourish within and exploit; it also constituted a series of signs and wonders that invoked both the established idea of providential intervention and the ideologically charged ability to read what was happening in the contemporary world through the looking-glass of the Bible.

The apparent 'fall' of the kingdom recalled the cataclysmic events of the Book of Revelation, and observers lost no time in making this connection. Given this, it is no surprise that those who drafted the 1648 law sought to close down radical interpretations and beliefs as much as the reactionary, more traditional ones that had now become anathema.

The collapse of censorship in the early 1640s appeared to have lifted a lid on the forces of religious speculation and ferment. While it was possible to feel paranoid about imagined menaces, tangible evidence of these would regularly break the surface, especially as the war dragged on. In an attempt to escalate the Parliamentarian war effort, Oliver Cromwell instigated the professional and motivated New Model Army. This was an elite force of fiercely motivated troops, generally inspired by an unrelenting religious zeal fed by constant interaction with the Bible and Scripture. Their contemplation would be neither predictable, nor by any means conventional. Many self-consciously splintered off from the Church of England to become, in their own minds, Independents. These comprised a range of groups, including those arguing for total devolution of religious government to independent churches and chapels – a position we would in modern times call Congregationalist. It would also include those who espoused adult-only baptism, the less extreme descendants of the Anabaptists. Although these groups had caused trouble in the previous century, it was other groups spawned from this ferment that would be of more concern to the authorities.

The first group of considerable concern was a very loose association of individuals that the authorities came to call the Ranters. This group had spotted the apparent flaw in the Calvinist doctrine of predestination. If the eventual fate of all was predetermined (or predestined) then behaviour in this world had no bearing on the eventual salvation, or damnation, dealt out to the individual. This led Ranters to actively avow the positive virtues of a dissolute life – with a deliberate emphasis on excessive smoking, drinking, nakedness and sexual licence among men and women alike. This theological position has come to be known as Antinomianism.

Many of those in authority who were fearful of this supposed 'sect' also noticed that these Ranters took a considerable delight in swearing and blaspheming. Some of the ringleaders were even reported as having sung blasphemous songs in taverns to the well-known tunes used for psalms. This was not vice for them, but instead positive and shining virtue, because they believed only those elected by God for salvation could legitimately act in this way without it being sin. Part of this also came from their perception that the world was positively drenched in sin and that, if this was the case, then sin itself must clearly serve another function.

One conclusion was that Christ's atonement had been so complete that humankind was in a state of grace on earth, as though it was in fact heaven itself. The sense of the immanence of heaven was a cultural constant of this century, driving many interpretations of Scripture that found parallels in the tumultuous events of the period. Seen in this way, within their precise context, the Ranters become more plausible and explicable; but also more wilful and dangerous.

What lay behind this collection of beliefs was the idea that these individuals possessed some sense of the inner light of God. This gave them individual authority to act as the saved, true and only recipients of God's grace. They saw the Second Coming not so much as an event prophesied by the Bible, but as a metaphor, and they firmly believed that this wondrous transformation had happened within themselves. This was also a rejection of the providential notion of God that we have often met before. Ranters (and actually all who believed they had the inner light) rejected the idea of a God external to themselves acting upon the universe. If God was within believers, then it was they who controlled providence.

All this may have been fine and a devoutly reverential experience if you were on the inside of this equation. But if you were on the outside, it looked delusional, selfish, mad and presumptuous. Not only this, it attacked the majesty of a deity that also still controlled the providence that affected your own life. It also looked like these lewd and disreputable men and women were constantly commanding God, itself a regular component of the crime of blasphemy. Again, we will meet a still more powerful manifestation of this phenomenon of the inner life, and what it felt like to be excluded from this, in due course.

The Ranters were a positive nightmare for authority to deal with. Indeed, almost all attempts to silence them from the contemporary world – and from history proper – have been successful, indicating that the full oppressive machinery of censorship was brought to bear. Their ideas were dangerous but the harsh reaction of the authorities perhaps hints at a fear that such ideas were potentially more wide-spread than had been thought. The Ranters may have looked like the tip of an unruly, anti-authoritarian iceberg. If they were imprisoned and asked to recant their beliefs, they would sometimes do so and seek release, only for a premeditated relapse to occur. Of course, refusing to be bound by their word was simply another sin which the elect could commit without it, in fact, being sinful. Indeed, their act became still more virtuous because it was done to appease an authority for which they had no respect and towards which they felt no duty – an authority whom everything in the Ranter belief system instructed them to undermine and oppose.

Ranters were also enemies of conventional intellectual structures, objecting to the possession of language and ideas claimed by the country's two universities. Structures of power and wealth also came in for fierce criticism, as Ranters sought to uphold the rights of paupers and beggars in the face of ill-gotten wealth and materialism. One of their pamphleteers, Abiezer Coppe, writer of the widely circulated pamphlet *The Second Fiery Flying Roll* in the portentous year of 1649, denounced the rich, declaring:

> Your gold and silver, though you can't see it, is cankered, the rust of them is a witnesse against you, and suddainly, suddainly, suddainly, because by the eternall God, my self, it's the dreadfyl day of Judgement, saith the Lord, shall eat your flesh as it were fire.[3]

They even went so far, in some cases, as to deny the idea that the Bible was the literal truth of God's word, doubting the account of individual immortality in a heaven presided over by the Almighty. Ranters thus destabilized authority, mocking it with their ideas and riotous actions; they posed a challenge to a society desperately trying to hold onto, and indeed redefine, an acceptable moral standard.

The imperative to proceed against the Ranters and their works meant the machinery of censorship swung into action with impressive speed and efficiency. Coppe found himself pursued by the authorities who stated that the work contained 'horrid blasphemies'.[4] They moved swiftly and all located copies of this pamphlet were burned. Two other compatriots, Joseph Salmon and Andrew Wyke, were arrested in Coventry for blasphemy. Wyke openly boasted of his pride at having blasphemed, placing him doubly in defiance of the – to him – spurious authorities.

Parliament was so concerned about the menace posed by the Ranters that a committee was put into action intent upon legislating against them. The result was a hasty attempt to modify the 1648 legislation against blasphemy. The provisions of the 1650 Blasphemy Act make it obvious that the Ranters were the target. Thereafter, it became a crime to undermine morality and what the Act described as 'righteous behaviour' – a clear assault on the dissolute and reckless antinomian lifestyle adopted by the Ranters. The Act listed adultery, incest, sodomy, murder and fornication as despicable practices it sought to remove – clearly indicating the level of both suspicion of and panic at precisely what the Ranters were getting up to. It was also illegal to suggest that God lived within individuals, animals or objects. A first offence would result in imprisonment, the second in banishment and a third transgression would result in a capital sentence. In framing such legislation the authorities hoped to initially discipline the uncommitted, and would only then resort to removing them from conventional society if they persisted in their lewdness and error. It was also doubtless hoped that the death penalty was the ultimate deterrent and would almost certainly not be used, since who would be likely and willing to come back from banishment to face the executioner? This legislation did capture a number of Ranters in its net, notably Jacob Bauthumley for his pamphlet *The Light and Dark Sides of God* (1650). Bauthumley was tried by a military court for publicizing blasphemous ideas and was court-martialled – eventually receiving the customary punishment for serious infractions of blasphemy: boring through the tongue.

We get a further flavour of what it was like to encounter such a defendant in a case against a Muggletonian woman tried at the Old Bailey. The Muggletonians were another curious religious sect who were in some respects an offshoot of the Ranters, with many moving into their ranks after the main surge of Ranterism had passed. In July 1678, this woman – referred to in the courtroom as 'The Maid' – was asked several questions which led the court to conclude that she had committed the transgression of 'having taken upon her to be God'. On this occasion, the court sent her back to prison and hoped she would reconsider her declaration. When she appeared in court a month later it was clear that she had thought better of her belief, but scarcely in a way envisaged by the court. She came back into court and declared that she had revised her opinions and now declared that 'she was indeed the Third person in the Trinity, and that her Father was that Christ, who was with God at the Creation.'[5] In exasperation the court decided she should now be whipped to break her of the persistent poor habits she had acquired. Attempts to stamp out the Ranters and the antinomian heresy they promoted were never wholly successful, and traces of their beliefs could still be found in the late eighteenth and early nineteenth centuries.

The Ranters were individually rebellious, but society had also to cope with another group, the Fifth Monarchy Men, who saw it as their duty to bring about the violence of the last days foretold in the Book of Revelation. Their attempt at an armed uprising was something of a shambles. Samuel Pepys walked past the execution of one of its senior leaders, Major General Thomas Harrison, in October 1660, noting his calm demeanour which served to indicate a willingness to embrace the mantle of martyrdom. Although the Fifth Monarchists were a very worrying inconvenience for a short time, of longer-term significance was the approach and attitudes of one of the radical sects that have survived and flourished into our own time: the Quakers.

In most respects, the Quakers are today a conformist and respectable shadow of their once radical and highly disruptive selves. Like others, this group avowed that they were in receipt of the inner light, but it burned far more brightly for them. While Ranters wanted to go their own way – that is, to be substantially left alone – the Quakers actively courted trouble. They regularly disrupted church services, since all other religions and denominations were considered by them to be the Antichrist. Although the Cromwellian authorities had technically established full and expansive religious tolerance, they were faced with a perpetual problem of how to tolerate groups and individuals who themselves held intolerant beliefs and, indeed, were prepared to undertake intolerant actions to further the cause of their faith. Quakers represented a considerable problem for the government of the day, since they were serially disruptive of both religious space and the wider social peace: they disrupted church services, but their impact upon areas of secular life could, at times, be spectacular.

Several Quaker leaders were imprisoned for what seemed outrageously inflammatory acts. One in particular became notorious, and both his actions and those of the government against him, cata-pulted him into the folklore of blasphemy in England, ensuring his story would be repeated by subsequent generations. This man was James Nayler, another dissident personality who had been shaped by the turmoil of the 1640s, and the tide of inquiry and seeking it had unleashed. Like many others whose religious zeal overtook their earthly lives, Nayler had been radicalized as an officer in Cromwell's army. It is reasonably certain he was a Quaker, since he was arrested for the kind of publicly provocative act that was their stock-in-trade. Among a group of followers, Nayler had attempted to enter the city of Bristol on a donkey, in imitation of Christ's entry into Jerusalem. It was widely assumed that the inner light had actively persuaded Nayler that he was himself Christ incarnate. Indeed, on his arrest, magistrates found on him a letter declaring 'Thy name shall no more be James Nayler, but Jesus.'

These magistrates, confused about their precise duties and powers under the Cromwellian Instrument of Government, opted to pass responsibility for dealing with Nayler on to London. Since the Best and Biddle cases, the establishment of the Commonwealth of 1650 had effectively created a new situation: Parliament was now regulated, but individual members still sought to redefine its role. By now, growing confidence in Parliament allowed it to consider itself the appropriate tribunal to rule on important religious matters that also affected the peace and stability of the country. Nayler was arrested and brought before the House of Commons, which now assumed the full judicial responsibility to try him for blasphemy. Although it seemed a harder line was being taken, it was still the case that the House of Commons remained divided on the issue.

This divide in Parliament seemed to represent the whole nature of religious turmoil in England throughout the middle years of the seventeenth century. Those who had a narrow sectarian inter-est found most other religious denominations questionable or even anathema, while some who had fought for religious freedom were wary of letting it fall to despotic forms of censorship and control. These arguments were faced by those who argued that, while toler-ation was fine, in practice it should remain within limits. They had never envisaged that tolerance would be extended to anyone like the Quakers, or indeed any of the other dangerous sects that were straining for religious freedom.

Elsewhere there were also those who simply failed to be convinced by hard-line arguments in which the appropriateness of legal procedures vied with conceptions of divine will and the preservation of the godly commonwealth. What focused the minds of many was the presumption that whatever action Parliament took it would be liable to cast the country and government into unknown territory. In a world where time-honoured precedents had been hastily torn down, some were extremely worried by the establishment of dangerous new norms. Many argued that such powers were a step too far for Parliamentary sovereignty. Likewise, they went on to actively question whether this probing into the minds of men, even to preserve the ideals of the Christian Commonwealth, was a tyrannous violation.

Nonetheless, it did seem obvious to all in the House of Commons that Nayler needed to be heard and dealt with; thus he was brought before the House in December 1656. Nayler was unrepentant and openly spurned the authority of the House by refusing to kneel or remove his hat, both standard forms of Quaker defiance of authority and a blatant method of assuming this same authority for themselves. Nayler admitted his actions and confirmed his identification with Christ – clarifying that this was only in as much as Christ was within him (again a standard Quaker pronouncement) and that he did not assent to being worshipped. There remained differences of opinion on both Nayler and his beliefs in the House of Commons, which still contained factions manoeuvring for position and for the dominance of their views. As such, Nayler was a tool for establishing precedent, for example of Parliament's right to inquire into religious affairs as the supreme authority, now that the ecclesiastical courts and the bishops had been removed. Procedures were up for discussion, but were in the end so fluid that Parliament incredibly accepted the fact of his guilt without trial or debate. This was scarcely enacted with one voice, and many questions about the wisdom of and reason for the pronouncement went around in circles. In the search for a legal basis to proceed on, all had to be mindful of the statutes and precedents they reached for. When some grasped for the old heresy statute *De Heretico Comburendo* of 1401, it was gently pointed out that this law would see practically everyone in the building sent to the stake – it had better not be resurrected as a hasty and ill-considered justification for action against Nayler.

While Nayler had undertaken a profoundly presumptive and controversial action, it was by no means clear precisely how he had blasphemed. He had not usurped the position of God, nor had he sought to command the Almighty. Some argued that his beliefs were the logical destination of the commonplace belief that God was everywhere manifested in his own creation. Some went back to the arguments of the Emperor Tiberius to claim that, if Nayler's offence had been against God, it was scarcely a crime for man to punish on the Almighty's behalf. Others wanted to circumvent legal and theological arguments to merely pronounce Nayler a deluded madman, but crucially a sincere one. This was a verdict to which nineteenth-century secularists would later refer in the midst of their own struggles against the blasphemy law.[6]

After pronouncing this makeshift verdict of guilty, Parliament moved on to determine and enact Nayler's punishment. The House took a vote on whether to pronounce a death sentence and this was narrowly lost by a vote of 82 members in favour but 96 against. The House now had no option but to consider a range of lesser punishments, but again had to think deeply about this. The proportionality of such punishments was important, not least because the arguments about the depth of Nayler's guilt remained unresolved. As we have seen, punishments for blasphemy had come to be both diverse and arbitrary. This explains why the eventual decision on Nayler's punishment reflected a desire to pile a number of these punishments together. His sentence also displayed very firm action in a range of localities that had experienced the disquiet he had produced, and targeted the actions of his fellow Quakers.

Nayler was to be placed in the pillory for two hours in two separate London locations and would be whipped through the streets in his passage to the second stocks at the Old Exchange. At this site he was to have his tongue bored through with a hot iron and have the letter 'B' branded on his forehead. After this, Nayler was to be taken to the scene of his crime in Bristol, where he would also be whipped and put in the pillory. From here he was to be returned to London where he would spend the rest of his days in the London Bridewell prison, put to hard labour and denied access to writing materials.

Although Nayler had escaped capital punishment, his sentence was seen by many as an exceptionally harsh catalogue of punishments in a case where liberty of conscience was at stake. The first parts of the London punishment were carried out with Nayler enduring the sentence of whipping with considerable fortitude. Even for the brave, the magnitude of such punishment was beyond endurance, and some of the London public petitioned Parliament to have the rest of the sentence suspended. Thirty were allowed into Parliament to press this case and to appeal to the question of individual liberty. When they had made their argument, Parliament again fell to debating many of the questions that the Nayler case had been stirring up from the very first. The petitioners attempted to go above the head of Parliament to petition Cromwell, the Lord Protector himself. Cromwell, in turn, asked Parliament to clarify why it had sentenced Nayler, but the eventual reply only confirmed the second part of the sentence, this time with a two-to-one majority. So it was that Nayler received the second part of the sentence, including the boring through of his tongue and the branding, which he endured, according to witnesses, with considerable courage.

In the middle of the following month, Nayler had to undergo the final public portion of his punishment. He was transported and made to sit on a horse backwards as he entered Bristol. He was then prepared for the whipping, but the local authorities allowed one of Nayler's compatriots to place his arm on the executioner's, to limit the force of the whipping he would inflict. After this Nayler was returned to London, where he commenced what promised to be a life sentence of hard labour. Parliament detained Nayler for a time, but in September 1659 chose to release him. Still defiant, he returned to the preaching he had practised before. This satisfactory ending, of sorts, was unfortunately short-lived; broken by everything that had happened to him, Nayler died little over a year later.

Nayler's story is a complex and protracted one involving confusion and mismanagement among Members of Parliament and equivocation from the senior figures who controlled the highest institution in the land. It also showed the determination of a faction keen to see blasphemy punished for their own advancement. As far as the law's victims were concerned, it showed the dogged resilience of those willing to embrace the martyrdom that came as an almost inevitable consequence of their religious views. The nineteenth-century philosopher Thomas Carlyle, as well as some subsequent historians, reached instinctively for the explanation that James Nayler had been patently insane, so that Parliament deliberating over him and his fate for a quite inordinate amount of time was unjust and inept.[7]

But this is a modern judgement that misses the implications of Quaker doctrine for the personality, and the full meaning of what the inner light was capable of persuading people to do. It also fails to explain precisely why Parliament, and all the other authorities involved in the case, took Nayler and his actions quite so seriously. Whatever else it did, what happened to Nayler, and the interminable wrangling to reach a decision, indicated not only fundamental problems with how parliaments operated under the Commonwealth, but the virtual collapse of effective and defensible legal procedure.

The Late Seventeenth Century – Security and Crisis

With the Restoration, the return of royal governance brought an end to the periods of confusion over belief and authority that had characterized the 1640s and '50s. Henceforth, pronouncements on what really should, and should not, happen to blasphemers and blasphemy became clearer, more coherent and (at least on paper) more authoritarian.

As a part of this striving for coherence and clarity, one pivotal moment that occurred in 1676 would shape blasphemy laws for two centuries to come. A blasphemy case was brought against a man named John Taylor who had declared 'Jesus Christ was a whoremaster and religion is a cheat'.[8] In many respects it is remarkable how regularly this particular phrase surfaces and resurfaces. At first sight it seems a simple insult to religion and the tenets of Christianity believed by the bulk of the population. It appears obviously disdainful and conceivably the product of malice, masculine bravado or drink.

But everything we have heard before this case offers a further explanation. The denigration of religious images and emphasis on the word at the same time as religious authority was being questioned meant that the previous tenets of the Bible were now open to a wide variety of reinterpretation. This had not simply produced Ranterism, but also subjected Scripture to the power of simple reasoning, devoid of devotion and reverence. From this perspective, according to the Gospels, Christ associated with prostitutes during his ministry and was especially close to Mary Magdalene. Such supposed 'inconsistencies' seemed never to have been intended to be exposed to plodding and simple explanations of the world as experienced by the common artisan. Yet here they were, being picked apart by one individual with an inquiring mind and some time on his hands.

As we have seen, such pronouncements were not entirely uncommon, but what was decided in Taylor's case really did break new ground. The presiding judge was Sir Matthew Hale, a man whom later commenters, hostile to the blasphemy laws, would waspishly cite as an unenlightened man who had burned witches.[9] In passing sentence upon Taylor, Hale seemed very obviously conscious that he was making an important statement about the Common Law and case law of blasphemy. He justified a blasphemy conviction from the idea that religion and the law were symbiotically linked and should emphatically always be regarded as such. The actual phrase he used was that religion was 'part and parcel of the laws of England'.[10] Hale argued that Christianity should be equated with the law of the land, and that attacks upon it should be regarded as expressing contempt for the authority which law represented. To attack religion was, by definition, to attack the laws of the country – something no self-respecting serving judge could reasonably be expected to tolerate. From this period on, the so-called 'Hale Judgement' would regularly be cited as a cast-iron justification for proceeding to law in cases of blasphemy – and for expecting a conviction.

It is worth unpicking the implications of this judgement. Religion in 1676 – and, most importantly, established religion – a mere sixteen years after the end of Cromwell's turbulent republic, was now, under a restored royalist regime, considered to be an absolutely essential support to government. It explained and underpinned the morals that kept individuals from challenging the political and social order – such attitudes would resurface in the early nineteenth century, after another turbulent revolutionary period. But for now, intense elements of the providentialism that we have previously seen characterizing attitudes to blasphemy came back into fashion. A measure of how far this revival had occurred is to contrast popular fears of the blasphemer manifest in the actions against men like Taylor with the swaggering, blaspheming confidence of Ranter individuals, secure in the knowledge that they had already been saved on this earth.

This retrenchment, fear and the particular providential circumstances conspired to bring about the death of the only man in the

British Isles known to have been executed for the specific crime of blasphemy. The entire episode is an unfortunate catalogue of mistakes and the exercise of ill will, driven by personality and the circumstances of a particularly dark context. As an historical event, it has never been quite forgotten, and has knitted itself into the cultural landscape of Scottish history and the wider history of human rights.

Thomas Aikenhead was an impoverished, but keen and attentive, medical student in the Edinburgh of the 1690s. The fact that he was impoverished, and without influential connections to plead on his behalf, would eventually seal his fate. Like many students, Aikenhead could get caught up in his own self-confidence, and would brag and display bravado beyond what was wise. On several occasions he uttered some extreme opinions about the truth and benevolence of specific Christian teachings. It is quite difficult to decide precisely what motivated Aikenhead's outbursts. Some suggest this was youthful bravado colliding with misunderstanding. However, others have looked more deeply at Aikenhead's pronouncements and can see in them the germ of a coherent belief system.[11] This latter view would make him another seeker after truth, one motivated by an exposure to theological ideas that hurried past the reading public. This was all drawn by the twin locomotives of the Reformation and the printing press. It would also make him a descendant of the Ranters and Muggletonians, who were themselves confident enough to reconstruct the universe in the image they craved. Certainly the popular fear of such groups lingered on, and was manifest in censorship laws that hastily removed a great many philosophical and theological pamphlets from circulation. It would later emerge that Aikenhead had managed to gain access to many of these texts, and this in itself provided further justification for a fierce censorship regime.

Aikenhead's behaviour eventually came to the attention of the Edinburgh authorities. The timing of this was very unfortunate, since the General Assembly of the Kirk of Scotland had just enacted a law which was a sudden compilation of all the profane and immoral behaviour that they had been railing against for some years. One new element that had crept into this was an intense interest in curbing and removing blasphemy. This was now to be considered an entirely separate offence, rather than being lumped in with the general category of profanity – a change which again emphasizes the renewed seriousness of the offence. This was one circumstance that conspired to bring about the death of Aikenhead, but there were also others.

Several events of 1696 seemed to display God's wrath with and disfavour towards the Scottish nation, with a catalogue of woes and disasters befalling it. Declining Scottish trade had led to increasingly desperate attempts to revitalize the economy, eventually resulting in the Darien Venture – a project aimed at funnelling lucrative Pacific and American trade through a Scottish colony (optimistic-ally named Caledonia) on the central American coast near Panama. This 'Venture' was to eventually collapse with the unexplained death of a large number of the colonists, an English trading blockade, a siege laid at its gates by the disgruntled Spanish and its ignominious abandonment, all in quick succession.

Although this lurch to complete disaster took another three years, Scotland's desperation in the preceding three years had ensured that the Darien scheme attracted no less than 50 per cent of all the monetary wealth in Scotland, subscribed by rich and poor alike as they tried to save the country from its downward spiral. This inevitably meant that harsh economic woes really came home to the people of Scotland in 1696, and loomed large as a sign of God's providential displeasure. This was compounded by a year of poor harvests, which provoked panic buying in the city of Edinburgh. A further consequence of this perfect storm was that the government had empty coffers and could not provide sufficient funds to feed and equip the army – a situation which became critical when the capital was gripped by an invasion scare. The supposedly imminent arrival of invading French troops, amid impoverishment, starvation and despair, made for a uniquely toxic and dangerous atmosphere. In this febrile moment, individuals sought to appease God and the providence which had turned so violently against them. For those in the city of Edinburgh, the final straw appeared to be a fire outbreak in the Canongate area of the city, which may have destroyed as many as fifty dwellings. In the days after this, preachers reproached the population for their reckless behaviour, wasting no time in lecturing them on the terrible consequences of God's providential gaze upon them and their sinfulness.

Again, this points to the spectacularly unfortunate timing of Thomas Aikenhead's outbursts. He eventually wound up before Scotland's Privy Council, a matter of days after the Canongate fire. Aikenhead's recklessness had caught up with him, and he was now in considerable peril. The charges against him contained in the indictment were that he had declared the whole of theology to be a species of nonsense; he also actively doubted the truth of the Scriptures. With a phrase that many have picked out and noted from the case, Aikenhead became famous for allegedly describing the Old Testament as 'Ezra's fables', an epithet which both denied their truth and ascribed their fabrication to one writer – thereby doubly undermining conventional beliefs that such books were the word of God.[12] He also suggested that Jesus and Moses used conjuring tricks, and that Man's own industry and ingenuity was at the stage whereby it could thwart or stop the reach and power of divine providence. Aikenhead denied the power of eternal reward or punishment and also denied the Trinity – views which recall Ranter antinomian heresies.

Aikenhead's views, whether real or comprising words put into his mouth by the court, look like a compendium of almost all of the philosophical and theological positions considered blasphemous over the course of the seventeenth century. The last three accusations levelled at him, if true, serve to hint that Aikenhead's attitudes combined youthful scoffing with some more serious-minded reading and assimilation of quasi-blasphemous views. Both such sources of blasphemy would further have stoked the unfavourable attitudes that were rapidly building up against him from those in authority.

It seemed abundantly clear that Aikenhead should be made an example of. The fear of providential reprisal seemed to demand it and the seriousness of what was said, along with the implications of such words, seemed to lead in one direction alone. Aikenhead would have to contemplate undergoing some form of severe punishment, although at this stage it was not entirely clear how severe this could or should be. For the time being, he was imprisoned in Edinburgh's Tolbooth, next to St Giles Cathedral. By November 1696, after a further hearing, it became clear that Aikenhead would have to face a capital trial, an occasion where his life would be in jeopardy. From here we can see that the odds were dramatically stacked against him. He was a young man without influence or influential friends, and was unprepared for what might happen in a courtroom.

Such fears must have been confirmed when it became obvious that the might of the Privy Council, and the legal advice it could gather, was ranged against him. As if this were not enough, Calvinist zeal and the fear of providence provided the extra motivation to secure an outcome that would please the Kirk before God. This assault on the young man in the dock was led by the Lord Advocate James Stewart of Goodtrees. In reading the indictment, the court noted that Aikenhead had freely voiced these views and had not stumbled into offering them on the spur of the moment. It further declared that his utterances were not only contrary to the recent law but also, significantly, to the law of 1661 in which the death penalty was a more obviously prominent punishment. This effectively redoubled the danger Aikenhead faced as the new emphasis on blasphemy covered by the recently passed law combined with the ultimate penalty contained in the older law. What may have had most impact was Aikenhead's supposed desire to see Christianity irreparably damaged, and the belief that he would continue in this project if exiled. In this, Aikenhead was recklessly threatening to become yet another dangerous providential enemy waiting in the wings.

It had not taken long for Aikenhead to realize the depth of his predicament, and he made every possible effort to conspicuously backtrack on the views he had uttered. In court he repeatedly said that the views ascribed to him were abhorrent and that he was repeating the ideas of others that he had read. Moreover, this had all happened as a result of others offering him books which had set ideas whirling around his impressionable young mind. Although his age was debatable, it seemed from this early juncture that Aikenhead was really stuck for anything resembling a watertight defence. Because of this he decided to throw himself, in various ways, upon the mercy of the court. From this point onwards the court heard witnesses that confirmed the substance of the things that Aikenhead had said about sacred doctrines and persons revered by the Christian religion. The stark fact of his guilt really seemed to be beyond doubt and it was no surprise what happened next.

The jury retired and, without much deliberation, soon delivered a verdict of guilty. Aikenhead was convicted of the most dangerous charges against him, namely 'railing' against God and Jesus, denying Christ's ministry and the Trinity, and lastly denouncing and scoffing at the Holy Scriptures. Being found guilty of this parade of charges was perilous in the context of a ravaged and frightened Scotland living in unlimited fear of what was to come next. The judge almost had no alternative but to pronounce a death sentence. This vividly conveyed how he would be taken to Gallowlee, between Edinburgh and Leith, to then be executed in the late afternoon.

Even at this stage, it was scarcely obvious that the sentence would be carried out, since most sentences at this period in Scotland were not completely binding, and it was not unusual for them to be changed. Certainly, Aikenhead himself petitioned the Privy Council in search of a reprieve – again quoting his youth and regretting his foolish propensity to be led astray by others. One school of thought quickly came to the conclusion that the harshness of the proposed punishment was going too far and was potentially unjust. One of the Privy Councillors, Lord Anstruther, had visited Aikenhead in his cell at the St Giles Tolbooth and became convinced that, although his opinions had been vile, he was not malicious, nor even, perhaps, beyond redemption. Anstruther's own version of events suggests that he was moved sufficiently to plead for mercy on Aikenhead's behalf and was able to convince close to half of those present at Council that a more merciful outcome was required. The vote tragically went against the petition for mercy by one vote, and Aikenhead was told to prepare himself for execution.

Aikenhead was led to the scaffold on 8 January 1697, and all present noted how he appeared to be sorrowful and repentant throughout. He paused before his execution to deliver a dying speech, something of a tradition at public executions before the nineteenth century. In most cases these were intended to display the guilt of the offender and how wilfulness, fate and poor morals had inextricably led them to the sorry situation they now found themselves in. Certainly Aikenhead was prepared to go along with some elements of this ritual. He expressed considerable sorrow for what he had done. He then strongly emphasized that his story was a stark warning to all those tempted to indulge in idle speculation on ungodly thought and ideas. In doing so, he could not help declaring such ideas were now appalling in his eyes as he was preparing to make his peace with God.

Despite this, there were other elements of what he said that were somewhat more disconcerting. Although sorry for all his other errant opinions, Aikenhead never apologized for his assault on the Trinity, and even affirmed this errant belief at the scaffold. But there was more. Aikenhead revealed that he was beset by doubts and lamented the apparent contradictions and difficulties that those trying to maintain orthodox Calvinist beliefs had to wrangle with. It was difficult for the young and impressionable who, thanks to the piecemeal inadequacy of the Scottish censorship regime, had been left open to turbulent ideas taking free rein in their minds. Why could not people perhaps save Aikenhead from himself and the pressures upon him? Who was to know whether these pressures actually put something of a strain upon all those who might have had a passing role in the case – from the determined Privy Councillor to the person in the street who watched Aikenhead's sorrowful progress to the scaffold?

Although some of this is speculation, there is quite good reason for indulging in it. As we have noted, the execution of Aikenhead was unique for the British Isles, and thus it stands out as a very significant milestone in the history of blasphemy. The singularity of this event led to its story having a vibrant and contested history in the four centuries since it happened. Unsympathetic commentators south of the border saw the execution as evidence of Scotland's enduring barbarism. More sophisticated views noted how it was the product of religious forces being allowed far too close to the centre of power. Still others saw the Aikenhead case as an event that signalled the closure of Calvinist despotism in Scotland. According to these latter accounts, the case brought to an end religious fear and darkness, and ushered in what would soon be revered as the Scottish Enlightenment.

Commentators with an eye to contemporary events within their own time have kept the memory of this unfortunate youth alive. They have profitably used it to castigate authoritarian regimes that indulge their own religious bias and prejudices. Aikenhead was a cause célèbre in his own time and the memories of his story have endured to become a powerful motif of the quest for religious toleration, and the duty to uphold the principle of equal human rights. In the twenty-first century, he has given his name to a human rights award and has been the subject of theatre productions and radio plays that continue to explore his thoughts and history – betraying our lingering fascination with this whole episode.

When we look back at Aikenhead's own time, we can readily see that he was perhaps representative of cracks and fissures that were appearing in the crusade for confessional orthodoxy.

Aikenhead demonstrated that he was the victim of the circulation of ideas, whether these came from books, pamphlets or the risqué and dangerous conversations that occurred in an age of growing sociability – conversations that could spiral out of control. He was also a victim of his own sense of self and a resultant feeling that he had a right to his doubts, as well as a solemn duty to actively explore them. Limiting this right, and where it might take such individuals, became a source of contention and struggle in the coming century.

The imperative to control and regulate opinion was similarly evident in the decision of the English government, shortly after Aikenhead's execution, to pass the country's only blasphemy statute. This enactment of 1698 (known as the 9 & 10 William III, *c.* 32, *An Act for the More Effectual Suppressing of Blasphemy and Prophaneness*) was part of a wider push for increased discipline, and its context had echoes of Scotland's Blasphemy Act, itself motivated by providential fear. William III's grip on the English throne could, at times, feel tenuous and this blasphemy statute appeared around a plethora of similar Acts that regulated and disciplined a vast range of behaviour in society – culminating at the bottom of the disciplinary scale by enacting legislation which ensured that beer was served for the first time in standardized pint measures.

While drinking habits were a minor moral concern, blasphemy had the potential to disturb the peace of the kingdom and its security. The statute declared it was illegal, if once professing the Christian religion, to seek to deny the Trinity, the status of the Scriptures as divinely inspired or the undeniable truth of Christianity itself. This was intended to protect the Anglican Establishment and to protect other moderate sects, while ensuring it vanquished the heresies of the Unitarians and Socinians. However, we can see this hybrid blend of moral and security concern demonstrated by the progressive nature of punishments contained within the statute. For an initial offence the offender would be excluded from holding office in an official institution such as the government, the army or the Church. For subsequent offences the miscreant would be barred from using the conventional accompaniments of standard citizenship. This meant they would be prevented from sealing public contracts with others, or from obtaining legal redress against any complainant or plaintive. A third offence would result in a prison sentence of three years with no opportunity for bail.

In many respects, this legislation points to how the archetypal State wanted to treat blasphemers at the end of the seventeenth century. Such people were a menace and were also antisocial, but their actions were no longer life- or soul-threatening in the way they had been conceived of in the medieval period and early Renaissance. Given that they were such a nuisance, the safest course of action was to render them non-citizens. In doing so, the law was demonstrating its reach and effectiveness to both the perpetrator and victim of blasphemous words, all the while also securing the peace of mind of rulers and governors.

In the event, the statute was scarcely more than this declaration of intent, since it was relegated to the background. As we shall see, it was precisely its codification and its status as a milestone that actively made such a statute somewhat less useful. In the end, the malleability of the Common Law and its application to specific instances by judges – which established precedent as they pronounced sentence – was to triumph. This flexibility turned Common Law into a much preferred tool in seeking to prosecute for blasphemy. It was this very malleability which, at least in England, was to ensure the exceptionally long life of the Common Law of blasphemous libel. This malleability came to be trusted by judges, and eventually by civil servants, who readily embraced credible solutions that could get themselves and the overzealous out of sticky situations. This worked both ways, since these same judges and civil servants also thought such a law was the obvious servant of public opinion – thus, it could be trusted to reflect the changing times and sensibilities of the wider religious community.

While England followed this course, the history of what happened in the American colonies was rather more fragmented. As we have seen, the colonists were predominantly religious radicals fleeing from oppression in Europe. However, with them being spread far and wide in a sparsely populated country, they began to devolve responsibility away from the pattern emerging in Europe, one of centralizing states looking for opportunities to extend the writ of their forms of government. The American colonies resembled separate small European states that adopted their own individual approaches to the law and, given that blasphemy was a religious crime, this became an explicit feature of the legal codes developed by what would eventually become states.

Given the range of responses we witnessed in among the ferment of revolution in England, it is no surprise to encounter a similar range flourishing within these colonies. Some took the opportunity to start anew by trying to create a godly state in the manner envisaged, and even realized, by Calvin. This exhibited the Puritan philosophy we have already encountered in all of its many, different guises. It meant that some states, such as Virginia, were constructed on one vision of the godly Commonwealth and readily prescribed the death penalty for speaking out against the Trinity, or what was considered to be the essentials of the Christian religion.

But there was no Established Church in the colonies, something which limited the capacity for the rigid enforcement of laws, and was thus more likely to mirror the confusion of the Commonwealth and the questioning of both motive and justification that went with this. Massachusetts managed to operate in the manner that Parliament had done with James Nayler, but did not have properly constituted legal descriptions and procedures. This again was one aspect that further emphasized the wide and diverse provision for punishment which appeared in these different colonies. While many of the usual punishments existed, there were novel ones that can generally only be found in the Americas at this time. These included being made to ritually kiss the earth, or to witness yourself hanged in effigy – both instances emphasizing just how much this was effectively still an early modern shame culture.

Massachusetts, however, also had to cope with an analogous challenge from Quakers and similar dissidents that existed back across the Atlantic. The most famous of these was Samuel Gorton (1593–1677), a man who held a noisy collision of views which echoed the by now familiar conviction of the inner light common to Quaker and Ranter beliefs. He was also notorious for having an abrasive and confrontational personality, which compounded things still further. He loudly proclaimed his opposition to the Trinity and saw the State as essentially corrupt and spiritually bankrupt.

Gorton led a group of followers to a section of land near Narragansett Bay, Rhode Island, and was later asked to produce his warrant of entitlement to colonize the area. Gorton's reply was an inflammatory denial of the rights of the civil government of the state. The many blasphemous passages which his reply contained resulted in his arrest and a sentence of imprisonment followed by banishment. Gorton was forced to leave for England, where he was also viewed with suspicion as a conspicuously dangerous blasphemer. A change of fortune, of government and of atmosphere in New England allowed Gorton to return to the American Colonies where he was able to recolonize the same land and settle to live out the rest of his days.

The vital change that had occurred proved to be a remarkable and stark exception to the biblical literalism that some Puritan thinking voiced in favour of the ever-purer godly state. This was the impact of the grant given to Roger Williams to establish the colony of Rhode Island, including the land on which Gorton had settled and later resettled. This was perhaps the concrete realization of the full religious toleration that Oliver Cromwell had, at least initially, hoped for. Roger Williams was a deeply religious individual who believed in an extreme version of religious tolerance, one which would even admit Catholics, something almost entirely unheard of in the English-speaking world. His tolerance was based on a belief that religions could, and indeed actively should, strive earnestly to live together. They could do this, he argued, while debating the rights and wrongs of their belief away from the tyranny of over-anxious authority and Established Churches with vested interests. Williams believed you could convince others of the rightness of your own beliefs when opposed by theirs, but he was equally clear that this would only happen if it was safe for all to be present and engage in such opportunities for conversion.

Williams also faced the same problems that Cromwell had in dealing with Quakers. Such individuals, convinced solely by their own inner light, unsurprisingly had little or nothing to say to believers in other versions of Christianity. They especially annoyed Williams because they insulted and breached his strict demand for civility and dialogue. Quakers, in his experience, wanted to be both rude and uncommunicative, the two most grievous sins against toleration as Williams saw it. Williams was forced to tolerate Quakers, driven by the logic of his own position. If he believed in toleration he had to stay his hand and withhold any desire for action or reprisal.

In effect, he had reached the logical conclusion that was to define the reaction of authority from the end of the seventeenth century forward. What precisely was the role of government and legislature in modern conceptions of governance, especially in matters of religion? Williams concluded that it had now become the role of such authority to referee and ensure fair play, even if some of those taking part seemed unpleasant and thoroughly objectionable. This had become the imperative of law and order that was to drive blasphemy into the modern world. No longer was it right to protect some monolithic edifice called 'religion' – one that everyone appeared to know about but could neither see nor adequately define. It was now the duty of government to protect what it saw as widespread and grass-roots religion, beliefs which it knew were actually cherished by the public at large. Only when the rights of these people were violated was it necessary for the State to step in and address the wrongs it had seen.

Blasphemy had been central to some of the thoroughly important debates that had characterized religion's relationship with government during these years. As such, it had become a catalyst for defining both the limits of State power and the rise of individual conscience. As the years moved on, it was this latter phenomenon that acquired an almost sacred character of its own.

FIVE

BLASPHEMY IN THE NINETEENTH CENTURY

Perhaps the central organizing principle of early modern society was the idea of authority. Wherever ideas, events or even personalities needed explaining it was necessary that an authority do so. This meant forms of authority were everywhere asserting, and even imposing, their explanations upon the world. So doctors had their particular explanations for how the human body functioned, and how this determined the character of individual behaviour. Likewise, morality rested its authority on Christian Scripture and its message of salvation through belief and either good work or predestination. But there were other forces that seemed to be part of the universe, and the quest to experiment had started to uncover these. Electricity, gravity, the nature of the human mind and even the nature of human government and politics were all potential sites for experimentation. Although Benjamin Franklin had experimented with lightning and excitedly written up his findings, nothing prepared the English-speaking world at the end of the eighteenth century for the electrical storm crashing around the political writings of Thomas Paine (1737–1809).

Thomas Paine – Ages of Reason and Blasphemy

Having been involved in strikingly formative events in both the American and French revolutions, Paine anxiously wanted similar events to transpire in Britain. His ideas and tirades rejected tradition, age-old structures and institutions that justified their own existence solely through their revered antiquity. He always made such feelings more than plain, and endlessly used forthright and clear denunciation of all he found corrupt: the monarchy, the gradual and slow crawl to modernity of England's antiquated system of government – seemingly immune to revolution – and an image of God ruined by the selfish and greedy churches spuriously erected in his name. All of these were targets of Paine's merciless gaze and fiercely critical writings.

However, something that set Thomas Paine apart was that he combined these forthright ideas with a studied and talented use of language and communication. Together these made an intoxicating and dangerously seductive mixture. The proof of this is in the reactions of its enthusiastic consumers at large, and of those who thought it dangerous enough to seek immediate prohibition of its pernicious effects. Paine's message was all-encompassing, led by a stridently independent and game-changing political element. An important part of this was the attraction of his assault upon organized Christianity.

Paine should be classed as a deist, one who believed merely in a supreme being. This deity was scarcely the fierce God of the Old Testament, nor the seemingly insipid God of love from the New Testament – both of whom regularly failed to practise what the deity's self-interested acolytes preached. Paine's central text of argument in this area was *The Age of Reason* (1794), a book written substantially in a French prison, ironically containing an attempt to persuade the Revolution to step back from the course of outright and destructive atheism. Removed from this precise context, it read rather differently to those living under a seemingly more conservative and still oppressive religious settlement. It was, in short, well written, beguilingly persuasive and contained a number of fleet and pithy turns of phrase. These galvanized and delighted – but most importantly they got straight to the heart of the matter and changed minds.

We can actively trace the almost seismic effect of this book upon a surprisingly large number of individuals in different parts of Britain. This is because the authorities started to take people to court for printing and selling it. But this was only the start of the inspired *Age of Reason*'s long and disruptive history as a blasphemous text. Indeed, it ranks as the most prosecuted single work in the whole history of Western blasphemy. This has also given it a contrary reputation as one of the most influential free-thought works. Its fame lies, significantly, in its role as an enlightening text that has been involved in the conversion of its readers to atheism or agnosticism well into modern times.

The first bookseller to feel the wrath of the authorities was Thomas Williams, who was really nothing more than an impoverished street seller who got caught red-handed with a number of copies of *The Age of Reason*. While he pleaded poverty in court, this was scarcely considered a legitimate defence and he received a prison sentence of one year with hard labour. Surprisingly, the prosecuting counsel, Thomas Erskine, took pity on the defendant, even going to the trouble of visiting and assisting his destitute family. This case prompted Paine himself to put forward further arguments that limitation of opinion was tyranny.

> Of all the tyrannies that afflict mankind, tyranny in religion is the worst. Every other species of tyranny is limited to the world we live in, but this attempts a stride beyond the grave and seeks to pursue us into eternity. It is there and not here, it is to God and not to man, it is to a heavenly and not an earthly tribunal, that we are to account for our belief.
>
> If then we believe falsely and dishonourably of the Creator, and that belief is forced upon us, as far as force can operate by human laws and human tribunals, on whom is the criminality of that belief to fall; on those who impose it, or on those on whom it is imposed?[1]

The Conservative World Fights Back

Alongside his display of compassion, Erskine was dramatically scathing about the participation in the prosecution of the Society for the Suppression of Vice. This organization of the concerned, moneyed and urban upper and middle classes was an offshoot of Evangelicalism, counting Lord Shaftesbury among its members alongside other members of the aristocracy and London merchant elite. Such organizations had sprung up in urban Britain towards the end of the seventeenth century. In many respects, they were a response to the periods of chaos and apparent lawlessness that characterized the century. In the initially cosy Restoration world, it quickly became evident that challenges to the status quo, and to the Stuart regime, lay around every corner. After the Monmouth Rebellion of 1685 and the dangers of the Glorious Revolution of 1688, the watchword became the maintenance of discipline throughout society.

Societies to police all sorts of vice emerged like flowers in spring, seeking to charm – and coerce if necessary – the populace at large into compliance and obedience. These societies became quite a culture in their own right, spawning a conservative literature providing moral instruction for their officers, and constables employed by towns and parishes. These manuals explained how to detect and police vice, and offered guidance for constables executing the minutiae of their duties. They were even available for the general public to read, in the hope they would perform the twin functions of deterrent and reassurance.

Constables were to observe the usual suspects with extreme caution. Detecting and suppressing blasphemous literature was precisely one of these duties. Thus drovers, carters, soldiers, sailors and all itinerants were to be watched and their misdemeanours reported to the magistrate, who would issue fines according to the transgressor's monetary means. All this was to be done for a variety of reasons, some of them very familiar to us from blasphemy's earlier history. As one of these pamphlets put it:

> Forasmuch as the horrid, impious, and execrable vice of profane cursing and swearing (so highly displeasing to Almighty God, and loathsome and offensive to every Christian), is become so frequent and notorious, that, unless speedily and effectually punished, it may justly provoke the divine vengeance to increase the many calamities these nations now labour under.[2]

The 'Vice Society', as it became known, took to this task with unbridled enthusiasm, galvanized by a little fear. Their actions suited the government admirably. Initially the Common Law of blasphemous libel was more easily and readily used against blasphemous writings than the Statute Law of 1698, which was already out of date. It was also true that having a private agency undertake the government's work was efficient, and ensured effort was neither wasted nor duplicated. Nonetheless, this did mean that the government was at the mercy of the Society's reputation and profile, as well as the competence of those it employed and relied on.

The assault on the private vice of individuals and wider political danger began just before the start of the 1820s. After the end of the Napoleonic Wars the economy fell into a steep decline, creating mass unemployment and distress. Calls for representation in Parliament and other reforms were resisted, with the symbolic touchstone event being the Peterloo Massacre of August 1819. This meeting of families who had come to hear Henry Hunt speak at a political meeting in Manchester was charged by the mounted local yeomanry with their sabres drawn. In the carnage that followed, eleven people were killed on the field and several hundred injured – others would die later in fighting that ensued as the crowd dispersed in confusion. Radicals never forgot this incident and the government maintained its pursuit of political radicalism with the passing of the Six Acts.

This legislation aimed to limit the circulation of politically revolutionary opinion by preventing seditious meetings, military drilling and the production of arms. The Acts also imposed a fourpenny stamp duty on newspapers and determined to single out blasphemous and seditious works for prosecution. The association between blasphemy and sedition had been completed by the fact that seditious ideas from France had come to Britain via Paine, with his particularly godless message. The conservatively minded in England inherited the zeal and nosiness of the Vice Society; they gave it a wider and more coherent identity by preaching that England's prosperity had been founded on isolation from Europe, and a populace more or less content with their lot in life and their supposedly elevated place in a cosy afterlife. Radical ideas that advocated the levelling of society, and preached against the fraudulence of an afterlife, were dangerous and pernicious. Above all, they were recklessly cruel in their desire to ride roughshod over the simple aspirations of the poor to reach for heaven. Although radicals argued this was self-interest on the part of the landed and rich in the here and now, this fear that heaven was lost for the poor, and the poor in spirit, was also genuine.

High Tory commentators like Hannah More (1745–1833) had a prolific record of producing tracts defending all manifestations of the Establishment, and More in particular occupies an important place in the moral and political history of these years. She tried to paint over the radicalism contained in reforming and revolutionary Jacobin pamphlets by distributing God-fearing ones of her own. One pamphlet of hers, entitled *Village Politics*, created the image of Britain and its constitution as a vast edifice that had been steadily maintained and repaired by its scrupulous and genuinely concerned ruling classes. In pushing these ideas she was joined by the gentry of towns up and down the country, who composed formal addresses of loyalty. These were hastily composed, printed and distributed after the reaction to Peterloo had given the propertied classes sleepless nights. The works expressed the extensive foreboding of the propertied at the conscious wavering of devotion to Britain's sacred institutions. Alongside support for the king, the blessings bestowed upon the country through the benign influence of the Church were contrasted with the evils and terrors of blasphemous Jacobin ideas. The loyal address from Norwich, for example, strenuously attacked 'doctrines that tend to overthrow the salutary distinctions of civilized life, to undermine and destroy the sacred influences of Religion, and to subvert the Established Government of the Nation'. Similarly, the speech from York deplored attacks upon the British Constitution 'by blasphemous and seditious Publications, and by the speeches and conduct of evil-minded Demagogues'.[3]

This was no longer so much a religious struggle, as an ideological and political one. But ironically, these loyal addresses told Jacobin blasphemers what the ruling classes were afraid of, and thus arguably gave them an immense series of clues and ideas about how best to frighten the Establishment, about where and how to strike the most effective blows.

Richard Carlile, His Compatriots and Blasphemy as Social Progress

Blasphemers were now no longer isolated individuals. They were fiercely confident products of the Enlightenment who had conscious beliefs about the universe that they publicized in lucid and engaging arguments. Indeed, their articulacy seemed to make them still more dangerous, and this was itself a product of their engagement with the requirements of popular writing. The most successful and noteworthy of these individuals was Richard Carlile. He had been a provincial tradesman who arrived in London and was radicalized by his experiences there. He had witnessed the events at Peterloo and had been caustic in his reporting of the atrocities that occurred. As a result, he was already considered an enemy of the government and the wide scope of the Six Acts meant he would regularly fall within their sights.

Carlile inherited Thomas Paine's ideas and his critique of society that saw the people robbed both of property and the ability to think for themselves. The Six Acts were, to Carlile and his compatriots, repressive measures removing the opportunity for free discussion – on matters of religion, politics and a host of other subjects – in the name of preserving a corrupt state. Being prosecuted for blasphemy was one particularly effective method of criticizing the law and its operation in Georgian society, which otherwise afforded almost no other method for doing so. This meant that the bouts of verbal fencing that Carlile and his friends undertook in court were clever, subtle methods of spotting the cracks and fissures in the edifice of Church, State and law acting as one. It also shows individuals exploiting glaring anomalies to demonstrate how the apparent strength of the eighteenth-century order (and its early nineteenth-century survival) was in fact fragile and flimsy. That line of thinking had been constructed for those operating the law by the logic of the Hale Judgement and its linking of law and religion that we learned about in the previous chapter.

Because religion and law were fused together in this area, in the case of blasphemy the stakes were considerably higher for the authorities. They went into these cases believing they were protecting religion. But, because of the Hale Judgement, they were surprised and disconcerted to discover they had to protect the law and its legitimacy as well. In some instances this last aspect only dawned on the authorities when it was arguably too late to prevent embarrassment – and even the stark appearance of tyrannical high-handedness.

Carlile was prosecuted for publishing Paine's *Age of Reason*, as we know one of the seminal free-thought texts of the nineteenth century. He moved swiftly to launch his own newspaper, the *Republican*, after the demise of *Sherwin's Weekly Political Register* on which he had worked. Carlile stood trial for blasphemy in the autumn of 1819 and was accompanied in court by many of the important radicals of the age, including Henry Hunt and William Hone. Two years earlier,

Hone had himself embarrassed the government when a blasphemy trial against him had ended in acquittal.

Carlile's defence involved reading the entire text of Paine's *Age of Reason*, supposedly as a means of obtaining greater publicity through press reporting of the sentiments contained within it. Some historians doubt that this occurred, but news that it was possible would have at least encouraged any who heard about it to believe that a defendant's day in court might not see their opinion silenced completely.[4]

While as defences go this idea was rather less than stimulating, it highlights that Carlile recognized the court as a centrally important conduit through which to promote the virtues of free speech. Convicted of blasphemy, the sentence of three years' imprisonment and a fine of £1,500 promised to remove Carlile from circulation for some considerable time. He refused to pay the fine and found his publishing stock confiscated. Despite this, he resolved to continue radical publishing and passed the day-to-day running of the paper to his wife Jane. When Jane herself was imprisoned, Carlile's sister Mary Ann took up the post. This became an ongoing agitation as each individual, cornered by the authorities, found their place taken by another willing volunteer, each prepared for prosecution and imprisonment.

The campaign against Carlile also involved the activities of a number of private organizations that concerned themselves with rooting out blasphemers and bringing them to justice. Chief among these was, unsurprisingly, the Society for the Suppression of Vice, which took a particularly uncompromising line with Carlile and his works. Carlile likewise developed a lasting antipathy for this Society, linking it to an overarching conspiracy to deny free speech and free discussion of religious matters. This was something which he saw as the essence of freedom – a right which should not be denied within a world regulated by nature and natural laws.[5]

This reference to natural laws is fiercely contrasted here with the artificial and fabricated law associated with the Christian social order. Importantly, this stance echoed the idea of freedom touted by the philosopher Jean-Jacques Rousseau (1712–1778); and it is no surprise to see Carlile's approach, methods and ideas appealing to twentieth-century anarchists in England. The confidence in free speech arguments appeared early in Carlile's propaganda, so that he really believed that exploring and advocating his opinions was a guarantee of social progress – an idea which would crop up time and again in the ideas and court defences of both him and his compatriots. He told the Vice Society:

> The publication, I admit, may be offensive to some, but not to the virtuous and well meaning part of the community; it is offensive to those persons only who are interested in supporting the corruptions and abuses of the system we live under.[6]

The report of the trial of Mrs Susannah Wright for publishing the writings and correspondences of Richard Carlile gives us a first encounter with one of his accomplices. Wright was arrested as a result of the raid in February 1822 on the premises from which Carlile had been operating. Like the rest of Carlile's compatriots, Wright offered a firm and strident defence, seeking to convince anyone who would listen of the pure motives behind, and morality of, her actions. She commenced with an unambiguous accusation that Christianity was false and 'gross and cruel in its origin and progress', and further pleaded for the people to have representative government.

Wright denied having malicious motives, turning the accusations against her on their head by suggesting that the legal system supporting Christianity nurtured an inequality of treatment between faiths. From this she cross-examined witnesses and uncovered that they had been reasonably well paid by the Vice Society to lodge evidence against her. Indeed, they were making something of a living from doing so. It also became clear in questioning that these individuals scarcely knew their catechism, so the law was aided by witnesses and accomplices who were ignorant of religion.

Wright returned to conclude her case, advising the jury to 'be firm and do your duty' and insisting that she both scorned 'mercy and demand[ed] justice'. The jury obliged, swiftly returning a guilty verdict. It would be four months before Wright returned to court for sentencing. This time her notoriety attracted more of the public gaze – in both crowd numbers and press interest. When offered the opportunity to address the court, in 'plea of mitigation of punishment', Wright instead challenged the validity of the guilty verdict, arguing that Christianity had no place in the law.[7] The Chief Justice issued repeated warnings to her to desist from profaning the law and the Church in his court. To the amusement of the crowded courtroom she retorted, 'You, Sir, are paid to hear me.'[8] Infuriated by her obstinacy, the judge sentenced Wright (and by default her infant child with her in the courtroom) to be confined for ten weeks in the loathed Newgate prison.

A year later further prosecutions were instigated, one of these against James Watson for having sold another copy of Elihu Palmer's *Principles of Nature* (1801).[9] This book was often seen as a counterpart to Paine's work, and it followed the trend of identifying knowledge with social progress. Watson saw moral and political revolution naturally springing from older forms of tyranny. In the 25th chapter of his book Palmer declares:

> It has been during the last century that these things have been accomplished; the force of intellectual powers has been applied to the development of principle, and the combination of human labours already constitutes a colossus, against which the storms of unequal and aristocratic governments may dash in vain. The art of printing is so universally known, or rather the knowledge of it is diffused in so many countries, that it will henceforth be impossible to destroy it. The present moment exhibits the most astonishing effects of this powerful invention in the hands of nations, by that universal diffusion of principle and collision of thought, which are the most substantial guarantee of the future scientific progress of the human race. An effectual stand has been made, and resuscitated nations at this moment bid defiance to the double despotism of church and state.[10]

Watson was later to gain fame as one of early nineteenth-century radicalism's most prolific publishers, agitating for a 'cheap and honest press' and becoming involved in the Chartist movement of the later 1830s and 1840s.[11] Like others, Watson was prepared to vouch for the morality of the works he was selling, noting that the supposed corrupting influence of Palmer's work could not be proved. Watson also delved into the work itself in search of material with which to defend himself. He was anxious to create an established pantheon of reason, something his extensive reading had inspired him to undertake. This listed and explained the fearful consequences of intolerance in previous ages, citing, for instance, the excommunication of Galileo in 1508. Watson doubted the value of a God who had devolved power to lesser agencies of oppression and thus he doubted the court's authority to act as God's representative. This case also emphasized that the fact of publication was material to the prosecution and in most instances undermined the direction of the defence offered by Carlile's shopmen and -women. Although ineffectual witnesses inconveniently demonstrated that they could not comprehend what blasphemy was – much to the embarrassment of the prosecution – cases tended to concentrate on the fact of publication, with the expectation that the book's blasphemy would effectively speak for itself.

Suggesting that the book would 'speak for itself' was a view politically, philosophically and culturally opposed to that of the blasphemy defendants. These were men and women who repeatedly argued that the court was a place within the public sphere where the justice, utility, veracity and reason behind all systems of rules and government should be debated and evaluated. These individuals wanted the issues to be debated in the cold light of day. In seeking to silence defendants the court had used the language of keeping things hidden and again the lineage to Paine's suggestion about the monarchy as a charade exposed when the curtain is drawn back to reveal the light of day.[12]

The trial of William Campion has left us one of the most detailed accounts of what it was like to be a defendant in one of these trials. Campion believed that his honesty of motive and the 'truth' together exonerated his actions. He defended the morality of the works of Thomas Paine, arguing they were superior to the Bible. Following others, as well as the lead of his ideological mentor, he stressed that his target was the spurious Establishment of priestcraft and not any actual deity. Lastly he offered a version of the standard 'Tiberian' argument, which stressed that an omnipotent God should be capable of exacting his own revenge, without recourse to the power, institutions and punishments of men. In trying to secure an acquittal he addressed the jury and unwittingly demonstrated the potential danger of his Jacobin ideas:

Do as you would be done by; tolerate Theists, that they may
one day tolerate you; and recollect, that many a Christian
priest, who, during the French Revolution expiated his
bigotry on the Guillotine, must have lamented, that he prosecuted philosophy, and that he kept the people in ignorance,
till suddenly enlightened, they dashed into all the excesses
of revenge.[13]

The court itself was caught in something of a dilemma, as what
happened next demonstrates. Prosecuting counsel Sir Claudius
Hunter whispered some words in the ear of the judge. The judge
said, in reply, 'I think he had better not be interrupted.' At this
instant, one of the jurors asked, 'Are we to sit, and hear all this, my
Lord? I am quite sick of hearing it.' The recorder said he was loath
to interrupt the defendant, 'because he knew what was generally
said elsewhere, upon such occasions, by those who were enemies
to everything in the shape of law, order, and religion'.[14] Thus the
court, the judge and the jurors were cleverly boxed in by the tactics
of Carlile and his shopmen and -women. Those in authority in the
courtroom were thus damned if they did and damned if they didn't.

The trial of Mary Ann Carlile, the sister of Richard, introduced
another dynamic in 1821. In the courtroom she had clashed with
the judge, who had sought to prevent what he saw as unwarranted
criticism of the laws of England. Prevented from offering what she
saw as a full and coherent statement of her position, the text she
had intended to read in court began to circulate as her 'Suppressed
Defence'. This was another unexpected coup for Carlile, his shopmen and -women and their campaign. It introduced an element of
sensationalism and rapidly inspired sales. Mary Ann Carlile's trial
text ended with an uncompromising indictment of the blasphemy
laws themselves. She declared:

Christianity, I am bold to assert, is totally undefinable, and
Proteus-like, has assumed every shape, therefore any attempt
to bring it within the verge of those rules which are said to
constitute common law is morally impossible.[15]

This group of blasphemers were a danger to the law because of
how the law had been codified by Sir Matthew Hale in 1676. They

realized this and became adept at using the court to demonstrate the illegitimacy of the law and the religious dogmas which underpinned it – as Christianity, and the law made its instrument, were visibly and suitably disgraced. The link between religion and the law was seen in the eighteenth century by thinkers such as Edmund Burke as a mark of strength and continuity. This link was now exposed within its own institutions as potentially untenable and weak precisely because it was draconian.

As such these blasphemers used the oxygen of publicity in a manner that Thomas Paine (their ideological progenitor) would have wholeheartedly approved. These were the fledgling arguments for modern versions of free speech in England and beyond. These defendants were very effective in noting how the law restricted discussion because it had a vested interest in doing so. Because of this, it is no surprise to see Carlile, and his shopmen and -women, mentioned in modern reformulations of free-speech arguments, notably one produced during the Salman Rushdie affair, to which we will turn in a subsequent chapter.

Blasphemy in Europe and America after the Enlightenment

Despite the threat of the Jacobin revolution being exported to England, France still had blasphemy laws that sought social peace, even during the revolutionary period. The provisions of the revolutionary government of 1795, and later the Napoleonic Code of 1810, accorded religion at least an acceptable role within the emerging societies that were so different from the *ancien régime*. Both of these statutes placed a significant emphasis upon the crime of disrupting religious worship. A later Act of 1822 – under the restored monarchy – specified a prison term of up to five years and a fine of up to six thousand francs for attacking the State religion. A clause within the legislation extended this protection to a number of other religious groups deemed acceptable.[16]

Across the ocean, America had something of a collision with the Enlightenment. As we have seen, in the seventeenth century many states developed their own religious settlements, ranging in character from intolerance bordering on tyranny through to a modern-looking, relatively permissive religious freedom. The break with England involved the drafting of a fully codified constitution that aimed to provide enabling structures for freedom of thought and practice. Remembering that religious intolerance had forced their ancestors to emigrate to America, the early colonists had let states decide upon their own religious settlement. However, the American Revolution catapulted the country into an Enlightenment-inspired proto-democracy, one that had constitutionally enshrined 'inalienable' rights, rather than granting them conditionally to the populace. Most histories see this as a beneficial and comfortable form of evolution, but inevitably it did not come entirely free of baggage.[17]

One example of this was that the Constitution created a new – and for some contemporaries artificial – separation of Church and State. This was welcomed as giving freedom of worship, but there were also consequences for the national government's apparatuses for legislating and protecting religion from harmful criticism. This came to be tested in a case against John Ruggles in 1811 – a case that seems to have jumped, virtually unaltered, from seventeenth-century England. Just like John Taylor, Ruggles had taken the Gospel accounts of Jesus' early life at their word and had drawn the same conclusions as his English forebear. In an echo of Taylor, Ruggles had spoken publicly of his profanely stated belief that 'Jesus Christ was a bastard and his mother must be a whore.'[18] Ruggles was convicted – perhaps inevitably – and was sentenced to a $500 fine and three months' imprisonment.[19]

As a blasphemy defendant, Ruggles was almost forgotten by the legal minds who preferred to concentrate upon the judge's ruling. Such lawyers wanted to be certain how and why the State had a right and duty to punish him. In this way, the case unwittingly raised some thorny issues. The State of New York had no blasphemy statute and it seemed that, in the opinion of many, Ruggles would qualify for protection under the First Amendment. The question thus arose as to whether he was, in fact, being punished with the pernicious, and now considered alien, influence of English Common Law – precedents that still clung to America's cultural and legal landscape. The presiding judge at Ruggles's appeal, James Kent, did his best to import the Hale Judgement into American law. He argued that all blasphemy contravened public morals and it was therefore the duty of any responsible legal mind to stamp on it unequivocally. But this view was not universally accepted and many saw the argument as the product of an out-of-touch generation. These same people then reminded themselves of Thomas Jefferson's wish to push religion much further back into the shadows than had actually occurred; indeed, some of these commentators even spoke of the fact that the American Revolution felt somehow unfinished, as though a glimpse at how so-called freedoms could become conditional once again was a matter for serious concern. Ironically, this fear of the centralizing State greedily grabbing the power to regulate opinion where it could, would be turned inside out by the time we reach the twentieth century, as we shall see.

Foote, Coleridge and Manner

In England, the case that really was a milestone in blasphemy prosecution occurred in the early 1880s. The atheist newspaper editor George William Foote looked on aghast at the ruthless treatment of the country's foremost atheist Charles Bradlaugh. Foote found himself more incensed by the day as he observed the animosity and legal challenges Bradlaugh received from the hostile forces ranged against him – ruthless opponents of his attempts to enter Parliament. There were threats to bankrupt and prosecute Bradlaugh at every turn, all with the goal of removing this dangerous atheist menace from late Victorian public life.[20]

Foote resolved to get himself prosecuted for blasphemy, in the hope that apparently medieval laws would be shown up for what they were by the 'spirit of the age'. He congratulated himself that his stand was principled, but it did also sell newspapers – especially when his periodical the *Freethinker* could eventually print on its cover that it had been 'prosecuted for blasphemy'. The paper tried all it could to push boundaries of taste, profanity and humour. It had often forsaken serious-minded criticism of religion in favour of cartoons that mocked the apparently ridiculous situations in several biblical stories. This almost instinctively reminded readers of the juvenile and ill-judged sniggering they may have indulged in when they were children. This was the Bible made fun of, pulled off its pedestal of sanctity and seriousness.

But Foote waited in vain. Complaints had started to land on the desks of civil servants and Home Secretary Sir William Harcourt, but nothing was done. Certainly Harcourt had a lot of other things on his plate. These included an illegal French pornography trade running out of control in the capital, Irish terrorists and a smuggling ring involved in whisking unsuspecting young women to inhabit dens of iniquity in Brussels. Foote gamely kept going and eventually got his wish.

Although the cartoons caught the imagination – not to mention the headlines – the authorities fought shy of airing this comic potential in court. Nonetheless, Sir William Harcourt's forbearance had snapped and eventually Foote was prosecuted for a much more serious-minded article written by a correspondent, William Heaford. This turned a stock Christian phrase around to ask 'What shall I do to be damned?'[21]

To cap it all, Foote carried on with the cartoons and illustrations. Eventually he surpassed previous efforts with his Christmas number of the *Freethinker* in 1882. This contained a 'Comic Life of Christ', which comprised amusing skits on verses from the Gospels, including Christ being annunciated by the animals in the stable and preaching the Sermon on the Mount from the upstairs room of a pub. Foote pointedly went for the jugular with these illustrations; and, whatever else he did, Foote did confirm something about viewing the Christian religion as a 'religion of the book'. To believe this to be the word of God, rationality and credibility had often to be suspended, something Foote was determined to prove was discomforting.

Thus Foote regularly tapped the shoulder of his sympathetic readership, and even those appalled by his ribaldry, and made them realize that central Christian beliefs and stories had almost unbelievable comic potential. What came to be seen as the most offensive depiction of all was Foote's recreation of the text of Exodus 33: 21–3, a text in which God attempted to show his 'back parts' to Moses. Foote interpreted this in juvenile fashion, portraying God's bottom clothed in a threadbare and patched pair of trousers, accompanied by the unnerving and scatological suggestion that flatulence emanated from it. Crude and disrespectful, the image had the desired effect and Foote's publishing stock was hurriedly seized. He received a summons alongside two partners in crime involved with him in the paper: William Ramsey and Henry Kemp.

From this point onwards the authorities made some very old-fashioned assumptions. They tried to argue that Foote's publication was detrimental to public morals, was obscene, was instigated by the Devil and that the espousal of such morals indicated the degraded social class of the accused. Foote countered these accusations with some new ideas that signalled a change of tack from previous defences and past, failed attempts to use expert evidence. Foote argued that the forthright vulgarity of Salvation Army evangelism was an affront to his sensibilities as an unbeliever and was thus, to him, a form of blasphemy. Certainly his cartoons and journalism had been full of this motif of the coarseness and apparent poor taste of Booth and his followers. Despite instruction to the jury by Justice North, who sought a conviction, the jury could not reach a verdict and was discharged, the case to be heard again a few days later. North then refused the defendants bail, which reinforced the popular belief that all three of them could be considered by the authorities, and this judge in particular, to be a danger to public morals. Foote and his friends saw this as a calculated form of oppression, one which also had the added inconvenience of damaging preparations for their defence at the imminent retrial.

Foote and his compatriots were not nearly so lucky at the second hearing. Their evidence fell on deaf ears and Justice North argued that attempts to liken the *Freethinker* to other publications and invoke its place in the 'spirit of the age' were kicked into touch. North maintained that the paper was unique and should thus receive similarly unique treatment. The jury was much less impressed by Foote and his defence this time, and they found him guilty without leaving the courtroom.[22] This was what Foote wanted, but he did not quite count on the treatment that North had in store for him, Ramsey and Kemp: Foote was sentenced to twelve months in jail, Ramsey to nine months and Kemp to three months.

While Foote had wanted to provoke, he surely did not have a sustained prison sentence in mind as a likely outcome. The courtroom was in uproar and very soon news broke to all astonished sections of liberal and intellectual England. Petitions started to arrive at the Home Office, and some influential individuals let their disquiet be known. One of these was the Archbishop of Canterbury Edward White Benson, who wanted neither martyrs for free-thought, nor the good name of Christianity and its quest for purity dragged through the mud.

A crucial facet of the Foote prosecution was the importance legal contemporaries drew from the case, as indeed did the defendant.

In pronouncing upon the last of these cases against Foote, the attitude of Justice John Duke Coleridge was much more sympathetic. He allowed the airing of expert evidence and went so far as to eventually concede that the prosecution of blasphemy could be considered an ill-considered use of a bad law. Eventually this jury, like the first, failed to agree and the prosecution dropped the case.

Coleridge was now able to pronounce upon the current state of the law and what should happen to this crime thereafter. He deliberated long and hard, and, through this, one piece of case law changed the course of blasphemy's modern history in the English-speaking world. He finally overturned the straightjacketed statute that had been created by Sir Matthew Hale in the 1670s. Coleridge concluded that there may be something in Foote's quest to elevate the 'spirit of the age'. He was now prepared to accept that Christianity was no longer 'part and parcel of the laws of England'.[23] The sundering of these two institutions meant that the legal and cultural landscape of blasphemy – how to think about it or deal with it – appeared empty and desolate. Coleridge's way forward was to construct some alternative edifice (some legal commentators such as James Fitzjames Stephen (1829–1894) would call it a folly) that would regulate religious behaviour. Coleridge lighted upon the concept of 'manner' and this would govern legal thinking in blasphemy cases for almost the entirety of the next century. Christianity, and the rigid sanctity of its doctrines, could no longer be realistically defended as something monolithic.

In the contemporary world, Coleridge wisely concluded, publication restrictions meant that the courts would be full to the brim with sceptics, and perhaps even the only mildly curious. This was a potentially alarming state of affairs. Coleridge now argued that lawyers had to think of how blasphemy might occur in real situations. His idea of 'manner' provided a means of thinking deeply not about how blasphemy was theorized and created by the blasphemer, but instead shifted concentration to the complainant. It was how the individual reacted to what they heard, or read, that now became crucial.

This shift actually fitted in quite reasonably to a world that was developing a more sophisticated public sphere. Discussions that had previously attracted prosecution, and punishment, could now happen behind closed doors among like-minded adults. This was considered fine, since no one's sensibilities were assaulted, nor was anyone subjected to having their sacred beliefs lampooned or ridiculed. However, conducting the same conversation in public was a different matter. Individuals had a responsibility to ensure their opinions did not offend. One could criticize Christianity, but actively insulting God opened the door to a blasphemy prosecution.

Coleridge, and the interpretation of law he offered, worked to ensure that the public recognized the difference between these two scenarios. This also allowed the authorities and those charged with policing to rest a lot easier. Trying to decide what was blasphemous and what was not was quite often beyond the average policeman, as Carlile and his friends had frequently demonstrated. Precisely establishing who sold a blasphemous periodical to a particular police constable – and quite whether this had damaged the latter's moral outlook – had for some years carried the whiff of farce.

So when and how might Coleridge and the authorities presume that blasphemy prosecutions and court cases would occur in the future? The answer was fortuitous, yet in its elegance it also seemed to exhibit elements of calculating genius. The law of blasphemous libel had always been English Common Law, leaving responsibility for bringing prosecutions in the hands of the public at large. With words like 'manner' and 'offensiveness' attached to the new legal philosophy of the crime, the authorities could safely take a back seat. They were then awaiting manifestations of the public's anxiety to bring what was deemed unacceptable to the attention of policing agencies.

This approach even felt quite liberal since silence meant that what was in the public domain and went unmolested was either wholly acceptable, or at least tolerated. The beauty of this situation was that the capacity for toleration, and the blissful silence that resulted from it, could be counted on to progress as public taste became more liberal. This whole approach became a part of Home Office folklore, advice that would regularly be dusted down to remind overzealous politicians and nervous police constables of why things were as they were. What is especially interesting is that its logic would be demonstrated with most zeal and urgency to would-be reformers and repealers of the law. This was because their meddling had the capacity to not only upset the balance but to damage society.

Some, such as the distinguished judge James Fitzjames Stephen, detested this solution, since it made both a bad legal principle and a bad law credible. Although a vehement opinion, more attention was paid to the accusation that this was a law biased in favour of the educated and the professional. The books and journals that used rhetoric and intellectually biting phrases would be left alone or actively ignored. In contrast, the rather coarser street-corner orator could easily fall foul of the passing public, and the attitude of policemen called to the scene.

As English Common Law this solution and its consequences spread into Britain's colonies and became the bedrock of case law on blasphemy in, for example, Australia until the last years of the twentieth century. Given the considerable degrees of licence that the law allowed, it is no surprise that in Britain this religious 'settlement', such as it was, would endure and (mostly) flourish for almost a hundred years.

Throughout this period, it never seems to have occurred to the authorities that they had been duped by George William Foote. He engineered their compliance in his martyrdom, and they in turn had furnished him with all the credentials to be the hero. He could scarcely have wished for more. Foote had considerably more than his day in court, he gave his histrionic defence speech reminiscent of Socrates at this trial, mentioning all the arguments he could reasonably think of. He allowed himself to upbraid the judge about the draconian nature of Christian punishment, and he received a relatively lenient, albeit perhaps unexpected, prison sentence. While the last of these proved discomforting, Foote was nonetheless quietly pleased that his punishment would be a relatively drawn out and public affair. This of course gave him the chance to write up his experiences and have them serialized in his own newspaper. The column functioned as a weekly drip that fed the indignation of his supporters and sympathizers. When he was eventually released it was, unsurprisingly, to a hero's welcome.

The aftermath of the Foote case seems to have taught both sides some important lessons, although these were not learned as swiftly as they could have been. Sir William Harcourt learned to listen with more discretion to his civil servants, and thereafter did his level best to ignore the *Freethinker* and its provocative images. He thus hoped it could no longer benefit from the publicity of regular irritating and counterproductive 'show' trials.

Foote himself continued to publish the biblical cartoons and waspish, atheist content in his paper, but it never again attained the same prominence. Hopes to extend the audience for sustained anti-clerical humour also resulted in some new ventures. While the higher-brow agnostic and atheist press steered clear of the kind of ribaldry that Foote became known for, his friend and former co-defendant Ramsey launched a comic satirical paper called the *Jerusalem Star*. In some respects it resembled a contemporary publication like *Viz* but in others *Private Eye*. It had a nose for the ridiculous alongside a sensitivity to the styles of the New Journalism of the late 1880s. This paper reinvented biblical stories to make them seem as though they were happening within the contemporary world. Thus they took seeing the funny side of biblical stories to an entirely new level, noting for example how insanitary Noah's Ark had become by the fortieth day. This juxtaposition of the Bible with the modern way of reporting news was a further attempt to make the Bible seem ancient, anachronistic and again ridiculous. Satirizing the growing phenomenon of newspaper advertising, the paper also offered its readers insurance against fire 'in this world and the next'. While a potentially great idea at the time, at least in the mind of Ramsey, it fizzled out after a few issues as the joke quickly grew thin.

Certainly public taste was fickle, but this also shows that criticism of the Almighty could have a more serious intent and form. Foote himself was scarcely averse to this and it seemed obvious to him that his more serious, hard-hitting attacks on the injustice and immorality of Christian doctrine could not be so easily prosecuted as the mocking and the ribald. While Foote and his compatriots were dedicated opponents of Christianity who demanded the right to say so, it was the actual mechanism of free speech itself that would take blasphemy in a slightly different direction – albeit one equally spawned by the consequences of the Enlightenment.

Religious tolerance meant that the story of Christianity was open to many and varied interpretations. This possibility of interpretation and reinterpretation multiplied further still when we consider that Christianity had many central figures within its story that exhibited human emotions and frailties. Removed from wholly divine status, at least in the thinking of some religious denominations, the opportunity to discuss the nature and motivation of biblical personalities seemed almost an invitation.

Writers, Artists and New Agers –
The Coming of Modern Blasphemy

So far we have met the religious professionals who juggled these stories and interpretations, as well as the atheists who had no time for them. What the end of the nineteenth century also gave us was the creative individual who found in Christianity – and indeed other religions – raw material to 'think with'. This pulled some individuals into areas such as theosophy and spiritualism, as well as the first wave of esoteric belief we would now characterize as New Age. This was an atmosphere of searching and seeking that would take on a new earnestness as the *fin de siècle* turned into the First World War. As part of late nineteenth-century counter-culture the Almighty and the nature of Christian ideas became something for writers and artists to draw inspiration from. If the religious radicals of the early nineteenth century had pioneered the right to say what they liked about God and Christianity, as the century wore on, it became the role of writers and philosophers to pull this in many different directions.

Matthew Arnold (1822–1888) quietly lamented the ebbing of his 'Sea of Faith', a metaphor frequently tinkered with by subsequent generations, as though he had self-consciously created a blueprint for something more profound with his *Dover Beach* of 1867. Meanwhile, George Eliot had read David Strauss's *Das Leben Jesu* (Life of Jesus, 1835), which reopened the question of Christ's divinity. Despite having lost her faith, her novels henceforth were filled with motifs of redemption and salvation, and how these were a problem for all contemporary protagonists. Thomas Hardy's (1840–1928) characters regularly fell foul of a universe that at best could be characterized as indifferent to their hopes and suffering. Hardy would be followed by more naturalist heirs like D. H. Lawrence, and more modernist ones like Joyce, who actively sought to pull Western man beyond his Judaeo-Christian heritage.

Others went yet further. August Strindberg, a man cynical about all bourgeois institutions, turned his jaundiced eye upon marriage and what humans might expect from it. In passing he had called the Eucharist 'an impudent deception' and tried to quantify its true value to mankind like a commodity that had a purely monetary worth.[24] He expected criticism from those who believed he had devalued marriage. Instead his remarks were considered anti-religious by the queen of Sweden. He was thence prosecuted by the Swedish Justice Ministry, which accused him of mocking the word of God. A tide of free speech advocacy ensured Strindberg was acquitted, but he fell foul of widespread reluctance to actually see the work in question go to print. Notoriety in the world of blasphemy could be a fickle beast and it could taint the careers of those who wished to be known for something else.

After the Foote case, the courtroom and dock were regularly used as platforms for the advocacy of free speech and the defence of unpopular views. This happened in the United States just a few years after Foote's trial with the 1887 trial of C. B. Reynolds, an American atheist missionary and later a congressman. Reynolds had preached his atheist message throughout New Jersey and, after receiving short shrift in one town, had produced a cartoon depiction of his poor treatment, which he circulated in another part of the state. This leaflet was considered blasphemous and he was prosecuted. The trial provided an opportunity for America's foremost celebrity atheist of the period, Robert Ingersoll, to address the court. He noted that religious ideas and the groups that advocated them were all oppressed in the earliest days of their existence, sometimes through the consequences of regime change. Catholics, Lutherans, Puritans, Episcopalians, Presbyterians and Unitarians all had to brave their way through oppression at some point in the past. It was this imposition of orthodoxy that was anathema to religious freedom. The absolutist nature of such thought made American society hypocritical and the American people hypocrites. Ingersoll argued that

> What is blasphemy in one country would be a religious exhortation in another. It is owing to where you are and who is in authority. And let me call your attention to the impudence and bigotry of the American Christians. We send missionaries to other countries. What for? To tell them that their religion is false, that their Gods are myths and monsters, that their Saviours and apostles were imposters, and that our religion is true.[25]

Ingersoll thus called for a renewed sense of humility in his declaration that: 'Every man who has thought, knows not only how little he knows, but how little every other human being knows, and how ignorant after all the world must be.'[26]

Men like Ingersoll, Reynolds and Foote all thought that they were writing the epitaph of blasphemy. They had entered the dock sure in the knowledge that they were fighting the good fight against tyranny and that human benevolence would tame the idea of God in the minds of men and women. After all, civilization had brought us to this juncture, and was it not time that the idea of God be rewritten and rethought to simply keep up with the age? In seeking to defend C. B. Reynolds against a charge of blasphemy Ingersoll forcefully argued:

Gentlemen, you can never make me believe – no statute can ever convince me, that there is any infinite being in this universe who hates an honest man. It is impossible to satisfy me that there is any God, or can be any God, who holds in abhorrence a soul that has the courage to express its thought. Neither can the whole world convince me that any man should be punished, either in this world or the next, for being candid with his fellow-men. If you send men to the penitentiary for speaking their thoughts, for endeavouring to enlighten their fellows, then the penitentiary will become a place of honour, and the victim will step from it – not stained, not disgraced, but clad in robes of glory.[27]

These views brim over with the liberal, progressive confidence that was forged by the struggles of Paine, Carlile, Ruggles, Foote and Reynolds. While the next generation hoped to be inheritors of an unrestricted free speech, the assumption that progress could continue unfettered, aided by modernism, would be sorely tested throughout the coming century.

SIX

BLASPHEMY IN THE TWENTIETH CENTURY

The hopes for unrestricted free speech seen in the last chapter evaporated rather quickly as the end of the nineteenth century witnessed a new threat to the Western world in the shape of political anarchism. This ideology challenged precisely the coercive nature of the State that had developed on the back of policing opinion and civil rights. It was, in fact, the very stuff that blasphemy prosecutions had been made of since the early modern period. Individual opinion found itself still doing battle with what it construed to be a coercive state that defended its own interests while enslaving people into spurious beliefs.

Modern Blasphemers, Anarchists and Political Dissidents

Political anarchism was a menace to governments throughout the first two decades of the twentieth century. It spawned dangerous people who wanted to disrupt society, with one American anarchist, Emma Goldman, declaring that 'Anarchism is the great liberator of man from the phantoms that have held him captive; it is the arbiter and pacifier of the two forces for individual and social harmony.'[1] As a part of their philosophy of direct action, anarchists saw the use of dynamite as a panacea for the ills of society. While violence and assassination, perpetrated by the most extreme adherents, took the headlines, there was also a less obvious, but nonetheless potent, all-out assault on Christianity. Religion still seemed to be the dominant ideology enslaving minds that otherwise would be free and, so the militants believed, inclined to anarchism's version of the spirit within. Anarchism's seductive draw was that it offered a remedy for social evils while promising freedom and an overturning of the social order, all at once.

In both Britain and America radicals with anarchist connections set about using blasphemy as a tool to undermine government support for Christianity. In England the chief miscreants were three individuals from Bradford – Ernest Pack, Thomas William Stewart and John William Gott. These were men who had actively stepped aside from the socialist movement in Britain, in the belief that it had been infiltrated, quite insidiously, by the agents of Christianity. To these three men, Christianity was a belief system that was far too nauseatingly benign and weak for any anarchist to stomach.

We get a flavour of this combativeness and the systematic choice of easy targets in one of the Bradford anarchists' most famous pamphlets, entitled *Rib Ticklers; or, Questions for Parsons* (1900). This was a satirical affair that deliberately sought to appeal to an adolescent audience, or one at least prepared to indulge its adolescent side. Yet there was equally a serious edge to the pamphlet. Gott, Pack and Stewart seemed to have unearthed anew the lesson that Thomas Paine had taught radicals a century earlier: the most effective assault upon authority was to treat it with disdain through humour. Laughing loud and long dismantled authority and its pretensions quicker than most things – Pack was to label this 'the sword of ridicule'.[2] Moreover, the comedic approach allowed *Rib Ticklers; or, Questions for Parsons* to draw from a considerable reservoir of popular humour centring around the failings of Christianity as an explanation of the universe – likewise, the failure of its practitioners to set a moral example was particularly targeted.

Gott's publication was framed as a sequence of rhetorical questions which conjured up a humorous image of hapless clerics trying in vain to answer pointed remarks and jibes. Many touched on centuries-old accusations against the clergy. Their lasciviousness around impressionable young women and the regular abuse of their position and authority apparently made them 'purr round the ladies like black tom cats'. Their greed and willingness to profit financially at the expense of the people was exposed through noting that the Archbishop of Canterbury 'has refused to continue receiving £15,000 a year for preaching "Blessed be ye poor?"'[3] But there were also more hard-hitting questions, which undermined the Christian doctrine of salvation with the argument 'that while Christians consider that murderers are not fit to live with decent folk on earth they are quite good enough to mix with the saints in glory'. Similarly, the death of a mother in a fire with all her children was seen as a malevolent demonstration of God's mercy. The modern taste for evangelistic religion was similarly chided with the observation 'That "*now* is the day of Salvation" and that it has *now* been *now* for about 2,000 years.'[4]

The follow-up, *The Parson's Doom*, lampooned the attitudes of all Christian denominations, using their stances over contemporary religious education as they are observed arguing over the salvation of an individual 'boy'. Catholics emerged from this pasting as arrogant and still smarting from losing their dominant position as the established religion. The Anglican Church was in turn proprietorial and disdainful of both the Catholic and nonconformist threat. Meanwhile nonconformists prayed to smite the other two. The poor 'boy' left in the middle of this squabbling innocently argues that he has been forgotten by these vested interests which quite clearly cannot all be right. All this demonstrated a fierce and unrelenting anti-clericalism. These three individuals saw themselves in a strong radical tradition, and they were prepared to regularly invoke it in the minds of their readership.

Despite the inflammatory message of their writings, it was as much public order concerns that ensured that Stewart, Pack and Gott became a menace to Edwardian England. When these three men held public meetings they offered a three-cornered threat. As might be expected, their attacks on religion were inflammatory, and this also meant that the police had to contend with the potential for immediate threats to public order. Add to these factors that the public meetings provided opportunities for the three men to sell birth control literature and offer private meetings in which related advice was given, and the stage was set for a moral backlash. In some respects Stewart, Pack and Gott had bargained on placing the police in such a dilemma, actively revelling in the panic and discomfort they caused – in this respect we can see them as moral terrorists.

John William Gott had an especially novel method of spreading the message. He owned a mail-order clothing business and advertised 'bundles' in many of the free-thought and radical newspapers. These bundles included a range of clothing for all the family, with an enclosed parcel of what he called 'advanced literature', which was most likely secularist pamphlets but could possibly have contained birth control advice. He also undertook to employ and look after atheist men who had been turned out of their previous employment. Thus it is fair to say that Gott and his compatriots were fully embedded in a subculture that took aim squarely at the Establishment, and that they saw religion as a leading and vulnerable component of the dominant order. Moreover, Gott's 'parcels' delivered this menace right to the very centre of the contemporary family.

But how precisely did Christian England cope with these jibes, insults and unprovoked metaphorical assaults on its central beliefs? There is considerable evidence in Home Office files that senior policemen in the provinces were extremely concerned about the prospect of Stewart, Pack and Gott visiting their town and hawking their ideas and 'wares', while stirring up and worrying the local population. Yet their initial responses were largely inept. This became rapidly obvious when Gott and Stewart were taken to court in Leeds in 1903. This incident strongly emphasized the dilemma of policemen trying to decide what was blasphemous and what was not. The defendants capitalized ruthlessly on the various pitfalls such trials contained for the unwary prosecutors. It looked more than absurd for plain-clothes policemen to be queuing up to purchase Gott's publications, and still more so that the prosecution could not prove that the precise copy bought was the one that had been produced in court as a piece of evidence. A slightly comic note was sounded when the policeman concerned readily admitted he had not read the paper nor even glanced at it, but was nonetheless sure it was the same copy since he recognized the picture on the front.

After this testimony the case rapidly collapsed and the local police and town council were forced to reconsider. They were in a hole but embarrassingly refused to stop digging. The local town clerk, Percy Saunders, wrote to Stewart and Gott defensively arguing that they had no wish to interfere with their arguments, but instead had a duty to regulate the sale of the pamphlet. The pair had stopped selling the pamphlet and this had been the real reason for the withdrawal of the prosecution. Stewart and Gott understandably replied that the publication obviously must have contained their opinions, and that the reason given for the withdrawal of the prosecution was otherwise a smokescreen excuse to cover the ineptitude and bungling inexperience of the authorities.[5]

By 1911 lessons had clearly been learned. Stewart and Gott had never properly ceased their publishing programme, although almost all content was endlessly recycled. This time the prosecution, fronted by a Leeds clergyman, accused Ernest Stewart (now speaking under the borrowed popular pseudonym of Dr Nikola) of declaring at a public meeting that 'Christ was a dirty fellow'. When the cleric was unable to produce his original notes corroborating this, the case was hastily adjourned.

During the case Stewart was presented with a summons for a more serious offence that had rather more mileage than the previous attempts to stop him. During what we might now see as almost a comedy routine Stewart (as Dr Nikola) waspishly observed that God might 'throw him over the battlements' of heaven for refusing to believe in the Almighty and his apparent goodness, yet would be obliged to welcome in the recently executed Dr Crippen, who had received the last rites of a Catholic before execution. This was, in truth, the latest popularized version of the freethinker's assaults on the doctrine of forgiveness – something that seemingly operated an utterly anomalous conception of justice. This led Stewart to conclude 'God is not a fit companion for a respectable man like myself.'

This was seized upon as Stewart's most serious utterance yet. It was perhaps this, combined with the knowledge that Stewart and his compatriot Gott were determined and serial offenders, that led to the magistrate showing such a distinct lack of sympathy. He refused Stewart an adjournment, granting him a mere hour to prepare his case, which was inevitably inadequate.

Throughout, Stewart and Gott seemed to place considerable hope in the logic of the Coleridge decency test and its emphasis upon manner. Unfortunately for them the presiding judge, Justice Horridge, demonstrated his own interpretation of the law and its spirit. He emphasized in his summing up that both Gott and Stewart had singularly failed to take into account the context of where they were speaking. Sidestepping the question of the extent to which the words spoken constituted blasphemy, the judge argued that the opinions of the defendants were not as much at issue as their decision to air these in an open and potentially dangerous public place. Horridge stated that 'a man is not free in a public space to use common ridicule on subjects which are sacred to most people in this country; he is free to use argument.'[6]

The jury found the pair guilty without leaving the jury box, with Stewart receiving a sentence of three months without hard labour and Gott one of four months. Both Stewart and Gott had been clearly intellectually outmanoeuvred by Horridge, but this incident had also demonstrated that the police and authorities had learned to focus on public order issues. This made them feel considerably more at home than refereeing the collision between free speech and apparently objectionable religious doctrine. This free speech imperative led to further surveillance of Stewart, Pack and Gott and they received some custodial sentences handed out in other localities, such as Nottingham, for similar breaches of the peace.

None of this proved a deterrent and all three members of the group continued to offend into the 1920s, with Gott in particular serving a number of prison sentences during the First World War. Gott's most famous case was to prove fatal for him. In 1921 the *Rib Ticklers* pamphlet was reissued and this time Gott was prosecuted over a specific section in which Christ's entry into Jerusalem was likened to the actions of a circus clown. The depth of this precise insult led the judge to find that the pamphlet was liable to occasion a breach of the peace, and Gott was sentenced to nine months' hard labour. He was to pay a heavier price, however, with the death of his wife during the period of his imprisonment and his own premature death not long after his release in 1922. His misfortune thereafter became yoked to the cause for repeal, which linked seemingly draconian injustice to the sufferings of an ill-guided if determined campaigner. Few could argue that Gott had not striven to offend decorum and good taste, but his credentials as a campaigner for free speech and the dissemination of all opinion remained untarnished. This memory lingered, and would also reappear in modern summations of the law and its precedents, where it was noted that Gott's case marked the last occasion when the law of blasphemy overreached itself in England.

Gott had compatriots further afield, such as the Norwegian rationalist Jens Arnfred Olesen (1883–1958), who published material reminiscent of G. W. Foote's in his paper (translated from the Norwegian as *The Free Thinker*), for example outlining that Christmas holidays were a 'scam'. More famous was the case against Arnulf Øverland (1889–1968), who deliberately tested blasphemy laws by preaching a lecture entitled 'Christianity: The Tenth Plague'. The jury acquitted him, against the presiding judge's advice.[7]

Repeal or Reform – Blasphemy Laws in the Spotlight

A sense that the law of blasphemous libel was an anachronistic stain on the legal system – and, by implication, on British society – led to a series of campaigns to remove the law being staged through the 1920s and 1930s. While campaigners always hoped that successive Home Secretaries would be receptive and sympathetic, this never quite proved to be the case. Although hopes would be raised by each arrival in office of a more progressive Home Secretary such as J. R. Clynes, in practice there was little movement. In fact no Home Secretary in the first three-quarters of the twentieth century would lend their, or their party's, support to repeal. It does not require very much thought to uncover why this was the case. There was absolutely no party political advantage in any specific government taking the policy on as its own. Conservatives in both inclination and ideology had the Established Church to protect and saw Christianity as the central underpinning of morality. Liberals were still nominally non-conformist, while Labour politicians had in mind the vast swathes of God-fearing working-class voters who would be appalled by support for godlessness. Thus the quest to exert political pressure for repeal of the blasphemy law effectively got nowhere.

There was, however, one interesting development that looked forward to much more recent conceptions of the offence. In the early 1930s it was suggested that the law was embarrassingly partisan in its protection of Christianity. Critics argued that the law ought rather to more readily reflect what was already a religiously cosmopolitan empire. Civil servants certainly agreed to look at this, but their attitudes exposed the limitations of tolerance at this time. Throughout their deliberations the claims of Christianity were seen to quite obviously overwrite those of any other religion within the empire and, indeed, offered some quite disdainful and dismissive opinions about these latter. Yet these same people could still see the logic of extending the law and, more importantly, realized that British society would one day have to answer for the accusations that it was not as tolerant of other religions as it liked to pretend. Certainly it was vulnerable to suggestions that it was simply not prepared to move with the times. Very quickly these same civil servants concluded that an equalization of the law to encompass all religions was quite simply unworkable and would be storing up a veritable mountain of trouble for successive governments unfortunate enough to be left in charge of it.

Thus consultations almost fell at the first, albeit precipitously high, hurdle. Defining religion for the purposes of legislation obviously seemed to be impossible, such that even when the law tried to exercise something of a benevolent tolerance it could scarcely decide what counted as a religion and what did not. Attempting such a task presumed that the very definition of religion was a stable and static target. Who, for example, should be asked about what could legitimately be classified as a religion? Practitioners and believers would quite readily give a series of very partial answers that reflected their interests, while possibly undermining those of other denominations. If religious practitioners could not be trusted, then, was this a task for experts in the relatively young social science of comparative religion, or perhaps in legal aspects of religious belief and toleration?

Consultation of such experts might have proved acceptable, yet how credible could the findings be if the consultation process were to leave the religious out of the equation? Beyond whom to ask about a definition of religion, it also became obvious that laws in this field would have to be reappraised regularly, since the world of religion was itself in an almost constant state of evolution. But precisely when and how was government or the judiciary supposed to undertake such reappraisals? Given this obvious mess in waiting, these civil servants wisely decided to leave the situation alone, and advised the government to do the same. The whole episode, which emerges from a close look at Home Office papers for the period, can, in retrospect, be seen as a stark warning of the problems that would beset governments in the latter part of the twentieth century.[8]

Although the repeal movements and the Whitehall reconsideration of the law were prompted by what had happened to Gott and his contemporaries, the remainder of the twentieth century saw the retention and reconfirmation of blasphemy laws in Europe and the English-speaking world. For example, in the Polish penal code of 1933 blasphemy was considered punishable only if it could cause public disorder. The period also saw the laws against blasphemy reconfirmed in the Netherlands and the Republic of Ireland.[9]

The Religious as Inspiration – Blasphemy and the Modern Artistic Psyche

In terms of blasphemy, the rest of the twentieth century was primarily occupied by actions of various kinds taken against artists, writers and film-makers who found inspiration in the exploration of the divine and its possibilities. From the period immediately following the First World War we start to get the first sustained action against these representatives of a non-Christian counter-culture. In Weimar Germany the writer George Grosz (1893–1959) was prosecuted for his portrayal of some anti-clerical themes, and for a depiction of Christ wearing a gas mask, having been coerced into unwilling service in the Imperial German Army. The case eventually went through three tiers of court proceedings before the central court acquitted Grosz of blasphemy. The artist felt his actions had been justified as a stand for free speech.[10]

What this particular instance also indicated was that central courts in the twentieth century, like central authority of any kind, could afford to be more permissive and benevolent than local courts and jurisdictions were capable of being. By the end of the twentieth century, in America, this blatant mismatch of responses had been named the 'culture wars'.[11] Although this was a reductive stereotype, there was nonetheless some justification to the idea that the cosmopolitan, urban centres of the country felt they could impose their liberalism on the provinces, irrespective of their character and attitudes.

It took the Second World War to foreground the idea of inalienable human rights and to enshrine these in the Universal Declaration of Human Rights of 1948, the drafting of which was heavily indebted to the United Nations. The document stated clearly, at last, what had previously merely been an assumed and nebulous idea: that individuals had rights that governments had a duty to at least protect, if not to actively encourage and promote. The Declaration promised full religious tolerance to the individual, alongside similar support for their freedom of expression. We do not know to what extent those who drafted the document realized that these two responsibilities were likely to come into active conflict. The equal weighting of these two rights served to create an ongoing dilemma for social democratic systems – one that would effectively shape the second half of the century's human rights debates in the realm of religion and unbelief. For many years negotiating the tension in practice would generally come out badly for blasphemy laws. They could readily be made to seem anachronistic and unreflective of the 'spirit of the age' – just as secular campaigners from the nineteenth century had also regularly argued.

The first blasphemy law 'casualty' occurred in the United States in 1952 in a case examining objections lodged against Roberto Rossellini's film *The Miracle*. This was a film in which a woman believes herself to be the Virgin Mary after she is impregnated by a man whom the film hints is a St Joseph figure by his calling the divinity of Jesus into question. The film was banned by the authorities in New York (at this time named the New York State Board of Regents) after a wave of protest. In retaliation the film's distributor, Joseph Burstyn, lodged an appeal to have the ban lifted, principally by seeking to remove the State's power to license the display of films. Part of the case in the film's favour had been to note that it had not been considered blasphemous when shown at a film festival in Europe. The Vatican itself had disliked the film, but had refrained from invoking its Lateran agreement with the Italian government, which rendered the latter duty-bound to ban anything the Catholic Church disapproved of. Christian political parties in Italy seemed to object to the film's moral tone and its portrayal of illegitimacy, but did not seem to consider it blasphemous or sacrilegious. If Catholic countries declined to take action, what, asked Burstyn, was so different about the State of New York?

While some argued that this was simply a piece of popular culture and that no one should really waste too much time on the consideration of its merits, the judgement in the Burstyn case made clear that it took cinema and its place in twentieth-century culture and society very seriously, declaring:

> It cannot be doubted that motion pictures are a significant medium for the communication of ideas. They may affect public attitudes and behavior in a variety of ways, ranging from direct espousal of a political or social doctrine to the subtle shaping of thought which characterizes all artistic expression. The importance of motion pictures as an organ of public opinion is not lessened by the fact that they are designed to entertain as well as to inform.[12]

A significant factor in this case was the role of engaged and committed religiously minded literati, people prepared to defend the rights of film directors as much as the rights of the religious. When the furore erupted, Otto Spaeth, a prominent Catholic and director of the American Federation of Arts, gathered together prominent Catholics involved in the arts for a viewing of the film, with the intention of soliciting their comments. These were illuminating to say the least. William P. Clancy, a priest teaching at Indiana's Notre Dame University, concluded that 'the film is not *obviously* blasphemous or obscene, either in its intention or execution.'[13] The judgement also quoted earlier opinion from Clancy that 'itself questioned the wisdom of transforming Church dogma which Catholics may obey as "a free act" into state-enforced censorship for all'.[14] Writing in the *New York Times* the well-known American Catholic poet Allen Tate suggested that the religiously inspired laity were no longer prepared to accept the religious hierarchy speaking on their behalf, since matters of faith had now been democratized:

> The picture seems to me to be superior in acting and photography but inferior dramatically . . . In the long run what Cardinal Spellman will have succeeded in doing is insulting the intelligence and faith of American Catholics with the assumption that a second-rate motion picture could in any way undermine their morals or shake their faith.[15]

This was the latest version of the 'Tiberian argument' that now included the suggestion that all forms of authority that wanted to act on behalf of God were not only underestimating His powers, but were undermining the widespread faith of people at large – a faith that had now been leavened with the other considerations of a mature Western social democracy. In the event, the *Burstyn v. Wilson* case established that blasphemy prosecutions undermined the First Amendment right to free speech. This decision was seen as a major milestone in the removal of censorship in the United States; thereafter any attempt to prosecute would be an unconstitutional breach of these First Amendment rights.

In Washington it may now have been felt that the matter was settled, but in fact a new chapter of distrust between the central Federal government and the individual states had opened. While

Washington focused on the needs and demands of the Constitution, local authorities believed they had a right, and an implicit mandate, to censor that which challenged the fundamental morals of the community. This was a pitched battle between the grass roots and overarching institutions, with the latter in the driving seat – at least for now.

Europe also witnessed a number of cases where artistic expression was assessed in relation to both free speech and the offence a work caused. Many Finnish blasphemy cases from the 1960s turned on the meaning of artistic works. The first, a novel by Hannu Salama titled *Midsummer Dance* (1964), included a parody of a religious sermon that attracted the attention of the Lutheran bishop Martti Simojki. Salama was convicted and received a suspended prison sentence; he was eventually pardoned by the Finnish president Urho Kekkonen. In 1969 a Finnish artist produced an image of a crucified pig and was convicted and imprisoned. In Denmark the case against Jens Jurgen Thorsen's Christ film manuscript in 1976 was thrown out because it was not proved that the film intended mockery.[16] In Poland after 2000 the sculptor Dorota Nieznalska fought an eventually successful ten-year-long case to defend the artistic integrity of an art installation, *Passion*. This had a film loop of a man exercising next to a Greek cross with a photograph of male genitalia superimposed where the figure of Christ would be. A short while later in Greece a Belgian artist, Thierry de Cordier, depicted a penis ejaculating on a cross. The exhibit's curator was accused of using this controversial work as a means of drumming up publicity.[17]

As the government had learned, the Common Law of blasphemous libel still in force in England had given the moral and cultural power of the law to people at the grass roots. This sometimes worked to the detriment of the authorities and, as had been proposed in the arguments of the Burstyn case, of the cause of religion itself. This remained the situation as long as individuals or movements for moral rearmament did not seek to override this logic.

Blasphemy and Modern Moral Crusades

In England the outcome of the Gott case of 1922 and the various, though unsuccessful, moves for reform of the law seemed to indicate that the tide was running against the law's chances of survival. This seemed still further confirmed by the pronouncement in 1949 – by none other than Lord Denning, the recently appointed Justice of Appeal – that the law of blasphemy had become a 'dead letter'.[18] However, all this reckoned without the formidable power of Mrs Mary Whitehouse, who touched a profoundly popular nerve with her wide-ranging campaigns against the permissive society. This was something which she convinced people had become a creeping presence within British culture by the end of the 1960s. One particular line of argument, to which she returned time and again, was that those in charge of the media were simply not demonstrating sufficient levels of wisdom and responsibility in deciding what should and should not be made available for public consumption. This meant that successive director-generals of the BBC regularly received communications from Mary herself, as well as her allies and followers.[19]

Mrs Whitehouse had a keen ear for the blasphemous, and in the early 1970s had considered lodging a complaint about an episode of the BBC sitcom *Till Death Us Do Part*. Accounts disagree on how precisely Mary was introduced to a particular issue of *Gay News*, a periodical for the homosexual community in Britain. Most consider this to have been sent by a sympathizer, generally described as a 'probation officer'. Others believe the relevant copy was sent by Bill McIlroy, the editor of the secularist newspaper the *Freethinker*, effectively the ideological heir of George William Foote.

What is scarcely in dispute was precisely how Mrs Whitehouse would react to the contents of the 3 June 1976 issue of *Gay News*. The paper contained a poem entitled 'The Love that Dares to Speak its Name', which reworked the famous phrase about homosexuality uttered by Lord Alfred Douglas. The poem portrays Christ as a promiscuous homosexual who during the course of his ministry had managed to have sexual relationships with King Herod's guards, members of the Sanhedrin, Pontius Pilate, John the Baptist and Judas Iscariot. The poem goes on to describe the feelings of the homosexual centurion at the Crucifixion, as he held the mutilated body of Christ. After this it graphically outlines necrophilic sexual acts between the two of them. All was garlanded with an illustration of the naked, crucified Christ with his penis on display.

On the face of it this was entirely the sort of material that Mary Whitehouse had been campaigning against, and it seemingly vindicated her demands for more restraint in the media. The combination of blasphemy and obscenity seemed to justify her making a stand. Indeed, the combination of these in a single work appeared to justify all her previous crusades. Those who created media content would, she reasoned, if left to themselves, show no restraint. Moreover, in an atmosphere of unlimited permissiveness, they would be further encouraged in their transgressive behaviour.

However, there were counter-arguments that made this whole situation much less straightforward. The poem had been written by James Kirkup, a respected professor of English literature. The case could also be made for viewing the poem, and its message, meta-phorically. Moreover, Kirkup argued that it sought to open out the salvation of Christ to all, including those otherwise marginalized by society. Thus the simple morality of the grass roots entered a stand-off against the literary and liberal Establishment. Almost everyone believed that the latter would triumph. After all, who could doubt that liberal progress and an end to such anachronistic laws would carry the day?

The make-up of the defence team seemed to bear this out, with John Mortimer leading, supported by a younger up-and-coming lawyer, Geoffrey Robertson. The case they had prepared sought to prove that Kirkup's poem was in many ways demonstrating the 'spirit of the age' – an age of inquiry, imagination and exploration. The defence wanted to bring an array of witnesses to testify that the sentiments and ideas contained in the poem were quite in keeping with what even the religious were prepared to consider acceptable in the England of the late 1970s.

However, things rapidly went wrong for the defence. All the jurors took a religious oath and the judge sought to prevent both sides from bringing forward theological evidence. The second of these occurrences, in a strange way, sounded a note of modernity for the prosecution case. It also rendered the admission of expert literary evidence inadmissible, leaving Mortimer and Robertson with con-siderably less to work with. In the end they had to make do with character testimony to the newspaper's good intentions and serious intent, offered by Bernard Levin and Margaret Drabble. Even this backfired, since the prosecution wheeled previous editions of the paper into court and was able to ask damaging rhetorical questions about its past content, parts of which could be made to seem dubious in the courtroom.

Looked at from a distance it perhaps does not surprise us that the judge took this decision to skirt round what would have been a vast swathe of expert evidence. Mortimer and Robertson may have wanted to make a spirited defence of the poem and of the clear and inalienable right to free speech. But their strategy was miscalculated, and they similarly misjudged the history of how blasphemy had been dealt with by the authorities. Presiding judge Justice King-Hamilton was merely guiding the court to weigh blasphemy by its capacity to create breaches of the peace, a line that the authorities had been pursuing since the start of the twentieth century. The judge concluded that the poem was blasphemous and would therefore cause outrage – a sentiment he clearly voiced once the jury had returned a guilty verdict. The editor of *Gay News*, Denis Lemon, was given a twelve-month suspended sentence and a fine of £500. King-Hamilton's parting shot was to express his deep contempt for the poem, and to thereafter publicly state that he believed the hand of the Almighty had been guiding his decisions.

While the events in the courtroom demonstrated a lack of progress and of liberalization, the case resonated around liberal and counter-cultural England. A defence fund was organized and a great many fundraising events (including 'blasphemy discos') demonstrated that modernizers were still prepared to fight back. The defence team vowed to fight on, and the case was eventually taken as far as the House of Lords. When the appeal was heard by the Law Lords it was rejected by three votes to two. This was lamentable for the defence since one of those who voted to dismiss the appeal, Lord Scarman, used the occasion to argue that the law should actively be extended to embrace the beliefs of all religions. This was similar in effect to James Fitzjames Stephen's comments after the Foote case, in which he decried Justice Coleridge having made a manifestly bad and unsuitable law survive to have a longer and more dangerously fruitful life.

The immediate effect within society was obvious. Cinemas that had booked seasons of gay films began to think twice, and an atmosphere of retrenchment pervaded the country. Censorship increased and the confidence of those who wanted to censor was boosted by the decision. Even soft-core heterosexual porn titles such as *Mayfair* and *Men Only* were temporarily withdrawn from the shelves of W. H. Smith, purely as a piece of censorship. Encouraged by this atmosphere, the outspoken Christian moralist Chief Constable of Greater Manchester James Anderton conducted over three hundred raids in pursuit of obscene material. This vein of retrenchment was conceivably also behind the attempt to bring the Sex Pistols to court in Leicester for the title of their album *Never Mind the Bollocks, Here's the Sex Pistols*.

The Law Lords' verdict also had wider and deeper implications for the debate about the place of blasphemy laws in Britain. While Lord Scarman had looked forward to an equalization of the law to protect all religions, the effect of the verdict and the case law it created was instead a considerable step backwards. The removal of expert evidence from the case to concentrate on the suggestion that the poem had been objectively blasphemous had one crucial implication: Judge King-Hamilton had, wittingly or otherwise, kicked the whole issue of 'manner' into touch. This unravelled the protection for anti-religious opinion that Justice Coleridge had established with his judgement in the Foote case in 1884.

The law was taken back to the situation it was in before the judgement in the Foote case. This meant that all the prosecution now had to do was to establish the fact of publication. Manner, and all the niceties of what the public would accept, had been eliminated by the case law of the *Gay News* case. This was a quite astonishing development which dramatically bucked the trend that had been playing out through Europe and North America in the twentieth century. The crime of blasphemy was not only back in England, it had been given a considerable boost by the actions of one judge and those who upheld the dismissal of the appeal. This also rode roughshod over the sentiment expressed by Lord Scarman, who had expressed his wish for the modernization and extension of the laws. Indeed they were not extended but, on the contrary, were reworked to look like they did in the middle of the previous century. Although not crucial at the time, this decision was to have great implications ten years later.

Salman Rushdie and the Globalization of Blasphemy

In 1988 the author Salman Rushdie published his long-awaited novel *The Satanic Verses*. At the time he considered it a viable piece of fiction; it was a book that indulged the imagination to a quite astonishing degree. The product of five years' work, the book was described by the historian Leonard Levy as:

> a phantasmagoric, surrealistic, and absurdist book. It is huge, sprawling, opaque, nihilistic and kaleidoscopic. It is crammed with esoterica, allegories, parables, metaphors, Arab words, and word plays. It is inventive, exuberant and incoherent, if not crazy. Little in the book is as it seems, for a devil in one scene is an angel in the next, and heaven becomes hell.[20]

In short, the book reached out to the literary world. It made assumptions about the prior knowledge of its audience, whom the author hoped would be sufficiently steeped in a Western culture that distinguished the literal from the imaginary. This would be an audience who would appreciate and applaud literary tricks and allusions. While the book played with a range of themes and ideas from many different literatures and societies, it also contained passages that were directly offensive to some Muslims.

The book contained a reworking of the Prophet's name to make it echo medieval Christianity's pejorative dismissal of him as 'Mahound', and thereby a false prophet who deceived individuals with his revelation of a false holy book, another theme re-awakening medieval Christian stereotypes.[21] *The Satanic Verses* also contained references to twelve prostitutes who were identified with the twelve wives of the Prophet – themselves revered in Islam as the mothers of future believers. Rushdie also demonstrated what seemed contempt for the holy city of Mecca by calling it 'Jahilia' or place of darkness. The very title of *The Satanic Verses* seemed to imply the Koran itself was satanic and fundamentally in error. While the whole book might be said to chart Rushdie's own metamorphosis from a product of the subcontinent, fleeing Islamicization, to English literary doyen, this interpretation scarcely worked for all who encountered it – whether that was through the text itself or from the reputation which went before it. Rushdie might also have argued that his lengthy book was part of an elaborately constructed fantasy – and some certainly have, at least to an extent, appreciated this argument.[22] It is debatable whether Rushdie could have foreseen how this apparently toxic combination of motifs would look to other eyes outside of the literary Establishment. Several Muslim academics in disciplines beyond literature responded swiftly, seeing Rushdie's work and its attacks on the Prophet as attacks on an active force in their lives.[23]

Word spread quickly and Muslims began to protest throughout the world, culminating on Valentine's Day in 1989 with the pronouncement from Iran of a fatwa by the Ayatollah Khomeini. This invited Muslims to seek out Rushdie and execute him for his blasphemies. The academic and commentator Malise Ruthven has argued that the action taken by Khomeini was high-handed and, strictly speaking, reached beyond his legitimate power within Islam as a *mujtahid* (someone empowered to offer an opinion of the law). Khomeini appointed himself judge and allowed his followers to declare him an imam. This transposed his pronouncements on Rushdie's book to another level.[24]

At first Rushdie backed off from the controversy, initially believing the idea that an apology for offending religious beliefs was necessary. This view suggested that real religious beliefs trumped the unfettered exercise of freedoms, however hallowed or hard won the latter were. This course of action addressed rumours within some sections of the Islamic world that such an apology might be both desirable and effective. In reality Khomeini stood firm in his pronouncements and it became clear that Rushdie's options had diminished considerably.

Rushdie went into what would prove to be a lengthy period of hiding, his movements shadowed by armed guards. He had not foreseen the level of indignation and the lengths to which those maddened by the stories of the book's contents would go to seek redress. Violence against publishers and their agents, and the murder of a number of individuals associated with the book, highlighted the level of indignation and outrage.

From the public burning of Rushdie's novel in Bradford in January 1989 there has been a trail of bloodshed associated with opposition to the book. Individuals died as a result of protests and riots in India and Pakistan. Bookshops and the offices of the publishers of Rushdie's novel received threats of violence and experienced bomb attacks, while many other premises were offered security protection. In the Middle East several Western hostages were taken, allegedly in response to the publication of *Satanic Verses*. But more was to come. The Japanese translator of the novel, Hitoshi Igarashi, was knifed to death on the campus of the university where he was professor of Islamic culture. William Nygard, the book's publisher in Norway, was shot while getting into his car outside his home in October 1993. In Turkey a mob had tried to corner the country's translator of the book at a conference hotel. While the translator, Aziz Nesin, was able to escape, the mob entered the hotel and killed 37 of the conference delegates.[25]

Around the first anniversary of Khomeni's first fatwa, Rushdie attempted a further clarification of his position in an article entitled 'In Good Faith'.[26] This particular piece was a coup for the recently launched *Independent on Sunday*. In his substantial article Rushdie argued that reactions to his novel pinned motives to it that more readily belonged to a work of non-fiction, such as finding it polemical and purposeful. Rushdie pleaded for the book to be treated again as a novel, a work of imagination, rather than a work with impact on the real world. Whether idealistic or naïve, this view really emanated from a writer who was backed into a profoundly unpleasant corner.

But what became increasingly obvious was that Rushdie and his literary work had unwittingly revealed far-reaching and long-lasting problems. The religious and the secularly liberal found themselves engaged in what felt like an epic battle. The religious saw a decadent and swaggering conception of free speech, which ridiculed the non-rational and asserted abstract rights against the deeply felt real beliefs of real people. It was even argued that these attitudes had themselves elevated Western liberal free speech into a religion, something that demanded due reverence and worship. Liberals saw tyrannical obscurantist belief reaching out from the past to devour writers and authors with its quest to limit thoughts, opinions and freedoms. All attitudes in this matter became swiftly polarized, and it took a considerable passage of time for critics and commentators to step back and assess what had happened.

The results were not pleasant to read about or contemplate. The *Satanic Verses* affair was responsible for turning blasphemy into an explosive world issue. The swiftness of reaction, and the dramatic speed with which outrage and condemnation spread around the world, indicated communications media had turned the world into a global village. Moreover, it seemed this village emphasized elements of internecine feuding every bit as much as greater awareness of difference and implicit interdependence. As such, it ran against the tide of liberal narratives of integration and inclusion. This area of liberal thought was awkward for the liberal free speech lobby and sometimes appeared to be glossed over by it. As Malise Ruthven has put it, 'in the electronic age, the quarrels of frontier villages erupt into people's living rooms everyday.'[27] Other commentators have focused squarely on the legacy of the Rushdie affair being a lingering polarization of views. Kenan Malik wrote extensively about how reasonable responses singularly failed to take charge, handing headlines and perhaps even the history of the affair to the extremes and the extremists. Liberal host cultures, so Malik argued, in their obsession with free speech, ignored political, cultural and social developments:

> liberals have not just created a particular picture of the Rushdie affair, they have also ensured that Western societies have succumbed to the picture they have constructed. They have helped build a culture of grievance in which being offended has become a badge of identity, cleared a space for radical Islamists to flourish, and made secular and progressive arguments less sayable, particularly within Muslim communities.[28]

With supranational organizations like the United Nations seeking to observe and regulate the conduct of nations and their governments, it became impossible to consider your cultural products as existing in isolation. In other words, this greater contact and knowledge also meant greater capacity to offend, as many discovered to their cost. It alerted the world to the fact that conceptions of blasphemy existed in world religions other than Christianity. As such, Lord Scarman's plea for equality in this area no longer seemed the eccentric wishful thinking some had considered it to be ten years earlier, but rather proved to be a far-sighted observation.

The logic of this surfaced in Britain with an attempt to bring a private prosecution for blasphemy against *The Satanic Verses*. The case was heard at the High Court, where those present were startled to discover that they were the subjects of a death threat. While the incident is a curiosity for its having involved the Muslim barristers present being obliged to name the precise blasphemies that Rushdie had engaged in, this was the sum total of the hearing's lasting impact. Since blasphemy had failed to move with the times, and had failed to address the concept of religious pluralism as Scarman had wanted, the case was dismissed, preserving the law's protection for Christianity alone. Blasphemy, it was decided by the court, had leaned back on its historical roots as a carefully worded protection for the tenets and beliefs of only the established religion of England.

Blasphemy and the Arrival of International Justice

However, the clock had been set ticking by this event and the questions it raised were to grow increasingly pressing in the ensuing decade. In a globalized world where immigration had turned the populations of many countries into multicultural ones, sustaining protection for indigenous religions alone was unacceptable. The legacy of the Rushdie affair has scarcely left us. Both Western liberalism and Islam have subsequently felt insecure and episodically at the mercy of world events. Rebuilding trust and pursuing decisive action through international co-operation appeared the best way ahead; but the road was scarcely going to be an easy one.

Supranational organizations like the European Union (EU) and the United Nations wanted to see parity and equality of treatment for all citizens in all countries. Britain itself was given a further, worrying reminder of this when in 1995 film-maker Nigel Wingrove took the British government to the European Court of Human Rights. Wingrove's film of the visions of St Theresa of Avila (*Visions of Ecstasy*) had been refused a certificate by the British Board of Film Classification (BBFC) because it 'might' be blasphemous.[29] The film contained scenes that eroticized St Theresa's dreams of a union with the crucified Christ, with Him appearing to respond to her approaches. The action of the BBFC here contravened the principles of Common Law by operating prior restraint on publication. But it also served to demonstrate the heightened sense of concern and sensitivity operating in governing circles. Wingrove took his case all the way to the European Court and was initially successful, although he would eventually lose the case after an appeal by the British government. The judgement in this case allowed Britain to keep its law under what was known as the 'margin of appreciation', a clause of the Convention. This was effectively an intentional loophole in the Convention that protects and secures exemption for laws that reflect national cultural concerns and characteristics. Wingrove for a time bowed out of film-making as a result of this and the film only eventually became widely available to view in 2012.[30]

A very obvious quid pro quo came from the European Court ruling. Strong and unequivocal signals were given to indicate that Britain could no longer operate this law in its own sweet way in an unrealistic parochial bubble. Protection for one religion alone – indeed, in Britain, for only one branch of that established religion – was an unsustainable position which stood in contravention of the intentions and spirit of European law. At a time when the harmonization of British with European law loomed into view, this advice looked suspiciously like brinkmanship.

Thus the liberalization of the law – which had proceeded apace more or less throughout the preceding decades – was dramatically derailed by events at the end of the century. Blasphemy had gone from an anachronism lingering on through the existence of some legal curios, to become a worldwide, toxically corrosive phenomenon. The world, and arguably Britain in particular, was little prepared for this sequence of events. By the end of the 1990s Britain had secured its margin of appreciation at the European Court, and slunk back to its own more comfortable legal world. However, the ticking clock of overarching modernization was echoing in its ears, and this was to get progressively louder into the new millennium.

Just a few years later, blasphemy erupted again in an episode that had distinct echoes of the Salman Rushdie affair. In September 2005 the Danish newspaper *Jyllands-Posten* published twelve different cartoons of Muhammad that clearly associated the central figure of the Islamic religion with terrorism. Like the British government in the Rushdie affair, the Danish prime minister stepped away from taking action when requested to by representatives of the Muslim community within the country.

Again the swiftness of reaction was particularly notable. A number of Christian buildings were attacked in Muslim countries and over two hundred deaths occurred during rioting. Westerners in particular parts of the world came under threat of kidnapping once again. However, the liberal world and the profession of publishing was this time swift to mobilize itself in defence of free speech. Newspapers and Internet outlets throughout Europe rushed to republish the cartoons. This was an act of solidarity that expressed support for the ideals of free speech and for the freedom to act as critics. This was reasserting and valorizing the role of the journalist, while seeking to lay down a gauntlet to the forces of censorship – clearly indicating an ongoing ebb and flow of these two competing notions of 'belief' and 'expression'. It may even be argued that this strident backlash to defend *Jyllands-Posten* was itself a recognition that the champions of 'expression' had been far too slow in coming to Rushdie's aid over a decade earlier. 'Belief' had seemingly grown emboldened and increasingly powerful, as governments and individuals appeared to adopt self-censorship as the best and safest course of action.

But flashpoints would continue to appear. One of these was the furore that surrounded the West End musical *Jerry Springer: The Opera*. This portrayed a hard-pressed God who declared in song 'It's not easy being me,' while Jesus – in an interview session on a cosmic *Jerry Springer* show – admitted to being gay. A case could be made that this musical was satirizing the *Jerry Springer* talk-show format, but not everyone saw things that way. The organization Christian Voice was a prominent opponent, organizing protests and employing a variety of media to spread its message and pressurize outlets to shun the production. In 2007 the organization's leader Stephen Green attempted to prosecute *Jerry Springer: The Opera*, but the case was dismissed because the judge was convinced that there was no evidence that the play was explicitly aimed at Christianity. The judge argued it was just as likely to have been an assault on the confessional reality television show. Moreover it could not be shown by Green's case either that the play risked damage to society nor that it might provoke civil strife.[31] After this, low-level pressure was brought to bear on theatres and local authorities to boycott the musical throughout its tour around the provinces of Britain. Despite the court's favourable verdict, the tour was unexpectedly denied Arts Council support. At times it looked like the American tactic of denying 'tax payer's dollars to the culturally and morally "questionable"' was emphatically bearing fruit.

Alongside these developments, governments and international agencies were working to reframe the debate. Pakistan brought the first resolution against defamation of religion in 1999 to the United Nations Commission on Human Rights. After a review conference in Durban, South Africa, in 2009 – which moved on from defamation to talk about incitement to religious hatred – the Rabat Plan of Action was instigated. This was highly critical of blasphemy laws, declaring that they would damagingly stifle all religious debate.[32]

Elsewhere blasphemy laws mutated into incitement laws, and in some places reappeared as other laws under new names. This phenomenon can be noted in countries like Portugal, which seems to have a relatively undiluted form of blasphemy laws. Austria, on the other hand, may have repealed its blasphemy laws, but it retains offences such as the disparaging of religious doctrine and interfering with religious services.[33]

Yet when put on the spot, 'expression' still felt gratified that writers and journalists (writing in many languages) were themselves periodically emboldened enough to come to the aid of the apparently abstract principle of free speech. The contemporary world emerged from the globalization and migration of the end of the twentieth century as interconnected, but it also had efficient mechanisms of scrutiny. Writings and literature would be examined carefully, but equally the human rights attitudes and records of modern governments would be scrutinized. In both areas those whose behaviour was deemed to be deficient, dangerous or wilful would find themselves in the court of public opinion. This set of precedents, drawing on the cases discussed in this chapter, was itself to be reiterated and revisited as we moved into the contemporary age.

SEVEN

BLASPHEMY IN THE CONTEMPORARY WORLD

As we have seen, throughout the last two millennia, the idea of blasphemy has frequently been seen as anachronistic; yet there have also repeatedly been those willing to revive it for their particular time and place. The legacy of this series of revivals has been startlingly demonstrated in the contemporary era, which has seen blasphemy become a volatile political and religious question, prone to combust under the slightest provocation. As such, this last chapter cannot really claim to be any sort of ultimate conclusion, because our story is scarcely over. Indeed, as I write these words, new chapters of various kinds are being written by events in France, New Zealand, Denmark, Pakistan and the Republic of Ireland.

As we shall see later in this concluding chapter, it is perhaps the last of these that best illuminates the chaotic and troubled history of the idea of blasphemy in the twenty-first century. Recent events in Ireland have highlighted the problems of blasphemy laws in Western democracy. Like many other countries that inherited English Common Law, Ireland had been living with an aged concept of blasphemy that existed – as it had in England – locked away in dusty and forgotten legal texts. Yet, in the midst of what commentators had been telling us was a secular society – one that had walked away from, and indeed actively scorned, the opportunities offered by religion – surprising things were happening.

Suddenly, in the early 2010s, a number of international events and incidents made clear that the supposed death of religion in the Western world had been somewhat prematurely announced. Indeed, something significant had now happened to provide proof of this, because aspects of religion had now become central to identity. Increasingly the language of rights – which had originally been invoked by blasphemers seeking to disbelieve what they wished – seemed to have turned full circle. Confidence in the free speech narrative had inspired the practising of rights, and this had in turn been extended to religious ideas. This was partly an offshoot of the late-twentieth-century attitudes that came to be labelled multiculturalism. Effectively, this meant the definitive recognition of the rights of new populations and interest groups that formed in the wake of post-colonial populations arriving in Western countries. If the first wave of multicultural ideas revolved around ethnicity and race, it would take at least a generation before this would spread to accept, and meaningfully promote, the rights of the disabled and people of different sexualities and genders.

Responding to Modern Agendas – Tolerance and Hate

Increasing ethnic diversity in Western populations meant that a wider range of religions – many indigenous to the former colonies – were being practised, which in turn led to the demand that legal protections be extended to encompass these people and values. This self-conscious inclusivity is an especially pertinent aspect of multiculturalism for questions of blasphemy, not least because it seems set to undermine the privileged status of entrenched institutions, including established religions. This recognition of new religions as on an equal footing for the first time – replacing the condescension that had previously been the norm – was a natural part of extending full citizenship to new minorities in Western countries; moreover, it forced these countries to face up to the problems posed by their deeply partisan blasphemy laws. As we have discovered, policing and legal authorities in the West have always preferred to tackle this issue as one primarily about public order and maintaining the peace.

In the new millennium, the attitude to blasphemy laws displayed by international organizations continued to be fragmentary and even at times, contradictory; it would be a mistake to assert there was monolithic and unified opposition to blasphemy laws as such. The European Court of Human Rights seemed to frequently make declarations that upheld free-speech imperatives to protect even things that 'shock and offend'. But this same body's case law clearly displays tendencies to the contrary. For example, the judgement in the Otto Preminger Institute case arguably stopped full-scale liberalization of the law in its tracks.[1] The Council of Europe's Parliamentary Assembly was also regularly at odds with such judgements, preferring to be more forthright in seeking to defend freedom of speech. In this it was in accordance with the view of the Venice Commission (2009) and the Rabat Plan of Action (2012). Both of these latter organizations of legal experts have gone a stage further in recommending the full abolition of blasphemy laws.[2] In some respects this plurality of viewpoints might not be surprising, since declarations are perhaps more easily made than legal judgements on individual, awkward cases. We can note a particular irony that countries seem to back the removal of blasphemy laws when asked to subscribe to a worldwide consensus, but tend to act in quite the opposite way when faced with specific situations.[3]

To outsiders it seemed that many countries were ready to wrap up the issue of blasphemy with laws that would punish those whose actions went against this new world of equality. This legal ideology was to birth the modern concept of 'hate crime', which at its core aimed to stamp out racial attacks and the expression of opinions liable to occasion a breach of the peace. This was to be accomplished through strong deterrents against actions that stemmed from prejudices. Initially, then, the crime of hate speech was treated as an aggravating factor bolted onto public order offences such as assault and breach of the peace. At first, infractions were understood to target identity characteristics such as race and religion. Eventually, after criticism of their apparent partiality in protecting some minorities rather than others, the criteria have in recent years been broadened; for example, critics asked why UK legislation protected specific beliefs such as humanism and Scientology while animal rights protesters and Green advocates remained unprotected.[4]

Very quickly the idea of hate crime became a free-standing concept in its own right, becoming embedded in legal cultures and wider society in Western democracies. While the category of hate crime was the creation of authorities prioritizing the protection of public order, the link between this offence and blasphemy took time to become clear. This eventually became a more focused and specific offence of incitement to race, and latterly religious, hatred which also reflected the obsession with public order matters. Incitement laws seemed a convenient one-stop solution to many problems, not least because they identified specific characteristics to be protected. In particular, the legislation seemed better able to identify risks to religious and ethnic groups manifestly different from the established communities. Supporters of such legislation saw it as enabling, and some even suggested that it might provide a means of having done with embarrassing legal relics like blasphemy, which, they argued, looked completely out of place in a multicultural world.

But incitement laws themselves also contained a constitutive paradox. Generally speaking, they are intended to prevent hatred being stirred up, and are usually set up to protect more widely held opinion and ideas. The problem lies in the fact that ideas and opinions can lead to a hatred of beliefs. This is a lawful position, but incitement laws – and those that administer them – cannot always discern where the line gets crossed into a hatred not of beliefs, but of believers.[5]

This problem is summed up by John C. Knechtle's comment on how multiculturalism might yet win out over hatred: 'The challenge of the modern liberal landscape is to redefine the thinner, more general communal understanding of shared values so that the sense of belonging is stronger than the sense of alienation.'[6]

BY GETTING EVEN the liberal-minded to accept that there were limits to free speech, the advocates of incitement laws argued they offered a much-needed validation of every individual's religious status within their respective societies. The previously colonial Christian societies of the West now had no choice but to accept equality before the law with their Hindu, Jewish and Muslim neighbours. This also had the potential to kick into touch the problems so regularly identified by free speech watchdogs. Suddenly the arguments around religious speech no longer seemed so anachronistic – society now genuinely needed protection, once again, from the motivated individual who would damage the peace of the community.

Yet even with this broad principle of equanimity in place, it remained to decide what did and did not deserve protection. In England, the House of Lords Select Committee on Religious Offences reached back into history to examine the 1860 Indian Criminal Code for any contemporary relevance. The Code conveniently started from the premise of equalizing religious status throughout the Indian subcontinent (prior, of course, to independence and partition). This premise potentially offered a means of forgetting the history of inequality and the partisan privileging of one religion and to start again from scratch.

Yet the Indian Criminal Code remained a relic of the empire, and still appeared riddled with the condescension of a ruling administration in charge of a subordinate population. In a past age that associated the religions of the East with symbols, artefacts and buildings, the Indian Criminal Code was drafted to protect these specifically, rather than the values and rights of religious individuals. This approach once again focused minds on the public order aspects of the problem. In the contemporary age of interpersonal communication via television, email and the Internet, it quickly looked rather out of touch.

Neither the pressure to legislate in this area nor the logic behind one particular approach was accepted by all parties. The non-religious, and those opposed to this partisan recognition of religion, asked what was really so special about religion: why exactly should it be given privileged protection ahead of other aspects of identity – after all, there were certainly some groups who felt equally, if not more, oppressed than religious minorities. It was not simply opposition to the principle of incitement laws that proved an obstacle. The earlier provision of incitement-to-racial-hatred laws had thrown up unforeseen issues that provoked scepticism in many quarters. The enduring bugbear of how precisely to define religion as such remained, as did the problem of how to police any conceivable definition.

These obstinate questions did not dissuade numerous Western countries from seeking to resolve the multicultural imperative and logic of incitement laws. Any strategic approach to this seemed to involve repealing blasphemy laws and moving to put incitement laws in their place. Certainly this approach suggested itself to the British legislature, and the House of Lords Select Committee of 2003 convened with this particular plan of action uppermost in its mind. The Select Committee's members, which included lawyers and representatives of different faith communities, heard verbal evidence from the National Secular Society that blasphemy should be abolished with no replacement. By way of a reply, I watched the Select Committee fumble in folders and produce racist and inflammatory anti-Islamic leaflets that had been put through the letterboxes of Muslims in West Yorkshire. In effect, the committee was asking what precisely should be done about such attacks and provocation.

It could be argued that, with this question, the committee was suggesting that repealing blasphemy laws – while well and good in theory for the comfortable Western liberal mind – did not address the real problems at large in communities that they, as a law-making body, were compelled to tackle. This did not, however, amount to outright stonewalling; what emerged was a tacit suggestion that the Common Law of blasphemous libel would be repealed in England if the National Secular Society, and its supporters, would relent and allow an incitement-to-religious-hatred law to go forward.

By the time that the committee had heard the quite bewildering (and occasionally confusing) range of evidence, things seemed less clear than they had been. Vast numbers of the public at large wrote to the committee, voicing a broad gamut of opinion. Some argued the standard liberal free-speech line that blasphemy laws had no place in a modern society and globalized world – a place where communication and understanding were meant to transcend all such problems. But there was a remarkable range of opposition arguments, presented both by individuals and by some pressure groups. Some argued that Christianity deserved continued protection because it had always enjoyed this throughout history. Another argument echoes, almost undiluted, the thinking of previous centuries, by suggesting that the prosperity of the nation had been providentially granted to Britain and its empire largely due to its unswerving commitment to the Christian God. The Fellowship of Independent Churches argued that:

> The existence of a blasphemy law which defends the honour of the living God, the God of the Bible, is a strong signal that the United Kingdom is a country whose national religion is uniquely Christian, whose culture and values are built on the principles and practices of the Christian Faith, the source and inspiration of its heritage . . . Christianity is a Faith which has only ever been a beneficial influence upon the people who follow it, and upon societies which promote and encourage, it is fitting that the laws of our nation should uphold the honour of God by outlawing blasphemy

against the name and character of God, and of the Lord Jesus Christ.[7]

Some went further still, suggesting that the removal of the blasphemy law would contravene the monarch's coronation oath and added other providential messages of potential doom. The Elim Way Fellowship, a Pentecostalist organization in existence for over eighty years, wrote:

> When our sovereign Queen was crowned at her coronation 50 years ago she made a solemn commitment to the nation and before God to 'Receive this Orb set under the Cross and remember that the whole world is subject to the Power and Empire of Christ our Redeemer'. Our sovereign is also 'Defender of the Faith' (Christianity) and we believe this is fundamental for the on-going blessing and prosperity for our nation.[8]

What these various defences signalled was that blasphemy laws, however apparently old-fashioned, had a lingering appeal for a significant portion of the population. The laws were important symbols for the religious, but were also significant for those whose attachment to British Christianity in its various forms was more cursory.

Blasphemy laws gave the religiously committed real licence to speak for everyone who believed that the maintenance of morality was implicitly linked to the preservation of Christianity. Even if many people no longer went to church, or scarcely even believed, it seemed that they could nonetheless be persuaded that the health of Christianity in the modern world was still an imperative.

Given the argumentative sophistication displayed by parties on both sides of the argument, it is not surprising that the attitude of the House of Lords Select Committee began to waver. Its report evidences a deep quandary. The importance of free-speech modernization now felt as compelling as the arguments both for new forms of protection and for the retention of past forms of protection – with vocal sections of the public exhibiting a surprising fondness for these latter. In the end, the committee stepped back from making any positive recommendations for government action, effectively cautioning against repeal of the laws and retention of them. While this may have seemed unhelpful, it should be remembered that it high-lighted the dilemma facing all social democracies; in this instance the balance between free expression and the protection of minorities seemed best served by equivocation.

So, while perhaps a coherent response, the committee's report was inevitably less than helpful to the Blair government of the day, which had pioneered the concept of hate crime – an idea that policy advisors had brought back from the American courts. We might now recognize this as the most recent instance in a long history of government agencies feeling distinctly uneasy about decisive action in this area. Moreover, it also appeared that there was equally a reluc-tance to accept responsibility for the inaction. During the passing of the Racial and Religious Hatred Act of 2006, an amendment that would have removed the offence of blasphemy, tabled by the House of Lords, failed by 153 votes to 113.[9]

In the event the deadlock between Lords and Commons was solved by the actions of a single Member of Parliament. Evan Harris, MP for Oxford West and Abingdon, had previously demonstrated support for secular and humanist causes. He had been present at the Select Committee deliberations in 2003 and likewise had vol-unteered at a public commemoration to read a section of the famous and controversial poem 'The Love that Dares to Speak its Name', which had been prosecuted for blasphemy in the '*Gay News* case' in the late 1970s. Harris had also, by this time, become a vice chair of the All Party Parliamentary Humanist Group and an honorary associate of the National Secular Society.

Amid some surprisingly conciliatory noises from the Brown government and the Church of England, the atmosphere around blasphemy repeal seemed to be subtly changing. In January 2008 the government signalled it might be prepared to allow removal of the law. Shortly after, a letter to the *Daily Telegraph* urging repeal of the law of blasphemous libel was endorsed by leading Church of England figures, most notably the former Archbishop of Canterbury Lord Carey. In such company, government agencies could feel a little more comfortable when shunted into taking action on repeal. But progress still required the co-operation of Evan Harris for government to achieve resolution without concerted action from government ministers. When the Criminal Justice and Immigration Bill came before the House of Commons in 2008, Harris proposed an amendment that would remove the law of blasphemous libel from the statute books. This eventually became law on 8 July 2008, and became a cause for celebration for the National Secular Society, among others.

While this legislative action covered the situation in England and Wales, a similar amendment tabled in Northern Ireland a year later had to be withdrawn. Scotland's law appeared obscured by the mists of time such that, while no outright repeal seemed in sight, some remained convinced that due to its prolonged disuse, the law had effectively ceased to exist north of the border. A collision of past and present disabused people of this assumption when it was noticed that Scottish blasphemy law was tied up with the Act of Union of 1707, and that only repeal of this latter would finally draw the curtain on blasphemy legislation in Scotland.[10]

The vexed problem of religious hatred in England and Wales was tackled under the Racial and Religious Hatred Act of 2006. This amended the 1986 Public Order Act to create the offence of stirring up hatred against persons on religious grounds. This had subsequent extensions tailored to the situations in Northern Ireland and Scotland.

This concerted and decisive movement on the problem of blasphemy laws – especially after so many abortive attempts to grapple with the issue – looked like the beginning of the end. Countries in the English-speaking world had mostly found their own solutions to the issue. America, as we have seen, had a very different history as a result of its departure from the concept of a State Church and its very different histories of federal and local law. Australia and New Zealand had also managed, by now, to part company with the legal precedents that they had inherited from English Common Law. While blasphemy prosecutions, and even heated discussion of the offence, may have been unpleasant reminders of past religious conflicts, they nonetheless also served as important reminders that the issues were both serious and deeply complicated. The potential seemed yet sharper, now, for countries that had thus far experienced something of a smoother ride in this area to find themselves caught up in a sudden, unforeseen collision with blasphemy.

Ireland and the Anomaly of Modern Blasphemy Laws

Just such a collision occurred in the Irish Republic very soon after England had settled on the course of repeal. Ireland was a country that was confronted by a perfect storm when the failure to know, or define, the subject faced new imperatives and pressure from outside the country. Charles Haughey, when minister for justice in the early 1960s, had famously sidestepped the issue of defining blasphemy in the Dáil (the lower house of the Irish legislature), claiming – with both skill and obfuscation – that everybody in the country knew what blasphemy actually meant. This answer, while expedient, ensured that knowledge of the offence and its impact in fact eluded most of the Irish population and even some of the country's lawyers and lawmakers.

In this sense, Ireland could be characterized as sleepwalking into what happened next. The retention of a moribund law which supposedly 'everyone knew the meaning of' occurred alongside the sudden arrival from both the European Union and the United Nations of the new legal agenda of laws seeking to police religious hatred from Western societies. In the aftermath of England's repeal, Ireland's judiciary and its governing party, Fianna Fáil, felt compelled to investigate the legislative situation on its own shores, inquiring whether it was still fit for purpose. It became clear that the Irish Constitution of 1937 contained a statutory requirement that there be a clause concerning blasphemy. Although Christianity and the Catholic Church were central to the wording and spirit of the Irish Constitution, this by no means made the country a fully theocratic state.

European law, and the pressures for harmonization of human rights and expectations, loomed over the horizon, bringing with it the presumption that the Irish government would update its legislative stance on blasphemy. Before this point Ireland and its laws on blasphemy had been carried along with the evolution of English Common Law precedent. These precedents had been retained when the new Constitution of 1937 had been ratified. Indeed the handful of blasphemy cases that emerged in the second half of the twentieth century had readily reached for the same English Common Law precedents as lawyers dealing with the same issues across the Irish Sea.[11]

But even here cracks were appearing that would rapidly widen when subjected to the seismic shock of European law and its under-pinning logic. In 1999 the case of *Corway v. Independent Newspapers* floundered on the grounds that the blasphemy contained in the pub-lication (a cartoon suggesting Catholicism's days were numbered) would almost certainly not cause a breach of the peace. However, this drew attention to the flawed logic of Charles Haughey's pro-nouncement that the law did not need defining. Not knowing or discussing what it meant indicated an undefined law simply could not be implemented, and remained a hostage to fortune. The case was thus an uncomfortable reminder that these laws were opaque, bordering on useless. Of greater impact, however, was the assertion that the law needed modernization to offer protection to other reli-gions – this would make Ireland recognize its status and destiny as a multicultural and multifaith society.[12]

Ireland thus had to satisfy the needs of its Constitution as well as the pressures to modernize – which were coming from a bewil-dering number of directions. In response, the Irish justice minister, Dermot Ahern, brought a bill before parliament that sought to change the laws against blasphemy through amendments to the new 2009 Defamation Act, namely the construction of Articles 36 and 37. This move prompted considerable surprise, even among Ahern's fellow Fianna Fáil members. Surprise turned to concern as the bill was examined and began its progress through the Dáil. The provisions themselves looked comparatively strange, owing no debt to previous religious legislation in this area; but the bill did seem to steer legislative thinking in the direction of preventing hate crime. Perhaps it was because prevention was prioritized in this way that the provisions against blasphemy appeared so spectacularly ill-informed and ill-considered.

The articles made the 'publishing or uttering' of 'blasphemous matter' an offence liable to a fine of 25,000 euros. Leaving Charles Haughey's opaque obfuscation behind, the offence of blasphemy was finally defined here as something that was 'grossly abusive or insulting in relation to matters held sacred by any religion'. Next to this, Article 36 Subsection b created a test of offence as an 'intention' to cause 'outrage'. The police authorities were given powers to seize blasphemous material, to be stored in preparation for any court case that might result. But this decisive approach was tempered in the bill by a number of attempts to install safeguards and to appease potential criticism from the free-speech lobby. The latter sections of Article 36 detailed a number of defences that could be offered in court. With wider public order still the foremost concern, the law tried to judge whether the blasphemous material would actively offend 'a reasonable person'.

It was clear that the articulate and vociferous artist, journalist and academic communities would baulk at these restrictions, and provisions were made to protect these groups' creation and use of material that might otherwise be considered blasphemous. One of the legitimate defences listed turned on whether specific material could demonstrate 'genuine literary, artistic, political, scientific or academic value in the matter to which the offence relates'. Mindful of the fact that, left unchecked, the Articles could become something of a 'charter for the offended', the provisions tempered this possibility with exclusions against religions whose 'principal object … is the making of profit', or those that employed 'oppressive psychological manipulation'.

Although its creators (Ahern and his advisors) were motivated by the wish to cover a number of eventualities, it was clear to see that the Defamation Bill was hastily constructed and filled with controversial provisions. It was equally clear that many of these created problems that were difficult to resolve. For example, the description of blasphemous matter covered by the law required that it be 'grossly' abusive, with no further guidelines or definition of what precisely this meant. With no definition of 'grossly' it was inevitable that abuse of lesser severity – that is, an apparently legally acceptable abuse – was likewise left with no clear threshold. Further, despite its new reforming credentials, the acceptable defences provided for in the Act looked distinctly old-fashioned: offering protections for artists and academics, while silencing those such as comedians and bloggers – potentially the most articulate critics – harked back to outdated notions of status and the Establishment that had been satirized by blasphemers at least since the nineteenth century.

The problems of defining terms were also found elsewhere in the Act. How, for example, would the courts determine 'genuine literary, artistic, political, scientific or academic value'? What was 'genuine' and, equally, what precisely would constitute 'false' academic or artistic value? While the inevitably circular arguments might have offered a diversion to some pedants or the odd senior common room for an hour or two, there was a clear danger that these semantic arguments would have to be tested in full public view in court – likely with embarrassing results. As if this were not problematic enough, the legislation would also be asking legal authorities to define the characteristics of a 'reasonable person' – something particularly difficult to do in the endlessly controversial area of blasphemy law.

Other established and familiar problems reared their heads once again. Defining what constituted a 'religion' was largely evaded, and the attempt to distinguish such groups from 'cults' – clearly intended to be their illegitimate rivals – was likewise unclear. The suggestion that the latter could be distinguished as having the sole intent of generating income immediately fell foul of the age-old, and frequently voiced, acerbic anti-clerical objection to all mainstream religions. As such, there arose the even more embarrassing possibility of religions being demonstrated – in an Irish court of law – to be no more than cults.

With the passing of the bill into law, outside government circles all this seemed an unsightly mess – one in which the Fianna Fáil government had shown itself to be hasty and myopic in its legislation. Criticism gathered pace from the opposition and from external groups who were adversely affected by the new provisions. The pressure group Atheist Ireland published on its website a range of quotations that could be considered blasphemous under the new law, some of these from the Bible itself.

Remedial action only began to appear imminent following the election of February 2011 and the formation of a Fine Gael–Labour Coalition. Speaking in the Seanad (the upper chamber of the Irish legislature) in February 2012, Labour Party senator Ivana Bacik noted that this law had 'gone against the EU norm in adopting a new statutory definition of blasphemy based on a definition of offence'.[13]

As criticism mounted still further, the new government agreed that the provisions in the Defamation Act needed to be investigated and, if necessary, evaluated by the public by referendum. The government announced a Constitutional Convention, which eventually met just outside Dublin in November 2013. The Convention was tasked with investigating a number of ideas and proposals concerning the Irish Constitution.

In preparation the Convention established a website where individuals and organizations could make their views known to the Convention itself and to any other members of the public who cared to browse the site. In the days leading up to formal investigation of the current law and its function, the sentiments expressed on these pages were overwhelmingly dismissive of the Defamation Act and the very principle embodied by such blasphemy laws in the modern age. Many saw the law as unnecessary, and some felt that it stigmatized Ireland as a cultural backwater clinging hopelessly to the past – and perhaps an imagined past at that. It is, however, to be expected that opponents of the law were going to be the most vociferous respondents. What was less clear were the inclinations of the vast majority of people who simply did not make their feelings public – what did 'silent Ireland' think about all this?

Some tentative answers began to emerge as the Constitutional Convention picked apart the issue. Alongside government officials, the Convention also contained 66 Irish citizens from all walks of life to represent wider opinion, people who had been asked to advise the government on the issues at hand. On a cold Saturday morning in November the Convention heard a number of speakers from the legal, academic, religious and activist worlds, and excerpts from these found their way onto Irish television news broadcasts. One speaker argued against the provisions of the Defamation Act, citing the notion that laws enacted in a state should be deserving of respect and should thus be acceptable to all.

The Convention was initially asked the simple enough question of whether it wanted to retain blasphemy as a provision of the Irish Constitution. The Convention's vote returned a clear majority in favour of removing this provision, with 61 per cent seeking removal, 38 per cent wanting retention and the remaining 1 per cent un-decided. A subsequent vote indicated that a majority (53 per cent) thought blasphemy provisions should be replaced by religious hate crime laws, as had occurred in Britain seven years earlier.[14] This all seemed logical enough – blasphemy had seemingly been voted down as anachronistic, partial and counterproductive. The void left might best be filled by incitement-to-religious-hatred laws, which could be properly formulated to offer protection for all.

However, what happened next was unforeseen by many at the Convention and cast a strange shadow over proceedings. Those present were asked a third question: 'should there be legislative pro-vision for the offence of blasphemy?' This seemed to be backtracking. The wish to 'replace' it in the Constitution with hate crime legislation appeared to have sealed its fate. But this later question dragged blas-phemy back to the table by suggesting it was still apparently in some manner viable, since in Ireland laws exist that are not mentioned in the Constitution. This time a vote was much closer, with 50 per cent voting against a legislative provision for blasphemy and 49 per cent voting in favour. When the path for possible retention of the law was explored in a further question, 82 per cent wanted a 'new detailed law including incitement to religious hatred'. Thus blasphemy and hate crime laws were to augment each other, if these expressions of opinion were to be followed. To some it seemed that the discussions had gone around in circles, to eventually arrive more or less at the original departure point. However, thinking more deeply about what had transpired it was possible to draw some different conclusions. A majority had realized that blasphemy should be removed from the Irish Constitution. Yet after hate crime provisions had replaced it, at least in the mind, there was enthusiasm to bring back blasphemy.

This displayed something of a lingering affection for an offence that had seemingly stayed on the statute book without doing sub-stantial harm to anybody. To some it spoke of tradition and the maintenance of religion underpinning morality. If individuals genu-inely took this view there was an argument that blasphemy laws were part of the bedrock of Irish life, as well as a readily identifiable aspect of its Christian culture. Similar ideas had, as we have seen, surfaced in the debates surrounding the House of Lords Select Committee on Religious Offences in 2003. Certainly this is not the only line of argument from the Convention's website that the House of Lords Select Committee would have recognized, but that large repository of written opinion also contained variations specific to Ireland.

The Catholic Church itself had argued for repeal of the law, recognizing that making such laws viable hindered its mission in other countries that wanted blasphemy laws to use against Christian minorities. Conversely, a submission from a Catholic lay organiza-tion (the Order of the Knights of Saint Columbanus) argued to retain the law.[15] This was the latest episode in the long-running story of religious laymen being more conservative than their prelates, even suspecting the latter of the potential to sell them out, as numerous similar letters to the UK Home Office in the twentieth century had indicated.

We may never know the ultimate effect of the Convention's slightly confused outcome, and what immediate effect it may have had on government plans for action. Nonetheless, the Fine Gael–Labour Coalition government, with a rapidly approaching general election, decided to put the brakes on the issue. The volume of conversation about it dwindled and it was eventually stated that no action either on blasphemy or the Convention's recommendations would be taken in the current government's remaining term.

Charlie Hebdo and Explosive Violence

Despite this hiatus, action on the issue seemed inevitable and the problem would simply not go away. Sentiments that blasphemy was simply an academic and legal issue were not facing up to its presence in the wider world where it remained a source of violent conflict. This was reinforced in dramatic fashion when the *Charlie Hebdo* affair erupted in Paris.[16] On 7 January 2015 two armed men broke into the offices of the French satirical magazine *Charlie Hebdo*, unleashing a volley of bullets that left several dead and traumatized a whole society for a time. Since its founding in 1970 the magazine had often taken hard-hitting anti-clericalist positions; more recently it had published cartoons that lampooned the character and nature of Islamic sacred figures.

Before the massacre of January 2015 the magazine had attracted criticism from minorities it satirized, leading to courtroom disputes. Many similar depictions of the Prophet that were subsequently cited in 2015 were a component of a case brought against the satirical paper in 2007. More criticism of Islam in 2009 resulted in another case, and 2011 saw *Charlie Hebdo* back in court over a satirical assault on Christianity. In all of these cases, the presiding judges reminded plaintiffs that tolerating all religions involved tolerating criticism of them. The logic of this suggestion also argued that publications like *Charlie Hebdo* were not intended at all for those who had taken offence and that the latter were under no obligation, nor pressure, to interact with these ideas and opinions. They also reaffirmed that, in a secular society, such critical and challenging ideas were considered an important part of public debate and even potentially contributed to social cohesion.

The explosive nature of the shooting incident threw the contradictions and dilemmas faced by contemporary Western societies into sharp relief. Was a secular state the best guarantee of a neutral and functioning society? How far should the writ of free speech be allowed to dominate politics, society and religion? The events empowered the free speech lobby in the West, galvanizing many to invoke the 'Je suis Charlie' (I am Charlie) motto of solidarity, and energizing efforts for blasphemy law repeal.

Looking at the wider picture, some argued that the *Charlie Hebdo* attacks were not entirely about blasphemy but also highlighted the anti-Western frustrations of young Muslims who daily faced Islamophobia, post-colonial resentment and the high-mindedness of the liberal West. Another criticism of the *Charlie Hebdo* drawings argued that they were an unnecessary gift to extremists of both sides: they perhaps pandered to those who might consider inciting the hatred of the majority population against the minority depicted; and they could be used within minority communities to sway the views of the moderate toward the extreme.[17] Elsewhere commentators like the former Archbishop of Canterbury George Carey suggested that the chilling effect of the *Charlie Hebdo* shootings was to draw everyone into a worried silence that amounted to a de facto self-regulating blasphemy law.[18] While the incident momentarily made France question its founding ideals, this very quickly turned to veneration of those who had died in the massacre – including a courageous Muslim policeman, Ahmed Merabet, who was seen as a martyr for multiculturalism.

Ireland and the Gathering Pace of Opposition

At the UN Human Rights Council Universal Periodic Reviews of 2006 and 2016, France asked Ireland to withdraw its blasphemy law, and was joined by Sweden in the latter instance. It was noted by organizations like Atheist Ireland, albeit with trepidation, that the decisions and advice of the Venice Commission were being seen by the world at large as being especially applicable to Ireland.[19] The realization was beginning to dawn that the legislation Ireland enacted was no longer simply a distant noise offstage.

Other countries had also taken note of Ireland's new stance on blasphemy. To many it seemed paradoxical that Ireland's previous opinions on the matter had resolutely condemned new and innovative laws in countries considered oppressive. In 2009 Michael Martin, the Irish Minister for Foreign Affairs, had opposed attempts by a coalition of Middle Eastern states to make defamation of religion a crime at UN level, arguing that,

> We believe that the concept of defamation of religion is not consistent with the promotion and protection of human rights. It can be used to justify arbitrary limitations on, or the denial of, freedom of expression. Indeed, Ireland considers that freedom of expression is a key and inherent element in the manifestation of freedom of thought and conscience and as such is complementary to freedom of religion or belief.[20]

While accusations of hypocrisy might have been uncomfortable they might have been brazened out by some skilled diplomats. What was, here, of lasting damage to Ireland and the whole international stage was that the country, its government and its people had quite visibly changed their minds. Despite taking this progressive position on the international stage, whether by accident or design blasphemy was still a viable legal concept in Ireland.

The Organisation of Islamic Cooperation (OIC) in particular noticed that Ireland's new stance had focused on changes to the defamation law. This chimed with the OIC's continuing quest to gain support for extending the concept of defamation, something it had pursued since 2009. It had regularly requested acknowledgement of this demand at both the Human Rights Council and at the United Nations General Assembly.[21] Seizing upon the changed situation in Ireland, the lead voice of the OIC, Pakistan, actively drew on the wording of the Irish blasphemy law to propose a resolution on defamation of religion.[22] Beyond being something of an embarrassment to Ireland, the incident highlighted that Western criticism of such laws was not only hypocritical, but indicative of the kind of disdain for Eastern countries and their values that many commentators, such as Edward Said, had named 'orientalism'.

The situation remained in this unhelpful limbo. Irish politicians and civil servants now admitted in private that the attempt to solve a parochial Irish constitutional issue was misguided, miscalculated and ultimately myopic. While it was argued that the law had been drawn up with no intention of it being used, this assumption was tested and served notice that the determined would show the law up for what it was – indeed according to the taste or standpoint of its critics the law could variously be portrayed as a tyrannical gag or a domestic paper tiger with ironically far-reaching international impact. The misguidance and miscalculation could perhaps have been adequately handled, but even so, a certain inertia continued to hold off any resolution. The twentieth-century history of blasphemy had demonstrated that blasphemy consistently failed to be taken up as a party-political issue. Its 'appeal' and opposition to it refused to map on to party divides. Similarly, seeking to repeal laws around blasphemy offered little, if anything, by way of political advantage. As had proven to be the case in Ireland, waves of enthusiasm for repeal would falter and wane with the inevitable onset of another general election.

In 2015 Stephen Fry was interviewed by Gay Byrne for Irish television channel RTÉ for the tenth series of a show about life and faith. Towards the end of their discussion Byrne had asked his interviewee what he would do if after death he found himself at the gates of heaven and had to confront a God whose existence Fry had spent his life denying. Fry replied that he would rail against such a being – one who, for example, had visited bone cancer upon children – and he used a range of adjectives to suggest that He was not worthy of worship nor even anything resembling respect. In truth this was a polemic recapitulation of the classic atheist's argument on the 'problem of evil', which essentially holds that if God were omnipotent then it was in his purview to prevent evil, pain and suffering. Thus, if He existed, he had chosen quite deliberately not to do so, indicating that he was not a benevolent God but capricious and malevolent. After all, who, given the power to do so, would not seek to prevent evil and suffering? Given this paradox, so the standard argument goes, it was perhaps far better to accept no ruling power in the universe, thus providing natural and mechanical explanations for suffering and evil.

After the programme's broadcast on 1 February 2015, an individual walked into a Dublin Garda (police) station and reported this utterance as blasphemous and thus illegal under the country's constitutional provision for blasphemy. The duty officer asked whether this individual himself had been offended by the remarks and he replied that he was merely doing his duty as a citizen. He otherwise declined to comment. Shortly after this, RTÉ claimed that it had booked Gay Byrne into counselling for six months since he had felt faint during the course of Fry's reply. All this had the whiff of nineteenth-century melodrama about it, and reminded us that the reactions of prominent individuals could be described to enrage or reassure other audiences.

The Garda soon put the matter to one side, only to be reminded of the incident two years later, in May 2017, when the original complainant wrote asking what action was being taken. This briefly hit the headlines in the UK but more importantly it demonstrated that Ireland's blasphemy law could have international repercussions in yet another unexpected manner. Reports on the matter spread through social media platforms and other outlets syndicated across the world. As a result of 'the Fry case' New Zealand investigated its own legislative provision for blasphemy, and its parliament declared itself alarmed to discover that laws were still in existence and available for use. Hurried provision was made to repeal the laws and kick the matter resolutely into touch. In Europe, Denmark was similarly persuaded to re-examine its blasphemy laws and, after a debate in the first week of June 2017, it too removed them. A month later two members of the Dáil introduced Private Members' Bills to remove the offence of blasphemy from the Irish Constitution. Both were to prove unsuccessful.[23]

The Garda had dropped any plans to pursue prosecution on the grounds that they could not find a sufficient number of believers offended by Stephen Fry's remarks. Of course, no matter what grounds they might have cited for dropping the prosecution, they would be left open to criticism. And, indeed, the 'sufficient number' clause did cause anger in some quarters. As opponents of the law noted, perhaps those offended by such 'blasphemy' may well organize their complaints better next time the opportunity arose. Perhaps they would even ensure that public outrage and breach of the peace involving 'sufficient numbers' would occur. Did not the Garda's reasoning, these critics asked, turn the law of blasphemy in Ireland into an instrument of incitement?

More was to come, with the internationally known atheist commentator Richard Dawkins publicly challenging the Irish authorities to arrest him for blasphemy for words he had used at a lecture in

Dublin in June 2017. The legislation's status as a harmless and moribund law intended only to fill an awkward constitutional gap came increasingly into question. Deciding its capacity to be disruptive rather than placatory now lay in the hands of the people.

Ireland's political tradition of holding referenda, a hybrid version of asking for a people's mandate, regularly offered a method for government to 'test the waters'. These were held in order to consult the Irish people on issues central to the Irish Constitution – particularly on matters, like blasphemy, that tended not to neatly map onto usual party lines. The outcomes of these binding consultative ballots have led to significant and far-reaching legislative changes in Ireland – for example, in the years since the conclusion of the Constitutional Convention in 2012, separate referenda have allowed gay marriage in Ireland (2015), as well as a more hotly contested victory for legalizing abortion (2018).

For many, these changes have been seen as part of a wider project of modernization, fighting back against accusations of Ireland being a society riven by anachronism. For others the changes marked the passing of a dream of Ireland that De Valera had created. This latter could sometimes be portrayed as a religious and moral Ireland; one that had somehow withstood becoming European without surrendering too many of its essential characteristics. Put differently, this was a divide between a more cosmopolitan – and mostly metropolitan – Ireland determined to move (what it construed as) forward, contrasted with a more rural Ireland distinctly less convinced of the unlimited benefits of supposed moral modernity. As with many modern conservative causes, these latter attitudes often remained hidden; they are generally less often articulated, though certainly do occasionally break the surface, for example when the comparatively remote county of Donegal voted against abortion reform in the referendum on the issue in 2018.

The overwhelming success of these two referenda on gay marriage and abortion did have a noticeable effect on the attitude of the Irish government to the tide of moral reform. Although the Irish people were consulted, it never seemed clear whether the government was convincing the population at large of the need for reform or if it was actively responding to a growing tide. Either way, the government gained the confidence to announce plans for a referendum on Ireland's blasphemy law in the near future. The plans were confirmed in early 2018, and the date for the referendum on blasphemy laws was set for 26 October the same year. The government's decisions concerning the wording of the referendum question made it clear that their primary interest was in gauging public support for repealing the relevant clauses of the Defamation Act. Should the course of repeal be agreed upon by the public, it would give a mandate for the removal of all laws of blasphemy from Irish law; as such, it would bypass those complications around blasphemy being removed from the Constitution, yet retained in other laws, that had troubled the Constitutional Convention over a decade earlier.

So the autumn of 2018 became a backdrop to the campaigns leading up to the referendum. The biggest organizational presence on the campaign trail was Atheist Ireland, whose arguments accented the dangerous precedent Ireland's current laws had set. Its campaigning materials also contained information on a number of individuals imprisoned throughout the world on blasphemy charges. Chief among these was Asia Bibi, a Catholic Punjabi woman who had been accused of blasphemy as a result of a quarrel with a number of Muslim co-workers in 2009. She had been imprisoned and convicted and was awaiting the death sentence in a Pakistani prison. Her predicament was used to focus the minds of Ireland's voters on the implications of Ireland's current laws for the international situation around blasphemy.

These were powerful arguments and there was little that could be suggested to oppose their logic. Indeed, it became difficult to find anyone who would argue for the law's retention on the public stage. Initially this was something of a worrying issue because, as media outlets were duty-bound to provide balanced reporting – and to give equal time to both 'sides' of a referendum debate – the lack of oppositional voices meant their was a real risk of the whole issue being relatively absent from public consciousness. This provoked a fear among would-be repealers that the initiative was being handed to the opposition through a new way of encouraging the idea of silent Ireland – a concept evoked by those who claimed to speak on behalf of a majority whom they presumed would oppose change but were not inclined to speak out. There was similarly a slight fear that the success of the previous liberal measures would provoke reform fatigue, or perhaps even a backlash against an apparent juggernaut of change. One argument that had surfaced, which promised to be valuable for the repeal cause, was that the law in question was scarcely an ancient law. It was not a part of Ireland's religious heritage that it was being encouraged to give up, and thus perhaps it did not belong in the same category as gay marriage or abortion. The powerful and strangely enduring cultural motif of De Valera's Ireland was scarcely threatened here – indeed, repeal would restore an element of the Irish Constitution's earlier twentieth-century attempts to make blasphemy law less relevant to everyday life. The referendum, so the repeal argument went, was instead intended to combat an ill-judged and poorly implemented stopgap measure – one which had outlived its already very limited usefulness. Indeed, the Catholic Church in Ireland had begun to recognize that blasphemy laws could easily be wielded against all types of believer, not only those who professed no religion.

Fortunately (even if solely for the sake of debate) some individuals did eventually come forward to argue that the laws would keep the peace in a multicultural society and should be retained. Representatives of Ireland's Muslim community also argued that blasphemy legislation offered valuable protection against anti-religious acts. Some argued that Ireland had become obsessed with reform and that the cost of such a referendum could not be justified in the midst of the country's severe housing crisis. Despite these arguments, most commentators saw repeal as almost inevitable and began predicting a considerable victory for the repeal campaign. When speaking to people on the streets of Dublin, it was difficult to be precise about how the vote would eventually go. Those who had decided to vote for repeal were relatively vocal in their support of the cause, whereas those unsure of their opinion, or those who were possibly opposed to repeal, were remarkably adept at keeping their own counsel. As such, the leanings of the silent majority remained something of a mystery, and campaigners surely lost sleep not knowing how this group might decide when left in private with only their conscience and the ballot box.

In the event, the referendum took place, as planned, on 26 October 2018, alongside the presidential election. The result indicated that 65 per cent of the Irish electorate voted to have blasphemy removed from the Constitution and from elsewhere on the statute book. This was a more emphatic majority than the legalization of abortion referendum had produced, but a similar national voting pattern to that one could be observed throughout the country: the major urban centres of Dublin, Cork, Limerick and Galway delivered big majorities in favour of repeal that dwarfed the opposition vote. In counties close to these centres of population the 'overspill effect' of the cities and their influence could still be felt. Further away from these major conurbations, the numbers voting in favour of repeal gradually dwindled. Although all counties voted in favour, Donegal again came closest to delivering a 'hung' decision with approximately 52 per cent voting in favour.

Blasphemy's Afterlife

Ireland had voted to remove this dangerous precedent from the world stage, thereby undermining arguments, such as those that had been made by the OIC at the UN, about the rejuvenation of blasphemy laws in Western countries. As an interesting coda to this story, in the week following the Irish referendum Pakistan decided to acquit Asia Bibi on the grounds that the evidence was unreliable, and that she had faced intolerable pressure, having been made to confess in front of a mob demanding her death. This decision was received with considerable acclaim in the West, but not all of Pakistan's population agreed. In the wake of the acquittal the far-right populist party Tehreek-e-Labbaik Pakistan (TLP) instigated a concerted campaign against would-be and apparent blasphemers. While Asia Bibi was in hiding following her release, individuals and groups scoured the capital for her with malicious intent. A legal challenge to the Supreme Court's verdict was lodged, and while this was in motion negotiations between the government and the TLP delayed Asia Bibi's ability to leave Pakistan, causing further anxiety in the face of profound, ongoing hostility.

Eventually the Pakistan Supreme Court heard the appeal against her acquittal but upheld its original decision against the charge.[24] This cleared the way for Asia Bibi to go into a welcome exile, although her precise location remained unclear. Ireland's people may have voted to remove blasphemy laws but Pakistan's people demanded that they be reaffirmed. The prosecution of Asia Bibi demonstrated that, on occasion, people come to distrust official authorities and become wary of being 'sold out' by their representatives – a concern all the sharper where religious feelings are concerned.

Thus far in the twenty-first century, in the wake of the events outlined in this chapter, blasphemy laws have shaken off the caricature of anachronism that the modern era had arrogantly made of them. This dismissive logic has been replaced by a renewed interest in, and respect for, the oppressed religious groups and individuals. Blasphemy has been revitalized as a tool that individuals, and even nation states, might use to prop up minority identities that come under attack. This revitalization has arrived as an unwitting gift from some countries that, it seems, momentarily forgot that we live in a globalized world. So blasphemy had been rapidly transformed again into a credible law with more than credible advocates clamouring for its return and mainstream use. This is an occurrence that would have startled those who, over the previous century, had confidently predicted its quiet demise.

The long history of this concept and offence will no longer be characterized as one of progress from religious control through to Enlightenment tolerance; indeed, the assumptions of the Enlightenment now seem clouded and in question. Perhaps the enduring issue is encapsulated in John C. Knechtle's argument that

> Diversity in applying human rights standards to religious speech restrictions is already present in the world. This is what precipitates the debates. Diversity is a value espoused by liberalism, but of course, it is not diversity but diversity within liberal norms. The boundaries of liberalism may need to expand to account for acculturation, different balancing at the boundaries, changing demographics and political realities and the evolving nature of principles. These factors will decide the future iterations of blasphemy.[25]

Blasphemy, as contemporary society has discovered, still retains its role as a tool of control and regulation. After more than two millennia, blasphemy legislation is still reassuring the scared and threatened while also standing as a debatable constraint on the outspoken.

Concluding Remarks

Our history in this book is now up to date; but the history of blasphemy is scarcely over. Anyone who commenced reading this volume believing that the story of blasphemy was already concluded will probably have had their illusions shattered. The history of blasphemy seems to sit awkwardly when held up to the grand narratives that have supposedly governed its first two millennia. Developments like modernization, secularism and secularization have wrought only piecemeal change on blasphemy, and even then only for short periods. Orthodox religious observance retreats while religious 'feelings' seem to grow – at least as a tool of expression. Conflict appears followed by assimilation and belonging – only to erupt into conflict once more. Religious confidence alternates with species of religious fear. Government experts plan and execute legislative ways forward, only to be thwarted or to bow to unforeseen challenges. The right to determine what is blasphemous has been passed from the State to the individual and back to the State, and its role in creating feelings, identities and definitions of the State makes it a thoroughly contemporary presence. Despite the confidence of some that blasphemy would be left behind by 'progress', it is this very condition of society that is now making the phenomenon thrive.

We need to draw positives from this situation – whatever our beliefs, unbelief or life stances may be. Perhaps the only workable way forward is to never lose sight of blasphemy as an issue that affects all social groupings from the local to the global. This would mean ensuring that future generations will not have to keep rediscovering a phenomenon that seems past and remote. Blasphemy is not simply a part of our past; it is empathically here in the present and will surely persist into the future. Deeper knowledge and understanding of blasphemy, its effects and its histories may be the only thing that helps future societies to meet their particular challenges better prepared than any of us have been up to this point in history. Blasphemy laws are less fashionable than they used to be. But as we know the history of this offence has been fickle and less than progressive. Therefore further knowledge of blasphemy will hopefully enable those who favour it to think more deeply and carefully before so readily using a law with such consequences.

REFERENCES

Introduction

1 For more on the *Oz* trial and the *Lady Chatterley's Lover* case see Arthur Calder-Marshall, *Lewd, Blasphemous and Obscene* (London, 1972).

2 A reproduction of the poem and its accompanying illustration is available in Alan Travis, *Bound and Gagged* (London, 2000).

3 David Nash, *Blasphemy in Modern Britain: 1789 to the Present* (Aldershot, 1999).

4 David Nash, *Blasphemy in the Christian World: A History* (Oxford, 2007).

5 Peter Cumper, 'Blasphemy, Freedom of Expression and the Protection of Religious Sensibilities in Twenty-first Century Europe', in *Blasphemy and Freedom of Expression: Comparative, Theoretical and Historical Reflections after the Charlie Hebdo Massacre*, ed. Jeroen Temperman and András Koltay (Cambridge, 2018), p. 141.

6 See Talal Asad, *Genealogies of Religion: Discipline and Reasons of Power in Christianity and Islam* (Baltimore, MD, 1993) and Malcolm Lambert, *Medieval Heresy: Popular Movements from the Gregorian Reform to the Reformation* (Oxford, 1992).

7 Alan Cabantous, *Blasphemy: Impious Speech in the West from the Seventeenth to the Nineteenth Century* (New York, 2002); Francisca Loetz, *Dealings with God: From Blasphemers in Early Modern Zurich to a Cultural History of Religiousness* (Farnham, 2009).

8 Hypatia Bradlaugh Bonner, *Penalties upon Opinion; or, Some Records of the Laws of Heresy and Blasphemy* (London, 1934); Nicolas Walter, *Blasphemy Ancient and Modern* (London, 1990); Calder-Marshall, *Blasphemous, Lewd and Obscene*.

9 Leonard Levy, *Blasphemy: Verbal Offense against the Sacred, from Moses to Salman Rushdie* (New York, 1993).

10 Ibid.; Leonard Levy, *Treason against God: A History of the Offense of Blasphemy* (New York, 1981).

11 For the early Christian Councils see Mark Smith, *The Idea of Nicaea in Early Christian Councils, 431–451* (Oxford, 2018) and for a Catholic-influenced interpretation of the Councils and their role in creating the modern Western Church see Leo D. Davis, *The First Seven Ecumenical Councils: Their History and Theology* (London, 1988).

12 Neville Cox 'Blasphemy and Defamation of Religion Following *Charlie Hebdo*', in *Blasphemy and Freedom of Expression*, ed. Temperman and Koltay, pp. 53–83.

13 András Koltay 'The Freedom and Restriction of Blasphemy: Theoretical Perspectives', in *Blasphemy and Freedom of Expression*, ed. Temperman and Koltay, p. 239.

14 Levy, *Blasphemy*; see also Marjorie Heins, *Sex, Sin and Blasphemy: A Guide to America's Culture Wars* (London, 1993).

ONE: Blasphemy in the Ancient World

1 Chief among these is Tim Whitmarsh, *Battling the Gods: Atheism in the Ancient World* (London, 2016).

2 Ibid., pp. 123–4.

3 Quoted in Daniel Silvermintz, *Protogoras* (London, 2016), p. 24.

4 Whitmarsh, *Battling the Gods*, pp. 64–5.

5 P. J. Rhodes, *Alcibiades: Athenian Playboy, General and Traitor* (Barnsley, 2011), pp. 44–9; Walter M. Ellis, *Alcibiades* (London, 1989) pp. 58–60.

6 Plutarch, 'The Life of Alcibiades', in *Parallel Lives*, trans. Bernadotte Perrin (Cambridge, MA, and London, 1919), p. 15.

7 Thomas C. Brickhouse and Nicholas D. Smith, *Socrates on Trial* (Oxford, 2000).

8 Quoted in Whitmarsh, *Battling the Gods*, p. 126.

9 Plato, *Phaedo*, trans. Moses Mendelssohn (Bristol, 1789, reprinted 2004), p. 41.

10 Some suggest that the mention of jihad should be considered historically specific and not to apply to the lives of all Muslims thereafter. Others argue that there is no direct equivalent of blasphemy in Islam. See Neville Cox, 'Blasphemy and Defamation of Religion Following *Charlie Hebdo*', p. 75, and Peter Cumper, 'Blasphemy, Freedom of Expression and the Protection of Religious Sensibilities in Twenty-first Century Europe', p. 140, both in *Blasphemy and Freedom of Expression: Comparative, Theoretical and Historical Reflections after the Charlie Hebdo Massacre*, ed. Jeroen Temperman and András Koltay (Cambridge, 2018).

11 This is the view expressed in Zeeshan Hassan, 'Islam and Blasphemy Law', www.liberalislam.net, accessed 15 January 2019.

12 Khalid Zaheer, 'The Real Blasphemers', *Express Tribune*, https://tribune.com.pk, 2 January 2011.

13 'Blasphemy', in *Encyclopaedia of Islam and the Muslim World*, ed. Richard C. Martin (London, 2016), pp. 175–6.

14 Aslam Abdullah, 'Is Blasphemy Punishable by Death in Islam?', www.islamicity.org, 5 November 2018.

15 See Syed Ahmed Faisal Nahri, 'To Kill or Not to Kill? A Discursive Analysis of Colonial and Islamic Influences on Blasphemy Legislation in Postcolonial Pakistan', Master's thesis, University of British Columbia (2018), pp. 51–6.

16 Ibid., p. 56.

17 Verses in the Old Testament that mention blasphemy can be found in

Daniel 3:29, 7:25 and 11:36; Job 2:9; Ezekiel 20:27, 35:11–12; Isaiah 65:7; and 2 Samuel 12:13–14.

18 There is an extremely good account of the disagreements among biblical scholars in Leonard Levy, *Blasphemy: Verbal Offense against the Sacred, from Moses to Salman Rushdie* (New York, 1993), pp. 15–30.

19 'Definition of the Holy Great and Ecumemical Council, the Second in Nicea', quoted in Daniel J. Sahas, *Icon and Logos: Sources in Eighth-century Iconoclasm* (London, 1986), pp. 178–9.

20 The 1648 Statute of the interregnum expressly linked the concepts together in its title: *An Ordinance for the Punishing of Blasphemies and Heresies, With the Several Penalties Therein Expressed.*

TWO: Blasphemy in Medieval Christendom

1 Malcolm Lambert, *Medieval Heresy: Popular Movements from the Gregorian Reform to the Reformation* (Oxford, 1992), pp. 397–400.

2 See Chapter One of this book, where we see this exemplified in the differences between the Arians and the Nestorians.

3 Rev. Marcus Dods, MA, ed., *The Works of Aurelius Augustine, Bishop of Hippo*, vol. I: *The City of God* (Edinburgh, 1871), pp. 12–14.

4 Diarmaid MacCulloch, *All Things Made New: Writings on the Reformation* (London, 2017), p. 4.

5 Lambert, *Medieval Heresy*, p. 112.

6 For a general account of the pursuit and detection of the Cathars see René Weis, *The Yellow Cross: The Story of the Last Cathars, 1290–1329* (Harmondsworth, 2001).

7 Such punishments can be found across Europe with many of them also being transported to the American colonies.

8 Urals (Perm) Synod Court. Case Number 27_180 (1746–8). I am grateful to Marianna Muravyeva for bringing this case and the one in note 9 to my attention.

9 St Petersburg Secret Chancellery Court. Case Number 32_240 (1751).

10 Lars Grassmé Binderup and Eva Maria Lassen 'The Blasphemy Ban in Denmark', p. 431, and Helge Årsheim 'Giving up the Ghost: On the Decline and Fall of Norwegian Anti-blasphemy Legislation', p. 553, both in *Blasphemy and Freedom of Expression: Comparative, Theoretical and Historical Reflections after the Charlie Hebdo Massacre*, ed. Jeroen Temperman and András Koltay (Cambridge, 2018).

11 Anna Sapir Abulafia, *Christian–Jewish Relations 1000–1300: Jews in the Service of Medieval Christendom* (Harlow, 2011), p. 173.

12 See Jonathan Riley-Smith, *The Crusades: A History* (London, 2014) and Christopher Tyerman, *God's War: A New History of the Crusades* (Harmondsworth, 2007).

13 See R. B. Dobson, *The Jews of Medieval York and the Massacre of 1190* (York, 1974). See also 'York and Its Jews', www.davka.org, accessed 5 February 2019.

14 John Friedman, Jean Connell Hoff and Robert Chazan, *The Trial of the Talmud: Paris, 1240* (Toronto, 2012), pp. 44–9.

15 Abulafia, *Christian–Jewish Relations*, pp. 80–81.

16 Robert Chazan, *Fashioning Jewish Identity in Medieval Christendom* (Cambridge, 2004), pp. 115–17.

17 Lambert, *Medieval Heresy*, pp. 4–7.

18 Ibid., pp. 398–9.

19 Aquinas, *Summa Theologica*, Article 3: 'Whether the Sin of Blasphemy is the Greatest Sin?', Second Part of the Second Part L12 C4.

20 Guilhem Gil, 'Blasphemy in French Law from the Chevalier de la Barre to *Charlie Hebdo*', in *Blasphemy and Freedom of Expression*, ed. Temperman and Koltay, p. 26.

21 See David Nash, *Blasphemy in the Christian World: A History* (Oxford, 2007), pp. 52, 56 and 151–4.

22 William J. Connell and Giles Constable, *Sacrilege and Redemption in Renaissance Florence* (Toronto, 2005), p. 47.

23 Malcolm Barber, *The New Knighthood: A History of the Order of the Temple* (Cambridge, 1994).

24 Barbara Frale, 'The Chinon Chart: Papal Absolution to the Last Templar, Master Jacques de Molay', *Journal of Medieval History*, XXX (2004), pp. 109–34.

25 Cyrilla Barr, *The Monophonic Lauda* (Kalamazoo, MI, 1988), pp. 13–15.

26 Roisin Cossar, *The Transformation of the Laity in Bergamo 1265–c. 1400* (Leiden, 2006), pp. 135–6, 144–6 and 150–53.

THREE: Blasphemy and the Reformation

1 Carol Lansing, *Power and Purity: Cathar Heresy in Medieval Italy* (Oxford, 1998).

2 R. J. Moore, *The War on Heresy* (Harvard, MA, 1984).

3 Henry Kamen, *The Spanish Inquisition: An Historical Revision* (London, 1997).

4 John Calvin, *The Institutes of the Christian Religion*, www.ntslibrary.com, Book II, Chapter 1, accessed 24 October 2019.

5 See Javier Villa-Flores, *Dangerous Speech: A Social History of Blasphemy in Colonial Mexico* (Tucson, AZ, 2006), pp. 41–2.

6 See Maureen Flynn, 'Blasphemy and the Play of Anger in Sixteenth Century Spain', *Past and Present*, CXLIX (1995), pp. 29–56.

7 Alain Cabantous, *Blasphemy: Impious Speech in the West from the Seventeenth to the Nineteenth Century*, trans. Eric Rauth (New York, 2002), p. 83.

8 Diarmaid MacCulloch, 'The Council of Trent', in *All Things Made New: Writings on the Reformation* (London, 2017), pp. 70–77.

9 Villa-Flores, *Dangerous Speech*, p. 77.

10 Leonard Levy, *Blasphemy: Verbal Offense against the Sacred, from Moses to Salman Rushdie* (New York, 1993), p. 253.

11 Keith Thomas, *Religion and the Decline of Magic* (Harmondsworth, 1971).

12 Diarmaid MacCulloch, *Christianity: The First Three Thousand Years* (Harmondsworth, 2009), p. 624.

13 Hypatia Bradlaugh Bonner, *Penalties upon Opinion; or, Some Records of the Laws of Heresy and Blasphemy* (London, 1934), pp. 10–11.

14 William J. Connell and Giles Constable, *Sacrilege and Redemption in Renaissance Florence* (Toronto, 2005), p. 46.

15 See Elizabeth Horodwich, 'Civic Identity and the Control of Blasphemy in Sixteenth Century Venice', *Past and Present*, CLXXXI (2003), pp. 3–33.

16 Cabantous, *Blasphemy*, pp. 49–53.

17 Helge Årsheim, 'Giving up the Ghost: On the Decline and Fall of Norwegian Anti-blasphemy Legislation', in *Blasphemy and Freedom of Expression: Comparative, Theoretical and Historical Reflections after the Charlie Hebdo Massacre*, ed. Jeroen Temperman and András Koltay (Cambridge, 2018), p. 556.

18 Francisca Loetz, *Dealings with God*, trans. Rosemary Selle (Aldershot, 2009), pp. 56–60.

19 M. R. Baelde, *Studiën over Godslastering* (The Hague, 1935), pp. 109–10.

20 See Matthew 24:23–4: 'Then if any man shall say unto you, Lo, here is Christ, or there; believe it not. For there shall arise false Christs, and false prophets, and shall shew great signs and wonders; insomuch that, if it were possible, they shall deceive the very elect'; and Acts 17:24–25: 'God that made the world and all things therein, seeing that he is Lord of heaven and earth, dwelleth not in temples made with hands; Neither is worshipped with men's hands, as though he needed any thing, seeing he giveth to all life, and breath, and all things.' These were quite inflammatory texts, especially in this context.

21 Council of Trent, Session XXV (1563), www.thecounciloftrent.com, accessed 21 October 2019.

22 Christina Larner, *Enemies of God: Witch-hunt in Scotland* (Edinburgh, 2000).

23 Loetz, *Dealings with God*, pp. 123 and 183.

24 Ibid., pp. 113–15.

25 Christodoulos Stefanadis, Marianna Karamanou and George Androutsos, 'Michael Servetus (1511–1553) and the Discovery of Pulmonary Circulation', *Hellenic Journal of Cardiology*, L/5 (2009), pp. 373–8.

26 International Association for Religious Freedom, *Servetus: Our 16th Century Contemporary: A Brief Introduction to the Life and Teachings of Michael Servetus, a Pioneer of Religious Freedom* (Boston, MA, 2011), p. 4.

27 Jules Bonnett, *Letters of John Calvin Compiled from the Original Manuscripts and Edited with Historical Hotes* (Philadelphia, PA, 1868), vol. II, letter 324, p. 422.

28 H. Ashley Hall, *Philip Melanchthon and the Cappadocians* (Göttingen, Vandenhoek and Rupprecht, 2014), p. 124.

FOUR: Blasphemy and the Enlightenment

1 See Christopher Hill, *The English Bible and the Seventeenth-century Revolution: Uses of the Bible in 17th-century England* (Harmondsworth, 2004).

2 See Patrick Collinson, *The Elizabethan Puritan Movement* (Oxford, 1990).

3 Abiezer Coppe, *The Second Fiery Flying Roll* [1649], www.libertarianism.org, accessed 23 August 2019.

4 Leonard Levy, *Blasphemy: Verbal Offense against the Sacred, from Moses to Salman Rushdie* (New York, 1993), pp. 156–8.

5 Old Bailey Proceedings, 'The Maid. Royal Offences: Religious Offences' (ref: t16780828–14), 28 August 1678.

6 Hypatia Bradlaugh Bonner, *Penalties upon Opinion; or, Some Records of the Laws of Heresy and Blasphemy* (London, 1934), pp. 18–19.

7 Thomas Carlyle, *The Letters and Speeches of Oliver Cromwell*, ed. S. C. Lomas (London, 1904), vol. iii, pp. 18–19.

8 For a detailed examination of the Taylor case see Levy, *Blasphemy*, pp. 219–22.

9 Bonner, *Penalties upon Opinion*, p. 31.

10 Ibid.

11 M. Hunter, '"Aikenhead the Atheist": The Context and Consequences of Articulate Irreligion in the Late Seventeenth Century', in *Atheism from the Reformation to the Enlightenment*, ed. M. Hunter and D. Wootton (Oxford, 1992), p. 253.

12 For a contemporary appreciation of Aikenhead by modern non-religious activists see 'A Scottish Martyr', www.humanism.scot, accessed 11 November 2017.

FIVE: Blasphemy in the Nineteenth Century

1 Thomas Paine, *Letter to Thomas Erskine* (Paris, 1797).

2 *The Constable's Assistant: Being a Compendium of the Duties and powers of Constables and Other Peace Officers; Chiefly as they relate to the Apprehending of Offenders, and the Laying of Informations before Magistrates*, 3rd edn with additions (London, 1818).

3 *British Loyalty; or, Declarations of Attachment to the Established Constitution, in Church and State, opposed to Blasphemy, Anarchy, Sedition and Innovation. By the Merchants, Bankers, Civil Corporations and Parishes of Great Britain* (London, 1819).

4 For more on Carlile see Joel H. Wiener, *Radicalism and Freethought in Nineteenth Century Britain: The Life and Times of Richard Carlile* (London, 1983).

5 Richard Carlile, *Letter to the Society for the Suppression of Vice, on their Malignant Efforts to Prevent a Free Enquiry after Truth and Reason* (London, 1819).

6 Ibid., p. 3.

7 Richard Carlile, *Report of the Trial of Mrs Susannah Wright for Publishing, in his shop, the Writings and Correspondences of R. Carlile before Chief Justice Abbott and a Special Jury in the Court of King's Bench, Guildhall, London* (London, 1822), pp. 4 and 59.

8 *The Times*, 22 November 1822.

9 Richard Carlile, *Holmes . . . William Cochrane and Thomas Riley Perry: Being the Persons Who Were Prosecuted for Selling the Publications of Richard Carlile in His Various Shops* (London, 1825).

10 Elihu Palmer, *Principles of Nature*, Chapter 25: 'Commencement of the Nineteenth Century: Christianity; Deism; Reason: Science; Virtue; Happiness . . .' (London, 1819).

11 For more on this, see Patricia Hollis, *The Pauper Press* (Oxford, 1970).

12 For the original see Thomas Paine, *The Rights of Man*, Part 2, Chapter III.

13 *The Reports of the Trials of William Campion, Thomas Jeffries, Richard Hassell, John Clarke, William Haley, William Cochrane and Others for the Sale of Anti-Christian Publications in the Shop of Richard Carlile, 84, Fleet Street, London. Tried at the Old Bailey Sessions for June 1824, Before Newman Knowlys, The Recorder and Common Juries* (London, 1824), p. 23.

14 Ibid.

15 *Suppressed Defence: The Defence of Mary-Anne Carlile to the Vice Society's Indictment Against the Appendix to the Theological Works of Thomas Paine* . . . (London, 1821), p. 12.

16 Guilhem Gil, 'Blasphemy in French Law from the Chevalier de la Barre to *Charlie Hebdo*', in *Blasphemy and Freedom of Expression: Comparative, Theoretical and Historical Reflections after the Charlie Hebdo Massacre*, ed. Jeroen Temperman and András Koltay (Cambridge, 2018), pp. 31 and 36.

17 See Leonard Levy, *Blasphemy: Verbal Offense against the Sacred, from Moses to Salman Rushdie* (New York, 1993).

18 For reports see *People v. Ruggles*, 8 Johns (New York, 1811), p. 290.

19 See Levy, *Blasphemy*.

20 See Walter Arnstein, *The Bradlaugh Case* (Oxford, 1965) and David Nash, *Blasphemy in Modern Britain, 1789 to the Present* (Aldershot, 1999), pp. 109–66.

21 *Freethinker*, 21 and 28 May 1882.

22 For more on Foote's trial and confinement see G. W. Foote, *Prisoner for Blasphemy* (London, 1883).

23 Ernest Hartley Coleridge, *Life and Correspondence of John Duke, Lord Coleridge* (London, 1904), p. 291.

24 Michael Meyer, *Strindberg* (Oxford, 1987), pp. 130–42.

25 Robert Ingersoll, *The Trial of C. B. Reynolds For Blasphemy. Defence by Robert G. Ingersoll, at Morristown, N. J., May 1887* (Boston, MA, 1888), online at www.gutenberg.org, accessed 22 October 2019.

26 Robert Ingersoll, *The Works of Robert Ingersoll* (New York, 2009), vol. XI, p. 61.

27 Ibid., p. 110.

SIX: Blasphemy in the Twentieth Century

1 Emma Goldman, *Anarchism and Other Essays* (New York, 1910).

2 *The Truthseeker* (Bradford, 1911).

3 J. W. Gott, *Rib Ticklers; or, Questions for Parsons* (Bradford, 1900), p. 7.

4 Ibid.

5 E. Pack, *The Trial and Imprisonment of J. W. Gott* (Bradford, 1912), p. 3.

6 Home Office Papers, HO 45 10665/216120, item 216120/6.

7 Helge Årsheim 'Giving up the Ghost: On the Decline and Fall of Norwegian Anti-blasphemy Legislation', in *Blasphemy and Freedom of Expression: Comparative, Theoretical and Historical Reflections after the Charlie Hebdo Massacre*, ed. Jeroen Temperman and András Koltay (Cambridge, 2018), p. 558.

8 See David Nash, *Blasphemy in Modern Britain 1789 to the Present* (Aldershot, 1999), pp. 194–278.

9 Joanna Kulesza and Jan Kulesza, 'Blasphemy Law in Poland', in *Blasphemy and Freedom of Expression*, ed. Temperman and Koltay, p. 424.

10 E. J. De Roo, *Godslastering* (Deventer, 1970), p. 70.

11 Marjorie Heins, *Sex, Sin and Blasphemy: A Guide to America's Censorship Wars* (New York, 1993), p. 2.

12 345 U.S. 495(1952) *Joseph Burstyn, inc. v. Wilson, Commissioner of Education of New York, et al.*, no. 522 Supreme Court of the United States.

13 William P. Clancy, 'The Catholic as Philistine', *Commonweal*, 16 March 1951, pp. 567–9.

14 *Burstyn v. Wilson*.

15 *New York Times*, 1 Febuary 1951, p. 24.

16 Lars Grassmé Binderup and Eva Marie Lassen, 'The Blasphemy Ban in Denmark', in *Blasphemy and Freedom of Expression*, ed. Temperman and Koltay, pp. 431–55: p. 435.

17 Tuomas Äystö, 'Religious Insult and Blasphemy in Contemporary Finland'; Lars Grassmé Binderup and Eva Maria Lassen, 'The Blasphemy Ban in Denmark'; Joanna Kulesza and Jan Kulesza, 'Blasphemy Law in Poland'; and Effie Fokas, 'God's Advocates: The Multiple Fronts of the War on Blasphemy in Greece', all in *Blasphemy and Freedom of Expression*, ed. Koltay and Temperman, pp. 319, 435, 431 and 396–8.

18 Charles Stephens, *The Jurisprudence of Lord Denning: A Study in Legal History*, vol. III: *Freedom under the Law* (Cambridge, 2009), p. 23.

19 For an account of Mary Whitehouse and her crusades see Ben Thompson, *Ban this Filth! Letters from the Mary Whitehouse Archive* (London, 2012).

20 Leonard Levy, *Blasphemy: Verbal Offense against the Sacred, from Moses to Salman Rushdie* (New York, 1993), pp. 558–9.

21 Malise Ruthven, *A Satanic Affair: Salman Rushdie and the Rage of Islam* (London, 1990), pp. 38–9.

22 Ibid.

23 Ibid., p. 29.

24 Ibid., pp. 112–13.

25 Kenan Malik, *From Fatwa to Jihad: The Rushdie Affair and Its Legacy* (London, 2009), pp. 15–16.

26 This eventually became a publication for the experimental publisher Granta; see Salman Rushdie, *In Good Faith* (London, 1990).

27 Ibid., p. 163.

28 Ibid., p. 210.

29 Article 19 and Interights, *Blasphemy and Film Censorship: Submission to the European Court of Human Rights in Respect of Nigel Wingrove v. The United Kingdom* (London, 1995).

30 See Andrew Pulver, 'Visions of Ecstasy Cleared for Release after 23 Years', www.theguardian.com, 31 January 2012.

31 Mark Hill and Russell Sandberg, 'The Right to Blaspheme', in *Blasphemy and Freedom of Expression*, ed. Temperman and Koltay, p. 124.

32 Ibid., p. 115.
33 Ibid., p. 118.

SEVEN: Blasphemy in the Contemporary World

1 This case found against the Otto Preminger Institute, which had
   shown a film adaptation of Oskar Panizza's nineteenth-century play
   Das Liebeskonzil (The Love Council) – itself prosecuted when it was
   originally staged. The Institute argued that free speech protected the
   content of the film even though it shocked and disturbed. The verdict
   of the European Court of Human Rights was that such protection was
   unjustifiable and pronounced a verdict against the Institute. (*Otto-
   Preminger-Institut v. Austria* (13470/87).)
2 The Venice Commission Study 406/2006 on blasphemy, religious
   insults and incitement to religious hatred, adopted at the Commission's
   seventieth plenary session, 16–17 March 2007; *Rabat Plan of Action on
   the Prohibition of the Advocacy of National, Racial, or Religious Hatred that
   Constitutes Incitement to Discrimination, Hostility or Violence* (2012).
3 Jeroen Temperman and András Koltay, 'Introduction', in *Blasphemy and
   Freedom of Expression: Comparative, Theoretical and Historical Reflections
   after the* Charlie Hebdo *Massacre*, ed. Jeroen Temperman and András
   Koltay (Cambridge, 2018), pp. 4–6; and Robert A. Kahn, 'Rethinking
   Blasphemy and Anti-blasphemy laws', ibid., p. 178.
4 *Blasphemy and Freedom of Expression*, ed. Temperman and Koltay, p. xix.
5 Peter Cumper, 'Blasphemy, Freedom of Expression and the Protection
   of Religious Sensibilities in Twenty-first Century Europe', ibid.,
   pp. 155–6.
6 John C. Knechtle 'Blasphemy, Defamation of Religion and Religious
   Hate Speech', in *Blasphemy and Freedom of Expression*, ed. Temperman
   and Koltay, pp. 212–13.
7 House of Lords Select Committee on Religious Offences (2003),
   www.publications.parliament.uk, accessed 27 June 2017. Submission
   of Independent Christian Churches.
8 House of Lords Select Committee on Religious Offences (2003),
   www.publications.parliament.uk, accessed 27 June 2017. Submission
   of Elim Way Fellowship.
9 Mark Hill and Russell Sandberg, 'The Right to Blaspheme', in
   Blasphemy and Freedom of Expression, ed. Temperman and Koltay,
   p. 128.
10 See Callum G. Brown, Thomas Green and Jane Mair, *Religion in Scots
   Law* (Edinburgh, 2016).
11 This is discussed in Law Reform Commission *Consultation Paper on
   the Crime of Libel* (Law Reform Commission, 1991) Chapter One:
   'Historical Development of the Crime of Libel'. See also Constitution
   of Ireland, Article 40.6.i (Dublin, Stationery Office), p. 158.
12 Aodhán Ó Ríordáin, 'Dáil Éireann Debate – Thursday, 2 October 2014',
   www.oireachtas.ie, accessed 15 August 2019.
13 See 'Seanad Éireann Debate – Wednesday, 1 February 2012',
   www.oireachtas.ie, accessed 11 November 2017.

14 This concept was implicit in the deliberations of the House of Lords
Select Committee on Religious Offences. See verbal evidence given
18 July 2002 questions 220–238, online at www.publications.parliament.
co.uk, accessed 22 October 2019.

15 United States Reports, *Cases Adjudged in the Supreme Court at October
Term 1951, From March 10th (Concluded) through June 9th 1952 (End of
Term). Walter Wyatt (Reporter)* (United States Government Printing
Office), vol. CCCXLIII, p. 515.

16 See Cormac O'Keefe, 'Blasphemy Offence May Be Removed Next
Year', *Irish Examiner*, www.irishexaminer.com, 10 January 2015.

17 Temperman and Koltay, 'Introduction', p. 1; Guilhem Gil, 'Blasphemy
in French Law from the Chevalier de la Barre to *Charlie Hebdo*', pp.
46–9; Cumper, 'Blasphemy, Freedom of Expression and the Protection
of Religious Sensibilities in Twenty-first Century Europe', p. 147;
András Koltay, 'The Freedom and Restriction of Blasphemy: Theoretical
Perspectives', all in *Blasphemy and Freedom of Expression*, ed. Temperman
and Koltay, pp. 224, 248 and 250.

18 Erica Howard, 'Freedom of Expression, Blasphemy and Religious
Hatred: A View from the United Kingdom', ibid., p. 617.

19 Tarlach Mcgonagle, 'A Draft Obituary for the Offence of Blasphemy
in Ireland', ibid., pp. 472–3 and 477.

20 'New Blasphemy Laws – Free Speech is Not Up For Discussion',
Irish Examiner, www.irishexaminer.com, 1 May 2009.

21 Austen Dacey, *The Future of Blasphemy* (London, 2012), p. 2.

22 Clare Daly, 'Dáil Éireann Debate – Thursday, 2 October 2014',
www.oireachtas.ie, accessed 14 November 2019.

23 Mcgonagle, 'A Draft Obituary for the Offence of Blasphemy in Ireland',
p. 457.

24 See 'Asia Bibi Blasphemy Acquittal Upheld by Pakistan Court',
BBC News, www.bbc.co.uk, 30 January 2019.

25 Knechtle, 'Blasphemy, Defamation of Religion and Religious Hate
Speech', p. 221.

SELECT BIBLIOGRAPHY

Abulafia, Anna Sapir, *Christian-Jewish Relations, 1000–1300: Jews in the Service of Medieval Christendom* (Harlow, 2011)

Bonner, Hypatia Bradlaugh, *Penalties upon Opinion; or, Some Records of the Laws of Heresy and Blasphemy* (London, 1934)

Brown, Callum G., Thomas Green and Jane Mair, *Religion in Scots Law: The Report of an Audit at the University of Glasgow* (Edinburgh, 2016)

Cabantous, Alain, and Eric Rauth, trans., *Blasphemy: Impious Speech in the West from the Seventeenth to the Nineteenth Century* (New York, 2002)

Calder-Marshall, Arthur, *Lewd, Blasphemous and Obscene: Being the Trials and Tribulations of Sundry Founding Fathers of Today's Alternative Societies* (London, 1972)

Heins, Marjorie, *Sex, Sin and Blasphemy: A Guide to America's Censorship Wars* (New York, 1993)

Hill, Christopher, *The English Bible and the Seventeenth-century Revolution: Uses of the Bible in Seventeenth-century England* (Harmondsworth, 2004)

Hunter, Michael, and David Wootton, eds, *Atheism from the Reformation to the Enlightenment* (Oxford, 1992)

Lambert, Malcolm, *Medieval Heresy: Popular Movements from the Gregorian Reform to the Reformation* (Oxford, 1992)

Lansing, Carol, *Power and Purity: Cathar Heresy in Medieval Italy* (Oxford, 1998)

Levy, Leonard W., *Blasphemy: Verbal Offense against the Sacred, from Moses to Salman Rushdie* (New York, 1993)

—, *Treason against God: A History of the Offense of Blasphemy* (New York, 1981)

Loetz, Francisca, and Rosemary Selle, trans., *Dealings with God: From Blasphemers in Early Modern Zurich to a Cultural History of Religiousness* (Farnham, 2009)

MacCulloch, Diarmaid, *A History of Christianity: The First Three Thousand Years* (Harmondsworth, 2009)

Malik, Kenan, *From Fatwa to Jihad: The Rushdie Affair and Its Legacy* (London, 2009)

Marsh, Joss, *Word Crimes: Blasphemy, Culture, and Literature in Nineteenth-century England* (London, 1998)

Moore, Robert I., *The War on Heresy: Faith and Power in Medieval Europe* (London, 2012)

Nash, David, *Blasphemy in the Christian World: A History* (Oxford, 2007)

——, *Blasphemy in Modern Britain: 1789 to the Present* (Aldershot, 1999)

Plate, S. Brent, *Blasphemy: Art that Offends* (London, 2006)

Royle, Edward, *Victorian Infidels: The Origins of the British Secularist Movement, 1791–1866* (Manchester, 1974)

Ruthven, Malise, *A Satanic Affair: Salman Rushdie and the Rage of Islam* (London, 1990)

Smith, F. LaGard, *Blasphemy and the Battle for Faith* (London, 1990)

Temperman, Jeroen, and András Koltay, eds, *Blasphemy and Freedom of Expression: Comparative, Theoretical and Historical Reflections after the Charlie Hebdo Massacre* (Cambridge, 2017)

Thompson, Ben, *Ban This Filth! Letters from the Mary Whitehouse Archive* (London, 2012)

Travis, Alan, *Bound and Gagged: A Secret History of Obscenity in Britain* (London, 2000)

Tyerman, Christopher, *God's War: A New History of the Crusades* (Harmondsworth, 2007)

Villa-Flores, Javier, *Dangerous Speech: A Social History of Blasphemy in Colonial Mexico* (Tucson, AZ, 2006)

Walter, Nicolas, *Blasphemy Ancient and Modern* (London, 1990)

Webster, Richard, *A Brief History of Blasphemy: Liberalism, Censorship and 'The Satanic Verses'* (Southwold, 1990)

Weis, René, *The Yellow Cross: The Story of the Last Cathars, 1290–1329* (Harmondsworth, 2001)

Whitmarsh, Tim, *Battling the Gods: Atheism in the Ancient World* (London, 2016)

Wiener, Joel H., *Radicalism and Freethought in Nineteenth-century Britain: The Life and Times of Richard Carlile* (London, 1983)

ACKNOWLEDGEMENTS

Any author who has worked with this material for nearly thirty years will inevitably accumulate many debts to individuals and organizations that have helped along the way. Many have provided insight over the years as to the situation for blasphemy in Britain, America and Europe. These include Keith Porteus-Wood, Terry Sanderson, Lord Eric Avebury, John Cryer, Deborah Lavin, Willy Fautre, Bert and Ina Gassenbeek, Paul Cliteur, Chris Beneke, Christopher Grenda, August Hans den Boef, Jim Herrick, Callum Brown, Elizabeth Coleman, Peter Tatchell, Francisca Loetz, Gerd Schwerhoff, Geoffrey Robertson, Ted Royle, and Steve and Sean McEvoy.

I owe thanks to archivists and librarians in Oxford Brookes University Library; the Bodleian main, law and social science libraries; the University of Oxford Library; the British Library; the National Archives; South Place Ethical Society Library; Bishopsgate Library; the British Library Newspaper Collection; the International Institute for Social History (Amsterdam); and the Institute for Humanistik (Utrecht).

A number of history of crime colleagues, in both my institution and others, deserve thanks for engaging in numerous discussions and for providing a supportive and thriving research environment. These include Cassie Watson, Kate West, Shani D'Cruz, Sarah Wilson, Barry Godfrey, David Cox, Kim Stevenson and Professor Judith Rowbotham. I owe particular thanks to my close friend and writing partner Anne-Marie Kilday, who has always been a source of encouragement and deep understanding.

Members of Atheist Ireland made me very welcome on numerous visits there in the work towards referendum and repeal. In particular Michael Nugent, Jane Donnelly, John Hamill and Ashling O'Brien were especially important inspirations – providing insight, determination and further knowledge of what it feels like to argue against blasphemy laws in your own country.

Last, my family have endured much of my inconvenient absences and preoccupied presences over many years. Their tolerance is commendable so it is good to thank my wife Joanne, daughter Bella and our ginger cat George.

While these people have kept me sane and upright, all arguments and potential mistakes in this work remain my own. If it provides even the slightest insight into a murky, perplexing but important world then my task has been worthwhile.

INDEX

Act for the More Effectual
    Suppressing of Blasphemy
    (9 & 10 William III, *c.* 32)
    110, 118
Ahern, Dermot 11, 173
Aikenhead, Thomas 104–10
Alcibiades 25, 26
Alexandrians 37–8
Anabaptists 65–7, 92
Anaxagoras 23–4
Anderton, James Chief Constable of
    Greater Manchester 154
Anstruther, William, Lord
    Anstruther 108
Aquinas, Thomas 43, 50–51
Arians 37, 63
Arnold, Matthew 136
Arnoldists 40
Atheist Ireland (NGO) 175
Augustine of Hippo 41

Bacik, Ivana 175
Bauthumley, Jacob 96
Beguins 40
Best, Paul 89–91, 98
Bibi, Asia 184, 186
Biddle, John 91, 98
blasphemy
    and alcohol 62, 69, 73
    and anarchism 139–40
    and anger 60, 75, 81
    and art 136, 147–8, 150, 161
    and Calvinism 59, 71–2, 91
    and Christianity 12–18, 22,
        33–86, 168–9
    and Common Law 111, 118, 128,
        129–34, 150, 163, 168, 171–3
    and film 148–9, 159–60
    and the First Amendment
        (USA) 128–9
    and free speech 30, 109, 121–3,
        128–9, 135, 139, 147–8, 157–8,
        162, 167–8, 174
    and gambling 61, 69, 75–9
    and human rights 147–8
    and icons 43–5, 75–9, 87–8
    and iconoclasm 38, 59, 79–80
    and incitement laws 166–7,
        169–71
    and Islam 12, 31–3, 154–61, 178–9
    and Jacobin radicalism 120,
        125–8
    and Jesus 35–8, 40–41, 46–7, 102,
        151–2
    and Judaism 33–5, 45–9, 65–7, 71
    and literature 136
    and occupations 60, 118
    and the Reformation 38–9,
        58–86
    and the State 16–17, 20, 30,
        40–49, 62–4, 110–11, 113–14,
        166–71
    and the theatre 161
    definition of 12
    in America 14, 19–20, 62, 111–14,
        127–9, 137–8, 148–50, 154

in Australia 134, 171
in Austria 162, 165–6
in Belgium 60–61
in Denmark 45, 70, 150, 159–60,
    163, 182
in Eastern Orthodox 43–4
in England 7–11, 15, 18–20, 49,
    67–103, 110–27, 129–36, 139–46,
    150–54, 159, 161, 165–71
in Finland 150
in France 13, 46–9, 69–70, 163,
    178–9
in Germany 52
in Greece (ancient) 22–30
in Greece (modern) 150
in Italy 55–6, 58, 68–9, 75–9
in Mexico 60–62
in the Netherlands 18, 68–69,
    73–4, 146
in New Zealand 163, 171, 182
in Northern Ireland 171
in Norway 45, 70, 144
in Pakistan 161, 163, 180, 186
in Poland 146, 150
in Portugal 70, 162
in the Roman Empire 14, 34–5
in Russia 44
in Scotland 72–3, 104–10, 171
in Spain 18–19, 60, 61, 69–70
in Sweden 136–7, 179
in Switzerland 13–14, 71–2,
    80–82
laws 9–10, 13, 17–19, 49, 69, 91–2,
    104–5, 110, 145–6, 166–71
policing of 17, 67–86, 118–19, 164
punishments for 24, 43, 51–2, 68,
    79, 112
blasphemy in the Irish Republic 11,
    146, 163, 172–8, 179–87
Atheist Ireland (NGO) 175
Catholic Church opinions on
    blasphemy 177–8
Constitutional Convention on
    blasphemy 175–7
*Corway v. Independent
    Newspapers* 173
debates in the Dáil 172–4, 182
Defamation Act (2009) 173–6,
    184

Irish Constitution of 1937 172,
    185
Order of the Knights of Saint
    Columbanus 177–8
referendum on repeal 183–6
'Stephen Fry Affair' 181–3
Blasphemy Act (1648) 91–2
Blasphemy Act (1650) 96
Bogomils 40
Bradlaugh, Charles 129
Burstyn v. Wilson 148–50

Calvin, John 80, 82, 84–5
Campion, William 125–6
Carey, George, archbishop of
    Canterbury 170, 179
Carlile, Jane 122
Carlile, Mary Ann 122, 126–7
Carlile, Richard 120–27, 133
Carlyle, Thomas 101
Cathars 42–3, 65
Charles I, king of England 88–9
Charlie Hebdo 178–9
    Merabet, Ahmed 179
Clynes, J. R. 145
Coleridge, Justice John Duke 132–3
    'Coleridge judgement' 132–3, 143,
        154
confraternities 55–6, 78
Coppe, Abiezer 95
Cordier, Thierry de 150
Council of Chalcedon (451 CE) 38
Council of Nicaea (325 CE) 14, 37,
Council of Nicaea (787 CE) 14–15, 37,
    44, 59
Council of Trent (1545–63) 61
Court of High Commission for
    Ecclesiastical Causes 89
Court of Star Chamber 89
Coverdale, Miles 87
Cox, Neville 17–18
Cristofagia 19

Dawkins, Richard 182–3
De heretico comburendo 49, 99
Denning, Baron Tom 151
Diagoras of Melos 24
Diocletian, emperor of Rome 36
Diopethes 23–4

Dominicans 41, 48, 55
Donatists 36
Eleusinian mysteries 24–5
Eliot, George 136
Erskine, Thomas 117
Esti ludeos 46
European Court of Human Rights
    159–60, 164–5

Fifth Monarchy Men 97
Foote, George William 129–32,
    134–5, 151
Fraticelli 40
Freethinker 129–32, 134, 151
Friar Paul 48

Gay News case 8–10, 151–4, 170
Gnostics 36
Gorton, Samuel 112–13
Gott, John William 140–44, 150
    Parson's Doom, The 141
    *Rib Ticklers; or, Questions for
        Parsons* 140, 144
Green, Stephen 161
Grosz, George 147

Hale, Sir Matthew 103
    'Hale judgement' 103, 121,
        126–7, 132
Harcourt, Sir William 129–30, 134
Hardy, Thomas 136
Harris, Evan (MP) 170–71
Harrison, Major General Thomas
    97
Haughey, Charles 172
Henricians 40
heresy 13, 39–59, 65
homosexuality 8–9
Horridge, Justice Thomas Gardner
    143–4
House of Lords Select Committee
    on Religious Offences (2002–3)
    10–11, 15, 166–70, 177
Hunter, Claudius 126

Independents 93
Indian Criminal Code (1860) 166–7
Ingersoll, Robert 137–8
Innocent III, pope 46

inquisitions 41–2, 58–9, 61, 69
James I and VI, king of England
    and Scotland 87–8
    King James Bible 88
Jefferson, Thomas 129
Jerry Springer: The Opera 19, 161
Jerusalem Star 135
John of Leyden 66
Joyce, James 136
Jyllands-Posten 160–61

Ka'b ibn al-Ashraf 31
Kemp, Henry 130–31
Keyser, Thomas 67–8
Khomeini, Ayatollah 156–7
King-Hamilton, Justice Alan 153–4
Kirkup, James, 8, 152
Knights Templar 53–5
Knights War 66
Knox, John 72

Lady Chatterley's Lover case 8
Laud, William 89
Lawrence, D. H. 136
Lemon, Denis 153
Lollards 40
Luther, Martin 64–7, 83

MacCulloch, Diarmaid 41, 61
McIlroy, Bill 151
Malik, Kenan 158
Martin, Michael 180
Merabet, Ahmed 179
Molay, Jacques de 54
Monty Python's Life of Brian 34, 82
More, Hannah 119–20
Mortimer, John (QC) 9, 152–3
Muggletonians 96–7, 104

Nachmanides 48–9
National Secular Society 9, 167–8, 170
Nayler, James 52, 92, 98–102
New Journalism 135
Nieznalska, Dorota 150
North, Lord Justice Sir Ford 131

Otto Preminger Institute case 165–6
Organisation of Islamic
    Cooperation (OIC) 180

Øverland, Arnulf 144
Oz trial 8

Pack, Ernest 140–44
Paine, Thomas 115–17, 121, 124, 127
    Age of Reason, The 116–17, 121–2
Painter, Anthony, 73
Palmer, Elihu, *Principles of Nature*
    124
Philip IV, king of France 53–5
Pius V, pope 52
Plato 26
Polycrates 29
Porteus-Wood, Keith 9
Protagoras 23

Quakers 14, 52, 92, 97–8, 100–102,
    112–13

Rabat Plan of Action 161–2
Racial and Religious Hatred Act
    (2006) 170–71
Ramsey, William 130–31, 135
Ranters 93–7, 102–4, 112
Reynolds, C. B. 137–8
Rinaldeschi, Antonio 75–9
Robertson, Geoffrey (QC) 9, 152–3
Ruggles, John 128–9
Rushdie, Salman 154–9
    Igarashi, Hitoshi, assassination
        of 156–7
    'In Good Faith' 157
    Nygard, William, violence
        against 157
    Satanic Verses, The 154–9
Ruthven, Malise 158

Salama, Hannu, *Midsummer Dance*
    150
Salmon, Joseph 95
Saucer, Benjamin 62
Savonarola, Girolamo 76
Scarman, Lord Leslie George 154,
    158–9
Servetus, Michael 82–5

Sex Pistols 154
Six Acts (1819) 121
Society for the Suppression of Vice
    117–19, 122–3
Socinianism 63, 90
Socrates 26–30
Sophists 23
'Stephen Fry Affair' 181–3
Stephen, James Fitzjames 132, 134,
    153
Stewart of Goodtrees, Sir James 107
Stewart, Thomas William 140–44
Strauss, David, *Das Leben Jesu* 136
Strindberg, August 136–7

Taylor, John 102–3, 128
Tehreek-e-Labbaik Pakistan (TLP)
    186
Thomas, Keith 62
Thorsen, Jens Jurgen 7, 150
Tiberius, emperor of Rome 35, 100

Unitarianism 83
United Nations Commission on
    Human Rights 161
United Nations General Assembly
    180
Universal Declaration of Human
    Rights (1948) 147

Van Gogh, Theo 18
Visions of Ecstasy 159–60

Waldensians 65
War of the Three Kingdoms 89
Watson, James 124–5
Whitehouse, Mary 7–8, 9, 151–2
Whitmarsh, Tim 26
Williams, Roger 113–14
Williams, Thomas 117
Wingrove, Nigel 159–60
Wright, Susannah 123–4
Wyke, Andrew 95–6

Xenophon 30